WAR BABIES

The Generation That Changed America

WAR BABIES

The Generation That Changed America

Richard Pells

Other Books by Richard Pells

Modernist America:
Art, Music, Movies, and the Globalization of American Culture

Not Like Us:
How Europeans Have Loved, Hated, and Transformed American Culture
Since World War II

The Liberal Mind in a Conservative Age:
American Intellectuals in the 1940s and 1950s

Radical Visions and American Dreams:
Culture and Social Thought in the Depression Years

Cultural History Press

For Molly

because of her continuing faith in this book

CONTENTS

Preface

In 2009, I attended the fiftieth reunion of my high school class. We had graduated in 1959 from Southwest High School in Kansas City, Missouri—at the time one of the most highly-rated public high schools in the nation. Of my 400 classmates, approximately 250 showed up. Each of us contributed a one-page autobiography for a booklet commemorating our lives and adult triumphs.

All of us had been born in 1940 or 1941. We had been young children during World War II and the early postwar years, and teenagers in the 1950s. Most of us—men as well as women—had graduated from college in 1963, and then gone on to pursue careers in law, medicine, business, or teaching, while also raising families. In short, we had enjoyed reasonably successful lives.

It occurred to me, however, that no one had ever written about us as a distinctive generation. There have been plenty of books about the adults who suffered through the Great Depression and World War II, and then thrived in the late 1940s and 1950s (I've written two of those books myself). And the baby boomers—those born soon after the war, or in the 1950s and 1960s—have been chronicled endlessly, maybe more than they deserve. But for those who were born between 1939 and 1945, the people I call war babies, there is a notable absence of recognition of their special existence and a lack of analysis of their achievements.

So as I began to contemplate a book about the war babies, and started to do research, I was astounded by how many members of this generation became leaders in American cultural and political life over the past fifty years. The list of war baby luminaries who helped create or reshape modern America is illustrious.

In popular music, for example, the war babies include Bob Dylan, Joan Baez, Paul Simon and Art Garfunkel, Judy Collins, Joni Mitchell, Janis Joplin, and Barbra Streisand, as well as in Britain the Beatles and the Rolling Stones. Among the major film directors are Francis Ford Coppola, Martin Scorsese, and George Lucas, in addition to extraordinary actors like Robert De Niro, Al Pacino, Faye Dunaway, Harrison

Ford, Lily Tomlin, Christopher Walken, Harvey Keitel, Martin Sheen, and Joe Pesci.

In journalism, Bob Woodward and Carl Bernstein, Tom Brokaw, George Will, and Roger Ailes were all war babies. Jesse Jackson and John Lewis, both war babies, were indispensable to the civil rights movement, as were Mario Savio and Tom Hayden to the emergence of a new type of radicalism in the 1960s. Two of the war baby athletes, Muhammad Ali and Billie Jean King, transcended their respective sports and became transformative figures in the larger society. And among the war babies who have had a significant impact on domestic politics and American foreign policy are John Kerry, Dick Cheney, Joe Biden, Nancy Pelosi, Barney Frank, and Richard Holbrooke.

Given this roster, it is difficult to conceive of a generation that had a greater effect on America's music, movies, journalism, and politics. These were people who experienced as children the most global war in human history, followed in their adolescence by the Cold War and McCarthyism. As adults, they played crucial roles in the liberation of African Americans from a century of segregation, the opposition to the Vietnam War, Watergate and the destruction of a Presidential administration, and later American wars in Iraq and Afghanistan. Along the way, they revolutionized America's music and its movies. And they invented a culture and a politics that were more personal and individualistic than those of their parents. So the war babies are a special generation whose contributions to American life we have all come to share.

I do not intend this book as a sociological study of all the people born between 1939 and 1945. Instead, I am principally interested in those who were instrumental in altering the country's culture and politics during the past half-century. I want to show the elements in American life that influenced them as they were growing up in the 1940s and 1950s, and how they used those influences to change America once they reached adulthood.

Normally, "generations" are defined over a longer time span. Yet the conception of a generation need not always encompass fifteen- or twenty-year eras. The notion of a generation depends on what its members jointly lived through and accomplished. So the war babies constitute a unique generation not only because they were born during World War II, but because their experiences were different from their elders who endured the Great Depression or their children who emerged during the postwar baby boom, especially in the 1960s.

Moreover, the war babies were not simply contemporaries who happened to be born around the same time. Many of them were friends and professional associates (as in the instances of Francis Ford Coppola, Martin Scorsese, and George Lucas, as well as Bob Woodward and Carl Bernstein, or Nancy Pelosi and Barney Frank). Occasionally they were classmates attending the same schools who discovered they had similar interests and ambitions (like Paul Simon and Art Garfunkel). Or they were participants in the same political causes (like Tom Hayden, Mario Savio, John Lewis, and Jesse Jackson). Hence, the war babies matured during the same years, and worked intimately with one another as adults—whether in movies, music, journalism, or politics.

My book rests on four central themes. First, the war babies—not the generation of the Depression and World War II, or the baby boomers—produced the culture and the political attitudes we have all been living with ever since.

Second, the war babies were the architects of a value system that was less communal and more private, and more suspicious of the benefits of government policy, political power, and organizations of all types than were the members of what Tom Brokaw labeled the "greatest generation." For the war babies, the idea of community that had animated their parents became by the 1950s and 1960s the fear of conformity. Consequently, the war babies' efforts to change American society coincided with a quest for identity, an introspectiveness especially noticeable in the music of Bob Dylan, Joni Mitchell, Judy Collins, and Simon and Garfunkel. For the war babies, the realization of selfhood, the urge to distinguish oneself from the "lonely crowd," coincided with a desire to transform their country's institutions.

Third, the war babies' perspective on America was darker and more pessimistic than either their predecessors or their baby boom successors, yet it was precisely this skepticism that characterizes American culture and politics today. Fourth, the attitudes of the war babies were primarily exemplified in their movies, music, journalism, and politics, attitudes that the baby boomers and their descendants absorbed but did not originate.

I also want to make two secondary but equally important points. First, McCarthyism had a much more limited reverberation on American culture in the 1950s than historians customarily contend, a marginality that thereby permitted the war babies to experiment freely with their lives and ideas. Still, the McCarthy experience did inspire the war babies' suspicions about government agencies, a cynicism that led them later on to be the major critics of governmental conspiracies and deceptions in the epoch of Vietnam and Watergate.

Second, the changes in American life began not in the turbulent 1960s but in the calmer but no less vibrant 1950s, the years when the war babies moved from adolescence to young adulthood. In this sense, the war babies were never a "silent" generation—assuming such a phenomenon really existed in the 1950s.

In sum, the members of the "greatest generation" were chiefly survivors, both of the Depression and World War II. And they helped construct a prosperous postwar America. The baby boomers inherited that America, and confronted a blizzard of technological innovations, new waves of immigrants, the excessive accumulation of debt, and intermittent cataclysms in the stock market.

But the war babies were the champions of cultural and political renovation. Their art and their activities transfigured modern America. Because of what they attained, they were as decisive as any generation in the history of the United States. So I regard this book as a tribute to, as well as a critical examination of, the central role the war babies played in inventing a new America.

CHAPTER 1

A Child's Eye View of World War II

ON MAY 30, 2012, A LARGE PICTURE of Bob Dylan receiving the Medal of Freedom from Barack Obama appeared on the front page of the *Wall Street Journal*. On the same day, on the editorial page of the *New York Times*, the columnist Thomas Friedman had a long article on Paul Simon, celebrating Simon's contributions to global music. Both the photograph and the column affirmed the transformative effect that Dylan and Simon had on popular music, both in the United States and abroad.

Bob Dylan and Paul Simon were both war babies, each born in 1941. They were members of an exceptional generation, born between 1939 and 1945, exceptional because they and their wartime contemporaries reshaped American music, movies, journalism, and politics from the 1960s on. They were also, by the time they were young adults, colleagues, close friends, and in some instances lovers (as in the case of Bob Dylan and Joan Baez). They all knew one another and what each was accomplishing in their respective fields. In short, these war babies shared similar experiences as children, adolescents, and adults—experiences that inspired them to revolutionize modern American culture and politics.

I call this generation "war babies" because they were born during World War II. But the Second World War was by no means the only war they experienced. They watched the Korean War on television and in magazines and movies; and some of them served in Vietnam, either as soldiers (like John Kerry) or as foreign service officers (like Richard Holbrooke). Above all, they lived through the tensest, most terrifying years of the Cold War in the 1950s, when nuclear incineration was not an abstraction but a real possibility which they were aware of every day of their teenage years.

It is a commonplace, cited in innumerable books and essays, that the post-World War II baby boomers were the crucial generation in remaking America. This assertion has become too often an accepted cliché that bears little relation to the realities of the boomers' lives. First of all, the notion of a baby boom generation is too nebulous a concept to encompass people who were born from the late 1940s until the mid-1960s. It made a vast difference whether one was born in 1949 or 1961. The boomers who were born in the late 1940s or early 1950s had experiences that were quite dissimilar from those born in the late 1950s or early 1960s. Indeed, if you were born in 1960, you didn't experience the 1950s at all, and you were still a child during the turmoil of the 1960s.

But whenever a boomer was born, the simplest yet most important difference between them and the war babies is that the boomers were too young to have participated in the events or ignited the cultural changes that defined modern America. Most of the war babies entered college in 1958 or 1959, and spent their early adulthood during the Kennedy years, a more undamaged era, a different "cooler" 1960s than the tumultuous years of the Vietnam War. Nevertheless, they were old enough (as the baby boomers were not) to help galvanize the civil rights movement of the early 1960s. The boomers were too young to organize and speak at the March on Washington in 1963, like John Lewis who was chair of the Student Non-Violent Coordinating Committee (SNCC). The boomers were too young to endanger their lives in the summer of 1964 traveling to Mississippi to register African American voters (like Lewis, Tom Hayden, and Barney Frank). Nor did any boomers become murder victims that summer, like James Chaney, Michael Schwerner, and Andrew Goodman—all of them born between 1939 and 1943 (and in Goodman's case, a college classmate and friend of Paul Simon's). The boomers were also too young to have written the "Port Huron Statement" (as did Tom Hayden in 1962), the founding document of the Students for a Democratic Society and the New Left. And the boomers were too young to be at Berkeley in 1964, when the first student upheavals at an American university were led by a war baby like Mario Savio.

Culturally, the baby boomers were too young to have introduced a new form of popular music to America, starting in the early 1960s, as did Judy Collins, Joan Baez, Bob Dylan, Joni Mitchell, and Simon and Garfunkel. No boomer would have appeared at cabarets in New York or at the first Newport Folk Festivals, or began to make best-selling record albums in 1961 and 1962 like Judy Collins, Joan Baez, and Bob Dylan. Nor would a boomer have been asked (as was Paul Simon) to contribute his songs to the score for a movie like *The Graduate* in 1967, making it impossible to imagine that movie without "The Sound of Silence" or "Scarborough Fair," not to mention the chords for "Mrs. Robinson." Indeed, almost all the music we associate with the 1960s and early 1970s was created not by baby boomers but by war babies: Barbra Streisand, Janis Joplin, Carole King, Jim Morrison of The Doors, Jerry Garcia of The Grateful Dead, Grace Slick of The Jefferson Airplane.

Neither were the boomers old enough to start making movies of their own in the late 1960s, like Francis Ford Coppola, Martin Scorsese, and George Lucas. And then gone on in the 1970s to create a "new" Hollywood, an American movie renaissance filled with personal films like Coppola's *The Godfather: Parts I and II*, *The Conversation*, and *Apocalypse Now*; Scorsese's *Mean Streets*, *Taxi Driver*, and *Raging Bull*; Lucas's *American Graffiti* and *Star Wars*; or Michael Cimino's *The Deer Hunter*.

Politically, the boomers were too young to experience McCarthyism, either on television in the Army-McCarthy hearings or in real life (like Carl Bernstein). They were too young to have come home from Vietnam (like John Kerry) to denounce before the Senate Foreign Relations Committee the horrors the war was inflicting on both the Vietnamese people and on American soldiers. Neither would they have attended the first (unsuccessful) Paris Peace Conference in 1968 to negotiate a settlement to the the war with the North Vietnamese, like Richard Holbrooke did as an assistant to Averell Harriman. Moreover, no boomer—even one graduating from college in the early 1970s—had the opportunity (like Bob Woodward and Carl Bernstein) to work for the *Washington Post* and help unravel the most important political story of the twentieth century. And it is unlikely that any boomer would have spent enough time in Congress to emerge as the first woman Speaker of the House (like Nancy Pelosi), or served as the most powerful Vice-President in American history (like Dick Cheney).

Most of all, the baby boomers grew up in a very different America from the country into which the war babies were born. The baby boomers knew nothing but prosperity, in their youth and adulthood. But the war babies were still children in an America disfigured by the Great Depression. The impact of the Depression, as conveyed to them by their parents, served as a perpetual warning in their minds about the economic insecurities of the future.

It is true that by 1940, as America converted from civilian to military production, the Depression—at least economically—ended, and unemployment dropped by 1942 to one percent of the population. But none of these changes affected the daily lives of the war babies or their parents. They were all still living in a nation of scarcity, privation, and sacrifice, no matter whether they had jobs and were now earning decent incomes. There was very little to spend their wartime money on. You couldn't buy a new car or a new house (there was almost no residential construction during World War II), or indulge in an orgy of consumerism that typified American life after 1945. So the war babies were the inheritors of the Depression psychology—of the need to save, to avoid debt, to postpone material gratification, to constantly plan for a future that might be unpleasant—lessons they internalized throughout their adult lives, and which the baby boomers, born in a more affluent time, never absorbed.

Feeling poor, as did the war babies and their parents, meant living in cities in tiny apartments. Or in rural America, in farmhouses that were sometimes a century old. Feeling poor meant relying on mass transit to get anywhere. Feeling poor meant depending primarily on the radio for any connection to the outside world. In fact, the war babies were the last generation to grow up on and be entertained by network radio, still in its golden age, at least until the 1950s and the emergence of television. Feeling poor meant walking to a neighborhood movie theater to glimpse a different universe from the one you existed in every day. And being poor meant depending on yourself for whatever fantasies and dream worlds you yearned for beyond the boundaries of your constricted daily environment.

But out of their experiences as children and adolescents, the war babies discovered talents that they often developed on their own. And over time, they became the major filmmakers, actors, songwriters, journalists, and politicians in the America of the past-half century. Hence, they were an extraordinary generation whose childhood, adolescence, and adult activities distinguished them from their Depression predecessors and baby boom successors. In effect, the war babies were a generation as important as any in American history, creating a new more personal culture and a new more individualistic politics with which we all still live today.

The Birth of a Generation

Most of the war babies were born between 1939 and 1944. Thus they all had, once they became aware of it, a recognition that they were members of a similar generation, with comparable memories and ambitions.

I myself was born in 1941. A month before Pearl Harbor. At the time, of course, I didn't know I was a war baby. Like many members of my generation, I don't remember when I realized America was at war. But I do recall, probably when I was two or three years old, playing with toy soldiers and screeching "bang, bang, shoot the Japs."

Yet it wasn't the "Japs" that my parents or grandmother primarily cared about. For them, all Jewish, America was at war with Nazi Germany. Like the relatives of many Jewish war babies, my grandmother had fled the pogroms in Poland in the first decade of the twentieth century. She emigrated to Kansas City, Missouri, which was home to a substantial Jewish community, and where I was born. She encouraged her oldest son, my father, to become a violinist, and took him to Berlin to study, just before the rise of Hitler—not the most propitious moment to be a Jew, even an American Jew, in a land about to be enveloped in swastikas. My grandmother and father swiftly returned to Kansas City, but not without a foreboding of the slaughters to come.

My background was similar to those of other war babies—especially in the sense that most of us were the children or grandchildren of immigrants, or in some cases refugees from Nazi Germany or Eastern Europe. And the sensitivity to ethnic ties influenced our childhoods because we grew up among people in our families and neighborhoods who shared our immigrant heritage.

All my parents' friends, for example, were Jewish musicians, and most of them had Americanized their last names—for "professional" reasons I was told. My father, searching for work in New York in the 1930s, abbreviated his name from Pelofsky to Pells. Ultimately, with the help of a WPA subsidy, he was offered a position in 1938 with the Kansas City Philharmonic. Another violinist with the Philharmonic was originally Josef Lefkowitz until he became Joe Landes. The timpanist—a diminutive, wiry drummer whose legs and hands could never stop quivering, as if he were keeping time to an inner rhythm that only he heard—was once Benjamin Udelowitz before he turned into Ben Udell.

It was not simply my parents' generation that was sensitive to the prospect of their names sounding too obviously Jewish. Simon and Garfunkel originally performed in the 1950s as Tom and Jerry, as non-ethnic an appellation as one could invent. And Carole King was originally Carole Klein before adopting King from a telephone directory as a less Semitic stage name.

These alterations, at least in the 1930s and early 1940s, were motivated not just by the need for professional convenience. They were also a response to, or a premonition about, the risks of anti-Semitism in America. The Jewish executives who ran the Hollywood studios in the 1930s were similarly aware of the possibilities of anti-Semitism. So Jews as characters in movies were invisible, while Jewish actors like Emanuel Goldenberg reappeared as Edward G. Robinson, Melvyn Hesselberg changed into Melvyn Douglas, and Julius Garfinkle (the name he used when he was in the Group Theater in the 1930s) became John Garfield in the movies. At the same time, the head of MGM, Louis B. Mayer, originally a Jewish immigrant from Minsk, always asserted his Americanness by claiming—without any evidence—that he was born on the Fourth of July.

Beyond the reticence about Jewishness in Hollywood and among my parents and their friends was a larger tendency during the late 1930s and the war years for people of all ethnicities to try to identify with America, with the benevolence of the federal government under Franklin Roosevelt, and with the country's core traditions and values. This was an era filled with celebrations of America's past. One could see it reflected in the vogue of best-selling multivolume biographies of America's historical heroes, in the popularity of *Gone with the Wind* and Thornton Wilder's *Our Town*, in the Federal Music Project's rediscovery of nineteenth century folk songs and sea chanteys, and in the mythic small-town America commemorated in the paintings of Norman Rockwell. These images of cultural and political nationalism reinforced the notion, particularly during the war, that whatever our backgrounds we were all components of a nationwide community, with shared aspirations, shared freedoms, and in wartime a shared devotion to a national cause.

This spirit of cohesion among otherwise disparate groups and classes was also dramatized in Hollywood's portrayal of the multi-ethnic platoons that, at least in the movies, fought World War II. Even as a young child, I could recognize the images of national solidarity that pervaded the advertisements in the *Kansas City Star* and *Life* magazine, with their photos or drawings of soldiers smoking Lucky Strikes or swigging down Coca-Cola as a contribution, somehow, to the war effort. And I accompanied my parents, like so many other war babies, as they collected what was euphemistically called "scrap metal" (mostly discarded junk) to donate to the country's industrial production.

On a more serious note, my father—though a musician by trade—was exempt from the draft because he got a job as an inspector of airplane parts at a local Bendix plant. In that role, he really was an important factor in helping to win the war, his expertise a reminder that we were all participants—even as civilians—in the crusade against the Nazis and imperial Japan.

Meanwhile, for children like me who couldn't read the headlines or stories about particular battles, or understand the reports from war correspondents on the radio, World War II was an adventure experienced mostly through the maps that appeared in newspapers and magazines. Although the war in the Pacific was too difficult to follow, with struggles over islands none of us could locate or pronounce, the war in Europe was more easily comprehensible and more vivid. We could tell who was winning or losing the war by the colors on the maps that first showed the expanse of German conquest, and then the shrinking of the Nazi domain as "our" armies liberated Rome and Paris.

For succeeding generations like the baby boomers that lived through the war in Vietnam, or the protracted conflicts in Iraq and Afghanistan, there were no such maps that could illuminate the flow of victory and defeat. Which is why casualty figures and "body counts" became the sole indication of who was winning or losing. But those World War II maps were also the war babies' first introduction to the world outside the United States, the world my grandmother had left and to which Americans were now returning, eventually to try to recast Europe and Japan into our own national image.

I call the war an "adventure" for us because we did not suffer from the sort of devastation that ravaged civilians in Europe and Asia. Nor did we have any conception—even if we lost fathers or uncles in combat—of what World War II was actually like for those American soldiers who fought in North Africa, Europe, or the Pacific. We could sense from our parents and grandparents that we were born in and living through a momentous time. But unlike our contemporaries in London, Rotterdam, Stalingrad, or Berlin, we had no direct experience of bombs exploding, fires billowing, buildings disintegrating, rubble piling up in the streets, or armies thundering in tanks through our neighborhoods.

We—and this included all Americans on the home front—did not encounter the terrors of modern warfare, of cities and villages devastated, or of populations uprooted and terrorized by the specter of air-raids and death camps. So for the war babies, all we could do was view the war through the wide if not entirely innocent eyes of children, unaware that we were about to inherit a world fundamentally different from, and infinitely more complicated than, the one in which our parents had grown up.

The early experiences of the war babies—especially those who went on to exert a major impact on American culture and politics—were not necessarily identical to mine. But there were some uncanny similarities.

Most of the war babies who grew up to be artistic or political luminaries came from ethnic, if not always Jewish, backgrounds. Some were the children of musicians or artists. And many displayed an early talent for or fascination with the vocations that would mark their adult lives.

Francis Ford Coppola was born in Detroit in 1939. His paternal grandparents were Italian émigrés, though (perhaps as evidence of the family's Americanization) Coppola received his middle name in honor of Henry Ford. Coppola's father, Carmine, was like my father a musician—in his case a flutist first for the Detroit Symphony Orchestra and then (once the family moved to New York) for the NBC Symphony Orchestra under the direction of Arturo Toscanini. Carmine was also an aspiring composer who later worked on the scores for *The Godfather: Parts I and II* and *Apocalypse Now*. As a child, Francis contracted polio—the most dreaded disease of the first half of the twentieth century. Confined to a bed, he created a puppet theater, a traditional form of Italian entertainment, and one he reproduced in the early twentieth-century segment of *The Godfather: Part II*. The experience of polio also taught Coppola how to flourish alone, entertaining himself—an example of the reliance on one's own personality, instincts, and emotional resources, a trait that characterized so many of the members of the war baby generation.[1]

Coppola's childhood was not substantially different from that of Martin Scorsese, who was born in 1942 in Queens. Scorsese's grandparents on his father's side had emigrated from Sicily. As a boy, Scorsese like Coppola was ill; he had severe asthma (as did I) and was unable to play sports or engage in other physically demanding activities. Moreover, in the 1940s treatments for asthma (like allergy shots and vaporizers) were primitive and frequently futile. All a child afflicted with asthma could do was hope to be able to breathe without constantly panting for air. Usually, when the origins of a disease are unknown, doctors attribute the cause to a person's psychology. Certainly, asthma affects a child's temperament. So Scorsese was isolated from other people, a lonesome introvert spending much of his childhood staring out the window of his house and later his apartment in Little Italy in Manhattan (to which his parents moved after the war) at the street life teeming below. As an escape from his cloistered surroundings, his father often took him to the movies (as did my parents), where Scorsese first discovered a passion for an art form that shaped the rest of his life.[2]

In fact, Scorsese began as a young child to draw cartoons and then scenes from the movies he saw, almost as if he were creating story-boards for a film of his own. Like Coppola, Scorsese learned early on to depend on his own visual fantasies and imagination.[3] Consequently, Scorsese could not decide early in his life whether he wanted to be a painter, a filmmaker, or a priest. But what he did do, as an adult, was capture in his movies the vibrancy and violence of the streets in Little Italy.

Michael Cimino, another descendant of Italian-Americans whose father was a music publisher, was born in New York in 1939. Cimino was never as illustrious or as successful a filmmaker as Coppola or Scorsese. Early in his life, he hoped to be a painter rather than a film director. He did, however, direct one of the most emotionally wrenching movies of the 1970s, this one about another equally catastrophic conflict, the war in Vietnam. *The Deer Hunter* starred two other war babies—Robert

De Niro and Christopher Walken, both born in 1943. *The Deer Hunter* was only Cimino's second film, but he won the Oscar for best director, and Walken received an Oscar as best supporting actor.

Meanwhile, across the continent, George Lucas was born in Modesto, California in 1944, and in time became one of Francis Ford Coppola's protégés. In Modesto, Lucas soon developed a youthful infatuation with hot-rods and car races, an enthusiasm he later memorialized in *American Graffiti*. Like Coppola and Scorsese, Lucas used his childhood and the culture in which he grew up as a subject for his early movies.

Not every war baby associated with the movies became a director, though many of them did trace their lineage to Italy. Al Pacino was born in 1940 in New York to Italian-American parents (like Coppola and Scorsese). Pacino's parents divorced when he was two years old, and his mother moved to the South Bronx to live with her parents, who came from—if you can believe it—Corleone, Sicily. Robert De Niro was also born in New York, three years after Pacino; his background was both Italian and Irish, and he grew up (along with Scorsese) in the Little Italy section of Manhattan. De Niro's father, like Coppola's, was an artist, but not a musician; instead he was a painter initially influenced by the Abstract Expressionists of the 1940s and a sculptor, while De Niro's mother was a painter and poet.

Faye Dunaway came from an entirely different background than Pacino and De Niro. But like them, as well as Coppola and Scorsese, the patterns of Dunaway's life and personality were shaped early in her childhood. Born in 1941 in relatively impoverished conditions in Florida, Dunaway picked cotton as a child, all the while (at the urging of her mother) dreaming of a better life. From the beginning she had a difficult, painful relationship with her father. He was a career soldier who served in the war and stayed in the army afterwards, while also having affairs with other women, which meant that he was rarely at home. The closest Dunaway came to her father during World War II was by listening to battle reports on the radio.

All of these experiences inspired in Dunaway an early ambition to flee from her feelings of childhood alienation, to escape to the big city (preferably New York) and become a star, a celebrity. So she decided at the age of five that she wanted to be an actress and began taking dancing and singing classes, enthralled by the chance to perform on stage.[4] It was precisely these incipient influences that prepared her for the movie role of a lifetime in 1967, as Bonnie Parker in *Bonnie and Clyde*, another desperate, lonely young woman who hungers for fame. Bonnie became Dunaway's signature role, one that not only in fact made her a movie star but the most idiosyncratic actress of her generation. Indeed, Dunaway was born to play not only Bonnie but also Evelyn Mulwray, the woman damaged irreparably by her father (John Huston's Noah Cross) in *Chinatown* (1974).

While the majority of directors and actors (with the exception of Dunaway and George Lucas) were born or reared in New York, the war babies who became singers and composers had more eclectic roots. Judy Collins was born in Seattle in 1939. She started piano lessons when she was five years old, practicing Chopin and Debussy in the belief that she might some day become a serious classical pianist. But she also sang along with music on the radio, in her church choir, and for anyone who would listen. Like Faye Dunaway, Collins adored performing, cavorting on stage, watching the reaction of people in the audience. She was a child envisioning what it might feel like to be a show business idol.

Collins's interest in music was prompted by her father, who was blind but had started a dance band and sang in nightclubs in the 1930s, and had his own radio program during the early years of the war, playing records and interviewing musicians. Ultimately, in 1943, Collins's father was hired by NBC for a show broadcast from Hollywood. There he took Collins to meet or watch radio superstars like Bob Hope and Red Skelton.

Yet Collins had another cultural influence in her milieu, though in this case the stimulus was literary rather than musical. Her godfather was named Holden. He met J.D. Salinger in the army during World

War II, and Salinger eventually named his most famous creation, Holden Caulfield in *The Catcher in the Rye*, after Collins's godfather.

Like so many children in the 1940s, Collins caught polio, in her case at the age of ten, but recovered within two months.[5] My own parents were terrified of the disease and when my father spent the summer of 1946 in Corpus Christi, Texas, playing with a band after the symphony season in Kansas City ended, my mother refused to accompany him for fear that the South was a particular breeding ground for the virus. There was no evidence for this, but the anxiety was rampant nonetheless.

The panic about polio would not subside until the inventions of the Salk and Sabin vaccines in 1955 and 1957. Hence the baby boomers of the late 1950s and 1960s never had to face the specter lurking over them of paralysis, withered legs, and iron lungs, a specter the war babies lived with throughout their childhoods and adolescence.

In the meantime, Robert Zimmerman was born in 1941 in Duluth, remained healthy, and spent his childhood after the war in Hibbing, Minnesota. His paternal and maternal grandparents were Jewish refugees from Odessa and Lithuania, escaping the pogroms (like my grandmother) at the dawn of the twentieth century. Like many war babies who became filmmakers or songwriters, Zimmerman came from a musical background; his father played violin. Zimmerman's father also had polio but worked for Standard Oil so he was exempt from the war. Zimmerman's uncles, however, were soldiers who survived combat and returned home, though (as with most veterans) they were reluctant ever to discuss their often grisly experiences in the war.

Zimmerman himself, even as a child, was taciturn, remote, and secretive—qualities that would mark his persona as an adult. He devoted a good part of his youth listening to blues and country music on the radio.[6] By the late 1950s, as he embarked on his own singing career, Zimmerman renamed himself Bob Dylan, in honor of one of his favorite writers, Dylan Thomas.

Dylan's closest contemporary as a singer was Joan Baez, who nurtured his early career and was, episodically, his lover. Born in 1941 on

Staten Island to a Mexican father and Scottish mother, Baez soon moved with her parents to Menlo Park, California where her father studied at Stanford for a Master's degree in mathematics and taught military engineers during the war. Her father, though, was a pacifist who, despite his background in math and physics, refused to work on the atomic bomb at Los Alamos. His pacifism obviously influenced Baez who became a lifelong pacifist herself.

While in California, Baez began experimenting as a child with rhythm and blues on a ukulele. From childhood, she was also blessed with an exquisite singing voice—one she learned early to develop as a way of fitting in, as half-Mexican, with her white cohorts.[7] Though Baez was born in the New York area, along with many other war babies who became prominent singers and songwriters, her exodus to California meant that she met none of them until she moved to Boston in 1958, where she began by the early 1960s to achieve as much if not more fame than they did.

Among the most talented of the New York composers was Paul Simon. Born in Newark in 1941, Simon grew up in Forest Hills in Queens. Like Francis Ford Coppola, Simon came from a family of professional musicians. His parents emigrated from Hungary in the 1930s. Simon's father had been a first violinist with an orchestra on a Budapest radio station, and played bass with bands in Manhattan once he arrived in America, while Simon's mother gave music lessons on the harp both in Hungary and New York. Simon loved to listen to his father perform in bands, and was especially attracted to rumbas and sambas (increasingly popular in the 1940s). Simon would later expand on this fascination with exotic rhythms when he started experimenting with Latin American and African music in the 1970s.

But Simon had another passion as well—this one for the New York Yankees and particularly for Joe DiMaggio, one of the most elegant and charismatic of all the baseball players of the 1940s.[8] So it was not surprising that "where have you gone Joe DiMaggio" would become Simon's most famous lyric in "Mrs. Robinson" in 1968.

When Simon was eleven years old, he became friends with a class-mate, Art Garfunkel, also born in 1941 and living in Queens just three blocks away from Simon (although each had been aware of the other since the third grade). Garfunkel's grandparents had migrated to America from Romania, so both he and Simon came from similar Jewish backgrounds and harbored similar musical ambitions, which Garfunkel's parents (like Simon's) encouraged.[9] Once they discovered that they appreciated each other's voices in harmony, they started to perform as a teenage duo in the 1950s in school and before audiences, even making a recording—all this before they emerged in the 1960s as two of the most poetic singers of the war baby generation.

The ingenuity of their lyrics and compositions was matched by Joni Mitchell (whose name originally was Roberta Joan Anderson). Mitchell was not born in New York or in the United States, but in Canada in 1943. Nonetheless, she was a war baby with strong ties to America. Her father, whose ancestors came to Canada from Norway, served in World War II in the Royal Canadian Air Force, teaching pilots to fly. He was also an amateur musician (like Bob Dylan's father) who played trumpet and worshipped the swing bands of the 1930s. At the same time, her mother instilled in Mitchell a sensitivity to poetic language, especially as exemplified in Shakespeare.

Later, at the age of eight in 1951, Mitchell caught polio (like Francis Ford Coppola and Judy Collins), and began singing in the hospital. Her response to the disease as well as the musical and literary interests of her parents were the origins of her career as a sophisticated singer and composer who shaped American music as much as Dylan, and Simon and Garfunkel.

Indeed, foreign (especially British) singer/songwriters, all the same age as those across the Atlantic, had an enormous influence on their American counterparts. All the Beatles as well as Mick Jagger and Keith Richards of the Rolling Stones were born between 1940 and 1943. And so they became members of an international war baby generation, developing close personal and professional ties especially with Bob Dylan and Paul Simon.

As with most of the American war babies who became filmmakers or singers and composers, Carole King came from both an immigrant and a musical background. King's Jewish grandparents emigrated to Brooklyn from Poland and Russia. Her grandmother hoped that King's mother would become a classical pianist. King herself was born in New York in 1942, and the most valued piece of furniture in her home was a piano. King began making up songs on the piano when she was three years old, and started her first piano lessons when she was four. At the same time, King's mother took her, as a young child, to Broadway musicals, and collected cast recordings of shows like *Oklahoma!* and *Carousel*, to which King eagerly and repeatedly listened.[10] All of these childhood experiences were the catalyst for King's emergence as a major songwriter and performer in the 1960s and 1970s.

Similarly, Jerry Garcia had music in his genes. His father came to America from Spain and was a professional musician, playing clarinet in bands in the 1930s. Garcia's father named his son, born in 1942, after Jerome Kern as a tribute to the composers of what was then known as the great American songbook. Garcia's mother was an amateur pianist, while his grandmother loved listening to the Grand Ole Opry on the radio. So Garcia was exposed to all sorts of music as a child.[11]

What was crucial about the singers born between 1939 and 1943 was how much they modernized popular music in America, a music that had previously relied on the compositions of George Gershwin, Cole Porter, Irving Berlin, Jerome Kern, and Rodgers and Hart. Essentially, the war babies—particularly Judy Collins, Joan Baez, Bob Dylan, Simon and Garfunkel, Joni Mitchell, and Carole King—emerged as the new voices of the 1960s and 1970s, supplanting Frank Sinatra, Bing Crosby, and Ella Fitzgerald as the creators and interpreters of a different and more intricate American songbook.

In addition to their effect on movies and music, the war babies would ultimately have a profound impact on journalism. During the war, their parents depended on newspapers, magazines, newsreels in movie theaters, and above all the radio for reports of air raids on Britain and later on Germany, and for battles raging in North Africa, Italy, France, Russia, and the atolls in the Pacific. By the late 1940s, as children, we ourselves became familiar with the resonant voices and eccentric cadences of Edward R. Murrow, H. V. Kaltenborn, Gabriel Heatter, and Walter Winchell. They transported the world, whether in Washington, D.C., New York, London, Berlin, or Tokyo, into our kitchens and living rooms.

Winchell began his broadcasts by pressing urgently on a telegraph key before greeting his audience with the inimitable "Good evening Mr. and Mrs. America from border to border and coast to coast and all the ships at sea. Let's go to press." Out in South Dakota, one of Mr. and Mrs. America's children was Tom Brokaw, born in 1940, who could only imagine through the radio what it must have been like to be a denizen of Winchell's Broadway nightclubs.

Brokaw's parents, like those of other war babies, were shaped by the Great Depression. They were incurably thrifty; they recycled food, saved old clothes, and were reluctant (as were my parents) to buy anything that wasn't absolutely necessary. Brokaw's father remained a civilian in World War II but contributed to the military effort by working at an ordnance depot and as a construction foreman for the Army Corps of Engineers. Brokaw himself remembered the wartime blackouts in his hometown, even though there was no possibility that German or Japanese planes were about to bomb South Dakota.[12] The blackouts, all over the country, were really a way of reminding people on the home front that they too were at war.

Brokaw, from childhood on, admired the resilience and values of his parents and their contemporaries who survived the Depression and World War II, and built a more prosperous America after the war. It was Brokaw who later called them "the greatest generation" as the title of his best-selling book in 1998. Yet despite his esteem for his parents' fortitude, and his continuing affection for the rural remoteness of South Dakota, the experience of listening to the news on the radio eventually bred in Brokaw an ambition (like Faye Dunaway) to escape to the bright lights and urban exhilaration of Walter Winchell's world, and to some day become a journalist, or at least a media personality, himself.

Still as much as the war babies and their parents depended on radio for local, national, and international news, no form of information diminished the authority of print journalism, whether in newspapers or in magazines like *Time, Newsweek, Life, Look,* and the *Saturday Evening Post.* As a result of this influence, two of the newspaper reporters who gained fame untangling the political mystery story of the twentieth century were war babies: Bob Woodward, born in 1943 in Illinois, and Carl Bernstein, born a year later in Washington, D.C.

Unlike the team of Simon and Garfunkel, Woodward and Bernstein could not have come from more dissimilar backgrounds. Woodward's father was impeccably Republican, a lawyer and later a judge who commanded respect from his Midwestern middle-class friends.

On the other hand, Bernstein's parents, both Jewish, were embodiments of the Old Left in the 1930s and 1940s. Their politics were defined by the Depression and the threat of Nazism. Bernstein's mother raised money for the Loyalists during the Spanish Civil War from 1936 to 1939. Bernstein's father was committed to the trade union movement; he believed the unions would transform American society. It was natural, therefore, that Bernstein's mother and father joined the American Communist Party in the early 1940s because of the Party's support for the working class and for the civil rights of African Americans, and also because by this time the Soviet Union had become America's ally in World War II. Although Bernstein's parents were not involved in the inner workings of the Party (Bernstein's mother thought the Party's interminable meetings were mind-numbing), and they drifted away from the Party by the late 1940s, their activities later appeared treacherous during the McCarthy era.[13] So Bernstein had some experience as an adolescent with the intimidating power of the federal government long before Watergate.

Other war babies grew up to engage in political activities that were often deemed suspicious by local or state institutions. John Lewis, born in Alabama in 1940, was the child of sharecroppers. The poverty in which he was raised and the hard work that he as a child and his parents endured picking cotton and grappling with debt could have made his family characters in John Steinbeck's *The Grapes of Wrath* or James Agee's *Let Us Now Praise Famous Men*, Agee's monumental account of Alabama tenant farmers, published in 1941. Moreover, Lewis's world was implacably segregated; he saw only two white people until he was six years old and his parents taught him always to be wary around whites. Despite the unpromising prospects of his youth and his hatred of working in the fields, Lewis yearned for a better existence, which both his church and later school offered.

Lewis became instrumental (at the risk of his life) in the civil rights movement of the early 1960s, as did Jesse Jackson, born in equally bleak conditions as an "illegitimate" child in 1941 in South Carolina. Ironically, in view of the stirring speech-maker he was to become, Jackson stuttered as a child. Yet like Lewis, Jackson aspired to be a Baptist minister, in early recognition of how important black church leaders were in the civil rights movement.[14] Lewis ultimately became a Congressman from Georgia, while Jackson emerged as the first serious African American candidate for President, his campaigns in 1984 and 1988 a direct link to Barack Obama's election in 2008.

John Lewis and Jesse Jackson became successful civil rights activists, despite the difficulties they faced in their childhoods in an America divided by race. But perhaps no African American suffered more for his political and religious beliefs and actions than Cassius Clay. Clay was born in Louisville in 1942 in somewhat more comfortable circumstances than Lewis or Jackson, but in a city that was still segregated, obsessed with the differences between white and black Americans, an experience that shaped Clay from childhood on.[15] Clay, who later reinvented himself as Muhammad Ali, would ultimately be stripped of his heavyweight championship because of his refusal in 1967 to be drafted into the war in Vietnam. For that refusal, Ali became a global hero, as consequential an athlete for American whites and blacks as Jackie Robinson had been when he integrated major league baseball in 1947.

Where Lewis, Jackson, and Ali altered racial attitudes in America, Billie Jean King (originally Moffitt) helped transform the status not only of female tennis players but of women generally in American life. Born in 1943, King was the daughter of a conservative Republican, like Bob Woodward's father. Yet from an early age, she displayed little interest in acting like a traditional girl or woman, a nonconformity that intensified during her adolescence and adulthood.[16] This defiance of female stereo-types enabled King to confront the male tennis establishment as early as her teenage years, and to become a prime symbol of the feminism that emerged in America in the 1960s and 1970s.

Not all the political activists of the war baby generation were African Americans or women. Tom Hayden, born in Detroit in 1939, was the descendant of Irish immigrants. His father served in the Marines during World War II (though he was never sent overseas) and identi-fied throughout his life with ordinary people he thought were swindled by the malign power of American capitalism. Hayden himself emerged in the 1960s as a leader of the movement against the Vietnam War (and later as the husband of Jane Fonda). Three years after Hayden's birth, in 1942, Mario Savio was born in New York, the son of a Sicilian steel worker who also served in the war. Like Jesse Jackson, Savio stuttered as a child though also like Jackson he overcame this disability to become a major orator.[17] Savio wound up as a leader of the first student upheavals in the 1960s, at Berkeley in 1964 in what was called, reflecting the war babies' idealism of the early 1960s, the "free speech" movement.

Indeed, a number of war babies entered politics, to become prom-inent conservatives or liberals as adults. Dick Cheney, for example, was born in 1941 in Nebraska and grew up in Wyoming. His parents were resolute Democrats, though this seemed to have little impact on Cheney's career as a Republican ideologue. Nancy Pelosi was born in 1940 in Baltimore to an Italian-American family who were also (like Cheney's parents) long-time Democrats. Her father was a Congressman and then Mayor of Baltimore from whom Pelosi learned starting in childhood how to structure campaigns, serve local constituents, make deals, dispense and receive favors, build coalitions, and count votes as if she was a female Spencer Tracy in John Ford's movie version of *The Last Hurrah*.[18] These experiences formed her political outlook and tactics, helping her ultimately become the first woman Speaker of the House.

Among the most unconventional of the war baby politicians, however, was Barney Frank. Frank's heritage was somewhat dubious. He was born in 1940 in Bayonne, New Jersey to a liberal Democratic Jewish family whose ancestors were from Eastern Europe. But Frank's family also had vague mob connections; when Frank was a child, his father served a year in prison for refusing to testify before a grand jury in a bribery investigation against Frank's uncle.[19] Perhaps this is why Frank always sounded, even when I met him at Harvard in 1966, like a character in *The Sopranos*. But the experience of seeing his father resist the grand jury and serve time in jail also instilled in Frank a youthful suspicion of authority and an innate rebelliousness (traits common to many war babies) which he retained throughout his teenage years and into his political career. More important, Frank's announcement in 1987 that he was gay was not only an act of courage, but he made it increasingly respectable for gays and lesbians to become powerful participants in American public life.

John Kerry affected a more upper-class accent and demeanor than Barney Frank, although his family was not wealthy and he first rose to prominence as an anti-Vietnam War activist. As a child, however, Kerry had an intimate association with World War II. Kerry was born in 1943 in Colorado, the son of a high altitude test pilot in the Army Air Corps during the war who later became a foreign service officer. Kerry's mother was a wartime nurse. Kerry's immediate family was Roman Catholic, and his parents instilled in him a robust sense of public service. But his paternal grandparents were originally Jewish though they converted to Catholicism and emigrated to the United States from the Austro-Hungarian empire in 1905, adopting the name of Kerry by dropping a pencil on a map of Ireland, which fell on County Kerry. Kerry's great-uncle and great-aunt were not so fortunate; both perished in the concentration camps. Kerry did not learn about his Jewish heritage until he was preparing to run for President in 2003.[20]

The war baby, however, who was to have the greatest effect on American policy, at least abroad, did not grow up to be a professional politician although he turned out to be supremely adept at bureaucratic intrigue. Richard Holbrooke was born in New York in 1941. His mother's Jewish family had fled Hamburg in 1933 after Hitler came to power. His father managed to escape to the United States from Warsaw in 1939, just as World War II was beginning and where Poland would soon become the epicenter of the extermination of the Jews.[21] So Holbrooke, like many other children born during World War II, was exposed to international disasters and dislocations, even if he and they didn't fully comprehend the agony of the world they had entered. In Holbrooke's case, it was no surprise that he became in his adult years a diplomat coping with other global calamities in Vietnam, the Balkans, Afghanistan, and Pakistan.

Few of the war babies enjoyed an affluent or even much of a middle class existence. What the majority of war babies had in common was that they, like their parents, were scarred by the depression—economically and psychologically—as well as by the hardships of World War II. Unlike the more prosperous baby boomers of the 1950s and 1960s, the war babies' world was marked by shabbiness and shortages, by ration cards that limited what food and other products they could buy, by old cars and trucks in perpetual need of repair (since automobile production was suspended during the war), and by the cramped space of city apartments or rustic farmhouses in rural America.

The war babies learned at an early age from their parents that debt was abhorrent. You did not buy what you could not afford—a lesson the postwar baby boomers were either never taught or blithely ignored, with dire consequences for the American economy at the start of the twenty-first century.

In one sense, the war babies lived in a world of dreams. Dreams brought into their homes over the radio or in newspapers and magazines. Dreams of traveling to another neighborhood or another town on busses, streetcars, or subways. Dreams of journeying to far-away places, a reverie symbolized by the ornate railroad stations in their hometowns and by the streamlined passenger trains that sped through their cities and farmland (though passenger train travel was restricted during World War II). Dreams of a luxurious world they could sometimes see (once they were old enough) in the movies, especially in Hollywood's musicals where Fred Astaire, Gene Kelly, and Judy Garland sang and danced amid the splendor of nightclubs or spacious houses, a world somewhere over the rainbow where the land of Oz glittered with magic and miracles.

Perhaps the ability of the war babies to take comfort in their dreams and fantasies, in a universe of their own imagination, is what inspired them later on to become filmmakers, actors, songwriters, journalists, and politicians. This was a generation that had to learn, with the help of radio and movies, to entertain themselves, to make up games that only they could play, to depend on their inner resources for pleasure—a reliance on their own capacities that they carried with them into adulthood when they created a culture that emphasized personality and a glorification of self-expression.

So it is certainly remarkable, but not necessarily surprising, how many of the war babies surmounted the physical and economic constrictions of their childhoods to become among the most important artists and writers in America in the second half of the twentieth century. Their childhoods instilled in them, whether they were conscious of it or not at the time, a sense that they were members of a distinctive generation with dazzling talents to contribute to America and to the world.

In effect, the war years were the first formative experience for the generation of directors, actors, musicians, journalists, social activists, and government officials who emerged as the leaders of American culture and politics beginning in the 1960s. In addition, since most of the war babies sprang from immigrant origins, they had an intuition, even as toddlers, of the world beyond the borders of the United States. Their childhoods endowed them with an instinctive intellectual and artistic sophistication, almost an inherited cosmopolitanism, that allowed them to learn from and take advantage of the changes that occurred in America during the 1940s and 1950s, and to reshape American life once they became adults.

The End of the War

I recall my mother telling me when I was old enough to understand that 1942 had been the most perilous year of World War II, when it seemed as if America might well lose the conflict. But by the summer of 1944, especially after the successful invasion of Normandy in June and the horrific battles in the Pacific that gradually brought the American navy and marines closer to the Japanese home islands, it was becoming clear to our parents that America was nearing victory. Of course, Americans tended to discount or minimize the effects of the mammoth struggles in Eastern Europe between our Russian partners and the German army. Indeed, the very notion of the American, British, and Canadian "invasion" of Europe overlooked the fact that Europe had already been invaded by the Red Army. Nevertheless, as children, we could perceive that the war we had lived with for all of our earliest years was no longer going to persist forever.

Whether the war news was ghastly or good, we absorbed these experiences through the fluctuating emotions of our parents. In fact, despite the notion that wartime and postwar America was dominated by men, many of us (like Al Pacino, Faye Dunaway, Carole King, and Jesse Jackson) learned about the world from women, particularly if our fathers and uncles were away at the war. Our mothers, whether they remained at home or worked in wartime jobs, taught us our first lessons about how to cope with the crisis in our nation and our homes. They conveyed to us, not so much in words (which we would not have been able to grasp) but in feelings just how volatile were the times into which we had been born. So the idea that our adolescent lives in postwar America would be placid, a symptom of another cliché about the "silent generation" in the 1950s, never really took hold. We were always aware of danger and instability, of fear and disorder, which the Cold War only intensified.

It was also World War II that prepared us for the capriciousness of adult life. And for the melancholy that accompanied even so exhilarating an experience as winning a global war.

My first political memory was of the day that Franklin Roosevelt died. It was April 12, 1945, when Berlin was about to fall, the concentration camps were being liberated, and the war in Europe was reaching its gruesome end. I was walking with my mother on a street in Kansas City, close to our apartment, when a barber left his shop to whisper something to her. She immediately erupted into tears. I'm sure that what distressed me was not the news of Roosevelt's death but rather the spectacle of my mother crying. Yet my deepest remembrance is how profoundly Roosevelt's death affected her, her reaction as emotional as any I myself and every other war baby later had in response to the assassinations of John F. Kennedy, Robert Kennedy, and Martin Luther King.

Judy Collins's father felt "desolate" when Roosevelt died. But she and Tom Brokaw also remembered the celebrations they saw in their neighborhoods or heard on the radio, people cheering and dancing in the streets, when the Germans surrendered in May 1945.[22]

Ironically, Roosevelt's successor was a familiar figure in Kansas City. I recall seeing Harry Truman in person on several occasions during and after his Presidency—not at political rallies but in restaurants, in hotel lobbies, at the theater. This postwar proximity to a President reflected what was still a naïve era when Presidents were not surrounded by a phalanx of secret service agents, and isolated by the threat of terrorism from the citizens they served.

To Bob Dylan, Truman's voice and nasal Midwestern twang sounded familiar, like the country singers he listened to on the radio.[23] Yet Truman's ascension offered no solace, even in Kansas City, for the death of a giant who had dominated the government, the radio, and our parents' lives for twelve years. My mother's sorrow, I later realized, was shared by millions of Americans who had depended on Roosevelt's voice and his cheerfulness to help get them through the hardest times conceivable.

The war itself continued for a few more months, culminating in Truman's decision to drop atomic bombs on Hiroshima and Nagasaki in August 1945 (Faye Dunaway's father, stationed in Japan after the war, saw the smoldering ruins of the two cities).[24] The bombs ushered in the age of potential nuclear conflagration with which we lived throughout our teenage and adult years. But when World War II finally concluded, we could appreciate our parents' relief that the most cataclysmic event of their lives, next to the Great Depression, was finally over. What neither they nor we knew was that we were about to enter an era as psychologically stressful in its own way as both the Depression and the war.

CHAPTER 2

Growing Up in Cold War America

THE UNITED STATES EMERGED from World War II as the most power-ful and wealthiest nation on earth. Its armies occupied and were soon rebuilding Western Europe and Japan. Its economic influence was dom-inant in Latin America and the Middle East. At home, the Depression had evaporated and Americans embarked on an era of unprecedented prosperity marked by the acquisition of new cars, furniture, refrigera-tors, washing machines, and the first television sets, all of these purchas-es accompanying an exodus of the middle class to the suburbs. There was every reason to believe that America's charmed superiority, its seclusion from the troubles of the rest of world, would continue indefinitely.

Yet by 1946, one year after World War II had ended, the Cold War commenced with the Soviet Union bludgeoning the countries of Eastern Europe into totalitarian replicas of Joseph Stalin's Russia. The suppression of democracy in Eastern Europe culminated in 1948 with a Communist coup in Czechoslovakia and a year-long Soviet blockade of the roads leading to West Berlin. By 1949, the civil war in China—which had persisted since the 1920s, lapsing only during the years of the Japa-nese invasion—terminated with the triumph of Mao and the Chinese Communists. During the same year, the Soviet Union exploded its own atomic bomb, eradicating America's monopoly on nuclear weapons. In 1950, America found itself embroiled in another war, this time in Korea, a struggle that lasted three years and cost 44,000 American lives including soldiers missing in action (nearly as many as would die in Vietnam). By 1953, the Korean conflict had descended into an unrelenting, brutal stalemate concluding with an armistice, the first war since 1812 which the United States did not win.

Although the United States responded to these crises, especially in Europe, with the Marshall Plan, the airlift of food and supplies into West Berlin, and the creation of NATO, none of these strategies altered the division of the world into two implacably hostile camps. Thus, by the 1950s and early 1960s, America was ensnared in a fearsome global struggle—political, military, economic, and cultural—with the Communists that, given the danger of the Cold War escalating into a nuclear inferno, obliterated all the exuberance Americans felt at the close of World War II.

It was these jittery conditions that shaped the adolescence and early adulthood of the war babies. Most responded by trying to figure out how they wanted to live their lives in a perilous postwar America. A few, even as teenagers, launched the careers that eventually made them innovators, particularly in films and music. Still others became rebellious, disobeying parental advice to turn themselves into perfect organization men and women attired in grey flannel suits or flawlessly feminine sweaters and skirts. Instead, they too started to experiment with the artistic callings that enabled them to light up the firmament of American culture from the 1960s on.

What all of these war babies had in common, however, was a craving to pursue their own dreams, to define for themselves their own identities, to explore their private ambitions unscathed by what David Riesman called in *The Lonely Crowd* (1950) the "other-directed" society in which most of the young were growing up. For the war babies who became filmmakers, actors, musicians, journalists, and politicians, their teenage years were a time to delve into their own emotions, to search for alternatives to the blandness of ranch-house living, to the all-too-cheery milieu of television shows like *Ozzie and Harriet* and *Father Knows Best*. They aspired to a life not of conformity but of self-realization.

They may not have known words like alienation. But in differing ways they felt estranged from the affluent America their parents—still harboring memories of the hardships of the Great Depression—seemed to be relishing. And this emphasis on selfhood, this detachment from parental satisfactions, became the reigning value not only of the war babies but ultimately of the country they helped to transform in the last half of the twentieth century.

Choices: The Church, The Street, The Stage, and The Screen

After the steep decline in residential construction during the Depression and World War II, millions of Americans took advantage of the post-war boom in new housing during the late 1940s and 1950s to move to the suburbs, or at least to the more pastoral subdivisions on the outskirts of the major cities. This migration had physical as well as psychological consequences.

In 1949, for example, my parents left an apartment in Kansas City for a two-bedroom house in the suburbs. The house was small and the neighborhood was hardly opulent, but it was where my family put down their new roots (indeed, my parents lived in the house for the next sixty years, until their deaths).

However skimpy the house was, it offered more space than our former apartment. I could play in the back yard or escape into the basement, making up my own games, enjoying the leisure as an adolescent that most people, whether young or middle aged, had never had much time for during the Depression or the war. Life in suburbia—whether in Kansas City for myself, or for Paul Simon and Art Garfunkel in Queens, or Joan Baez in California—was neither monotonous nor humdrum. The suburbs—however nondescript—afforded the war babies who resided in them the opportunity to explore their own aspirations, and to imagine ways different from their parents to live their adult lives.

Yet many of the war babies who became artists or politicians remained in or later returned to the cities (especially New York, Boston, or San Francisco). For them and their parents, suburban houses were either too expensive or too remote from the vitality of urban life.

After the war, Martin Scorsese's parents moved back to Little Italy from Queens because they couldn't afford a house in the suburbs. In Little Italy Scorsese encountered a constant din of people, peddlers, and shopkeepers, as well as drab tenements and the constant threat of violence. So Little Italy—insular, filled with time-honored Sicilian customs, dominated by the Catholic Church and the Mafia—became the emotional touchstone of Scorsese's adolescence, providing memories he carried with him into adulthood and his films.

In fact, the priests and the wise guys became Scorsese's twin role models, both enjoying equal stature in the Italian community. On the one hand, as an asthmatic, he admired the brawn and physical charisma of the mobsters. Many of his young friends were juvenile delinquents who graduated into made men, the goodfellas of Little Italy.

On the other hand, the gangsters always respected the priests and the Church as equal repositories of power, no matter what mayhem the mob produced in the streets (as in the penultimate scene in *The Godfather: Part I* where Francis Ford Coppola cuts back and forth between Al Pacino's Michael Corleone attending his son's baptism and pledging his fidelity to God while his trigger men massacre his enemies in an urban bloodbath). Scorsese himself envisioned two conflicting career paths as an adolescent: he could become a priest (he went to mass habitually, fasted during Lent, and served as an altar boy before briefly entering a seminary) or he could join the Mafiosi.

One reason Scorsese was attracted to the Church and initially decided to be a priest was the theatricality of the Catholic sacraments and rituals, as if these were gaudy spectacles that could be reproduced on stage or in film. But his interest in the movies, sex, rock music, and the excitement of a secular life on New York's sidewalks made him unsuitable for the priesthood. He was expelled from the seminary after his first year, and he soon gave up his ambitions to be a cleric.[1] It was revealing of his skepticism toward Catholicism that Scorsese as the narrator at the beginning of the appropriately named *Mean Streets* (1973) should proclaim that "you don't make up for your sins in church. You do it in the streets. You do it at home. The rest is bullshit and you know it."

From childhood on, Scorsese worshipped all types of movies—whether made in Hollywood or abroad. The street life of Little Italy reminded him of an Italian neo-realist film by Roberto Rossellini or Vittorio De Sica. Yet Scorsese especially loved Michael Powell and Emeric Pressburger's British movie *The Red Shoes*, a film about a ballet dancer that seemed to Scorsese to capture the tribulations of an artist's existence. By the early 1960s, he was equally attracted to the French New Wave (the films of François Truffaut and Jean-Luc Godard). But Scorsese also adored Westerns (particularly the movies of John Ford) and the films of Elia Kazan—most of all, *On the Waterfront*, released in 1954, which Scorsese quoted in Robert De Niro's "I coulda been a contender" scene near the end of *Raging Bull* (1980).

Scorsese's fervor for movies, and his notion that making films could be a form of religious as well as artistic expression, supplanted his earlier attraction to the Church. By the early 1960s, he had ceased to be a devout Catholic, shunning mass and confession. Instead, just as universities began to establish the study of the cinema, Scorsese entered film school at NYU in 1960 where he was taught by his first mentor, Haig Manoogian, the virtues of the auteur theory—the idea that directors were the true "authors" of their movies, and that they should strive to make films that were personal, even autobiographical—lessons Scorsese incorporated in his own movies by the 1970s.[2]

Around the same time, Francis Ford Coppola (after graduating from Hofstra) entered film school at UCLA. Several years later, George Lucas enrolled at USC's film school where he met Steven Spielberg, the first and most successful of the baby boom directors, born in 1946. Scorsese, Coppola, Lucas, and Spielberg all became close friends and colleagues with an identical passion for movies, and they made crucial contributions to the American film renaissance in the 1970s. It was fitting and symbolic, therefore, that Coppola, Lucas, and Spielberg jointly presented Scorsese with his first Oscar, as director of *The Departed* in 2006.

It was also fitting that Al Pacino and Robert De Niro emerged as stars in the movies of Coppola and Scorsese since they were all contemporaries and came from similar backgrounds. Pacino and De Niro, like Scorsese, were tenacious New Yorkers—Pacino from the Bronx and De Niro from Greenwich Village though he frequently hung out with friends in Little Italy. Both displayed an early talent for acting, and sometimes for nothing else. At the age of ten, De Niro played the cowardly lion in a grade school production of *The Wizard of Oz* although it's hard to imagine him as a childhood facsimile of Bert Lahr. Pacino managed to flunk all his classes in high school except for English, and dropped out of school at seventeen, holding a series of odd jobs while nourishing the thought of becoming an actor.

Eventually, Pacino was admitted to the Actors Studio where he studied with the legendary Lee Strasberg, while De Niro studied with the equally famous Stella Adler, who in 1943 was Marlon Brando's first acting teacher. Strasberg and Adler had both been members of the Group Theater in the 1930s, and were advocates of what became known as the "Method," an acting technique originally developed by Constantin Stanislavski at the Moscow Art Theater in pre-revolutionary Russia. Although Strasberg and Adler differed, often heatedly, on what the "Method" meant, each emphasized the need for an actor to draw on his or her own psychological resources, on memories and past experiences, on an inner intensity in interpreting a role that typically transcended the words a playwright or screenwriter had composed. This focus on the personality of the actor turned out to be one of the distinguishing characteristics of the war babies' preoccupation with self-awareness in the Cold War years, and it helped affect the general tone of American culture from the 1950s on.

By 1947, after Brando's revolutionary performance on stage as Stanley Kowalski in Tennessee Williams's *A Streetcar Named Desire*, a role he repeated in the movie version in 1951, the Method became the model for American actors, the technique in which they were trained and the impetus for their performances in plays and the movies from then until now.[3] It is impossible to imagine the modern American theater or film without the Method-inspired style of actors like Montgomery Clift, James Dean, Rod Steiger, Paul Newman, Warren Beatty, Dustin Hoffman, Sidney Poitier, Sean Penn, Jane Fonda, Joanne Woodward, and Meryl Streep.

As actors, Pacino and De Niro were the "children" of Marlon Brando. They became compelling practitioners of the Method from the moment they began appearing in plays in New York in the 1960s and in movies by the early 1970s. Faye Dunaway too was one of Brando's children. Which was more than she could say of being her own father's child. The tensions in her family increased throughout her childhood and adolescence, with her father frequently absent. Her parents finally divorced when she was thirteen. Afterwards, she saw her father once, in New York, and then never again. This certainly affected not only the way she dealt with men in her adult life, but also in how she interpreted her roles—particularly in the dramatization of her relationships with men—on stage and in the movies.

Like De Niro, Dunaway appeared in school plays starting in the eighth grade. After she graduated from high school in 1958, she entered Florida State and then transferred to the University of Florida, but at both places she was serious about pursuing a career as an actress. Yet Dunaway, like Bonnie Parker, was never going to be content to remain in the South. For Dunaway, Manhattan and Boston were beacons of culture, the cities where she had to be if she intended to perfect her craft. So in the early 1960s, she enrolled at Boston University's School of Fine and Applied Arts to further study acting. Her most important part in a play at BU was as Elizabeth Proctor, the wife of John Proctor in Arthur Miller's *The Crucible*, a performance that Miller himself came to see.

Dunaway realized at BU, however, that she really didn't know how to act, how to draw upon her private feelings in creating a character,

and that she wasn't going to learn unless she was trained by one of the
era's incandescent directors of plays and films. She got her chance when
she was admitted to the new Repertory Theater at Lincoln Center, presided over by Elia Kazan.[4] Like Lee Strasberg and Stella Adler, Kazan
had graduated from the Group Theater as an adherent of the Method.
Kazan quickly became a successful director as well as a tutor of actors.
He founded the Actor's Studio in 1947, though he stayed only a year, be-
queathing the leadership of the Studio to Strasberg. By the early 1960s,
when Dunaway began studying with him, Kazan had directed the major Method actors in some of the most influential plays and movies of
the time: Marlon Brando in *A Streetcar Named Desire*, Lee J. Cobb in
Death of a Salesman, Brando again in *Viva Zapata!* and *On the Waterfront*
(along with Cobb and Rod Steiger), James Dean in *East of Eden*, and
Warren Beatty in *Splendor in the Grass*.

Kazan had an acute intuition about talented, if unformed, actors
like Dunaway. He also recognized that she had an incessant air of drama
and fretfulness about her that would drive some later co-stars and directors (like Warren Beatty and Roman Polanski) nuts. Nevertheless,
Kazan used Dunaway's personal agitation (as he did with the emotions
of many actors) to elicit the high-strung performances she gave for other
directors in movies like *Bonnie and Clyde*, *Three Days of the Condor*, *Chinatown*, and *Network*. Kazan thus prepared Dunaway for key roles on
stage and then in the movies, where she became the principal Method
actress of the late 1960s and 1970s.

The Cold War period, from the 1940s to the mid-1960s, were the
formative years for war babies like Coppola, Scorsese, Lucas, Pacino, De
Niro, and Dunaway. What they experienced and learned as teenagers
and young adults prepared them for the transformation of the American
cinema they would all help to bring about.

But while they were drawing on their childhoods and adolescence to
develop into directors and actors, other war baby artists were turning to
music as the keystone of their careers. What the singers and songwriters
absorbed from postwar American music, and what they disdained about

its syrupy lyrics and melodies, would prod them to instigate a revolution in music in the 1960s.

Music in the 1950s

For the war babies, one of the stereotypes about American music in the postwar years was its insipid quality—symbolized by Perry Como's crooning in a cardigan sweater on his television show and Eddie Fisher's lachrymose accolade to his mythical father in "Oh! My Pa-Pa." Yet the 1950s was also the decade in which Frank Sinatra released his greatest albums, all of them on Capitol records—*In the Wee Small Hours, Songs for Swingin' Lovers, A Swingin' Affair!, Only the Lonely,* and *Come Fly with Me.* In these albums, Sinatra paid tribute to the songs (many of them originally sung by Fred Astaire in the 1930s) of George Gershwin, Irving Berlin, Cole Porter, Richard Rodgers and Lorenz Hart, Duke Ellington, and Harold Arlen. Sinatra not only had the ability to sound as if he were singing just to the listener, but he was also a masterful interpreter of lyrics. Unlike his contemporaries on the radio hit list of top 40 records, Sinatra made a song's words resemble poems of love and loss.

Similarly, in the 1950s, Ella Fitzgerald recorded her series of "songbooks" featuring jazzy renditions of Gershwin, Porter, and Rodgers and Hart. Far from indulging in infantile emotions, Sinatra and Fitzgerald were offering modern interpretations of an American musical genre from the 1920s and 1930s that was suffused with verbal and melodic sophistication, and a considerable dose of cynicism. These were songs meant not for teenagers on their way to their high school prom but for adults who understood what it was like to want "someone to watch over me" but who found it more likely to be playing solitaire, uneasy in an easy chair or, alternatively, enduring broken dates or having a conversation with "flying plates." In the world of Sinatra and Fitzgerald, as in the world of Hemingway and Astaire, love and sex were activities fleetingly enjoyed not only by wised-up men and women but by Cole Porter's birds, bees, and educated fleas.

Still, American music did start to change in the mid-1950s with the emergence of rock and roll. In 1955, the movie *Blackboard Jungle* opened with Bill Haley and his Comets blaring "Rock Around the Clock." The song and the movie became gigantic hits with the young, as did another Haley song "Shake, Rattle and Roll." Both numbers seemed perverse to parents brought up on the swing bands of the 1930s and the effortless singing of Bing Crosby. (Frank Sinatra initially dismissed rock and roll as music by and for "cretins.") Yet rock sounded like a first announcement of a generation gap between parents and their children that began in the 1950s and would swell in the 1960s.

The lyrics of Bill Haley and his imitators were, in fact, relatively mild. But no rock singer seemed more alarming or more rebellious to adults than Elvis Presley. Presley exploded onto the music scene in 1956, first on records and in live performances, and then on television shows like *Ed Sullivan* and *Steve Allen*, his act cleansed for the audience by having him appear with shaved sideburns and a camera that shot Presley from the waist up so that no one in the comfort of their living rooms could catch a glimpse of his pulsating groin.

What appealed to those war babies who aspired to be singers themselves, like Bob Dylan and Janis Joplin, was Presley's amalgamation of African American rhythms, Southern blues, and country and western traditions. Meanwhile, on the radio, the young could listen to the disc jockey Alan Freed broadcasting from New York and showcasing white and black rock and roll artists like Jerry Lee Lewis, Chuck Berry, Fats Domino, Little Richard, and Buddy Holly.[5]

Rock and roll, though, coexisted with a revival of interest in folk music in the 1950s. For those war babies like Joan Baez and Judy Collins as well as Bob Dylan, the appeal of folk music lay in its rural roots, its diversity, its contempt for commercialism, and its astringent portraits of an unjust world (in contrast to the apparent teenage immaturity of rock and roll). Moreover, the folk music of the 1950s boasted legendary heroes dating back to the Great Depression: Woody Guthrie, Pete Seeger, the Weavers, and Leadbelly. Because of their association with the Communist Party, Seeger and the Weavers were blacklisted from television during the McCarthy era and into the early 1960s, a punishment which only made the folk singers more alluring to Baez, Collins, and Dylan.[6]

Indeed, the folk revival in the 1950s had much in common with the Beat movement (though the Beats were more enthralled with jazz musicians than with folk singers). Yet both the folk singers and the Beats were the harbingers of the counterculture that would surface in the 1960s. In the 1950s, the primary venue for folk singers and the Beats were coffee houses, especially in Greenwich Village, Cambridge, and San Francisco. The coffee houses were modeled on European-style cabarets and they featured not only music but poetry readings, foreign films, and book sales, with a clientele that seemed universally clad in black sweaters and skirts or blue jeans.[7] The coffee houses were the setting in which the war baby singers could initially perform, hone their skills, and prepare for the fame that would soon follow.

Joan Baez was the first of the war baby folk singers to become well-known. During the 1950s, she had lived in various suburbs in California, though she spent a year in Baghdad where her father had worked with UNESCO. It was in Iraq, where she witnessed the misery of the poor in the streets, that Baez developed a zeal for social justice that would mark the rest of her life. Her family moved back to California, to Redlands (where she gave her first stage performance) and then to Palo Alto in the mid-1950s. At Palo Alto High School, Baez heard Martin Luther King speak—an event which intensified her pacifism, her commitment to non-violence, and her opposition to the ubiquitous air-raid drills that were conducted all over America at the height of the Cold War, students plunging under their desks in case of a nuclear attack.

Meanwhile, Baez—influenced by singers like Pete Seeger—had taken up the guitar. In 1958, her father was offered a position at MIT, and the family moved to Massachusetts. Baez (like Faye Dunaway a few years later) enrolled at Boston University, in the School of Drama, but departed in her second semester to devote full time to a musical career.

She began to sing in Cambridge coffee houses, especially at Club Mount Auburn 47 which was rapidly turning into the most trendy site in the Boston area for folk singers, Beat poets, and budding intellectuals. With her silky black hair, exotic Mexican-American face, and shimmering soprano voice, Baez was becoming among the most magnetic singers in the Northeast. So it was no wonder that she was invited in 1959 to appear at the first Newport Folk Festival.[8] By this time, though she had not yet made an album, Baez was on the verge of stardom.

Baez's closest competitor among the war baby women folk singers was Judy Collins—though they always regarded each other as friends and colleagues rather than as rivals. In 1949, Collins's family moved from Hollywood to Denver, where her father launched a radio program and then a television show featuring music and interviews. In Denver, through her father, Collins met Steve Allen and the jazz pianist George Shearing. And as Collins continued to study classical piano, her piano teacher introduced her to Arturo Toscanini. Throughout the mid-1950s, Collins gave piano recitals in Denver; as far as her parents, her teacher, and her audiences could tell, Collins was headed for a thriving career as a concert pianist.

Yet Collins was becoming increasingly interested both in singing and in folk music. She recognized that modernist composers like Igor Stravinsky and Aaron Copland had incorporated folk themes into their ballets and concertos; one could hardly listen to Stravinsky's *The Rite of Spring* or Copland's *Appalachian Spring* without hearing the folk elements that were the foundations of both works.

Collins was also attracted to the political significance of folk music, particularly as performed by Woody Guthrie and Pete Seeger. Soon, she taught herself to play guitar and gradually surrendered the dream of becoming a pianist, much to the consternation of her parents and teacher.[9] After graduating from high school in 1957, Collins began singing in any club in the Denver area that would invite her to take the stage. Gradually, she was becoming increasingly recognized as a dulcet interpreter of folk music.

In the audience at one of Collins's performances in 1960 was a scruffy patron, traveling across America like a character in Jack Kerouac's *On the Road*, who turned out to be Bob Dylan. In later years, Dylan liked to cultivate the myth that he had been a hobo, an itinerant farm hand, part Native American, and in general a person without any fixed roots. But the truth about Dylan's background was far more conventional.

After the war, in 1947, Dylan's family had moved from Duluth to Hibbing, Minnesota—a mining town inhabited by Eastern Europeans and Scandinavians. Dylan's Jewish family was middle class, and fit in with the rest of the population of what was essentially a typical small Midwestern community. Dylan himself dutifully underwent his Bar Mitzvah in 1954. Yet Dylan regarded himself as an outsider in Hibbing and among his fellow Jews—a perspective that would endure throughout his adult life.

The Cold War, however, reverberated in Hibbing as it did in the rest of America. Dylan recalled the constant air raid drills, and was terrified by the prospect of nuclear extermination. His refuge was poetry and music, especially the tunes he heard on the radio in the 1950s. Dylan's tastes were eclectic: he was drawn to jazz, rhythm and blues, and rock. He admired singers as varied as Frank Sinatra, Bing Crosby, Bill Haley, Elvis Presley, Little Richard, Chuck Berry, and Fats Domino. But he was also impressed by Bertolt Brecht and Kurt Weill's *The Threepenny Opera*.

Yet increasingly, Dylan—like Joan Baez and Judy Collins—was influenced by the folk music of Woody Guthrie, Leadbelly, Pete Seeger, and the Weavers. So he taught himself how to play piano, the harmonica, and guitar. By the time he graduated from high school in 1959, Dylan had determined that he would be a folk singer, like his idol Guthrie.

First, though, Dylan entered the University of Minnesota and even joined a Jewish fraternity in his freshman year—Sigma Alpha Mu, more familiarly referred to as Sammy. The idea of Dylan as a member of a fraternity was ludicrous to begin with, and his buttoned-down "brothers" with their ambitions to be lawyers or businessmen asked him to leave within a year on the grounds that he was too "aloof" and eccentric for their tastes. Thereafter, Dylan spent most of his time not attending classes at the university but in a Bohemian enclave of Minneapolis called "Dinkytown," where he started to sing at coffee houses.

Soon, Dylan dropped out of the university and (prompted by Woody Guthrie's autobiography, *Bound for Glory*) decided to ramble around America. His eventual destination was New York, arriving in Greenwich Village in 1961. Dylan immediately started visiting and singing for Guthrie who was hospitalized in New Jersey, suffering from Huntington's chorea, a degenerative disease that left him increasingly unable to move or to speak. Otherwise, Dylan frequented the coffee houses and jazz clubs in Greenwich Village, becoming known for a distinctively coarse singing voice that, at least at the outset of his career, seemed to imitate Guthrie's own style.[10] By the early 1960s, Dylan was not yet famous but—like Baez and Collins—he was about to transfigure American music.

Paul Simon and Art Garfunkel were already singing together at Forest Hills High School in the 1950s. Physically, they were a peculiar pair. Simon was five foot two inches, and always self-conscious about his diminutive appearance; he sometimes thought he looked like an elf. Garfunkel, on the other hand, was tall and handsome, with blonde curly hair and radiant blue eyes, as if he were a teenage Adonis. But what they shared was a superb sense of harmony and voices that together sounded perfectly synchronized, much like their adolescent models, the Everly Brothers.

Both Simon and Garfunkel were bored by what they considered the conformity of suburban life in the 1950s. As with so many other war baby singers, they gravitated initially to rock and roll; their musical deities were the standard 1950s rebels: Elvis Presley, Chuck Berry, Jerry Lee Lewis, Little Richard, Fats Domino. And like Judy Collins's parents, Simon's father was appalled by what he thought of as his son's primitive taste in music—another example of the generation gap that was starting in the 1950s—even though Simon was also becoming an excellent guitarist. Nor was his father mollified when Simon and Garfunkel, calling themselves Tom and Jerry, recorded their first hit, "Hey, Schoolgirl," in 1957, and were invited to appear on Dick Clark's national afternoon television show, *American Bandstand*. Yet despite the success of the record, "Tom and Jerry" never duplicated their initial success until they re-emerged as Simon and Garfunkel in the mid-1960s.

At heart, Simon was as much a lyricist as a composer. More than any of the rock and rollers he admired in the 1950s, Simon resembled Cole Porter, Lorenz Hart, and Stephen Sondheim in his infatuation with language and complex rhymes. After graduating from high school in 1958, Simon entered Queens College, majoring in English (while Garfunkel enrolled at Columbia to study architecture). Simon came to revere James Joyce, T.S. Eliot, Emily Dickinson, and Robert Frost (the last two of whom showed up in his lyrics for "The Dangling Conversation" in 1966). As his fascination with these writers suggested, Simon was increasingly drawn to themes of alienation, regret, and sadness which were reflected not only in his songs but also in his personality.[11] But it would not be until after he graduated from Queens in 1963 that he and Garfunkel resumed their career as a duet, this time under their own names.

One of Simon's classmates and friends at Queens was Carole King. Yet they never wrote a song together because Simon was not a collaborator.[12] His songs were his own, whether he performed them with Garfunkel or later as a solo act.

Along with Bob Dylan and Paul Simon, the other most intricate lyricist of the war babies was Joni Mitchell. As a child, Mitchell (like Judy Collins) studied classical piano, and was attracted to the modernist music of Debussy, Ravel, and Stravinsky. Once she entered adolescence, however, she grew more interested in painting, poetry, and jazz. Her musical icons were Miles Davis and the French singer Edith Piaf (whose melancholy songs Mitchell's own compositions resembled when she became an adult). Having switched from piano to guitar, Mitchell started out performing in clubs in Western Canada that featured folk music and jazz, before she moved on to Toronto and then to the United States in 1965 where her career as an idiosyncratic singer and recording artist took off.

Despite their affection for rock and roll in the 1950s, Baez, Collins, Dylan, and Simon and Garfunkel never tried to be rock singers themselves. Once they began to write or record their music, their songs were personal manifestations of their inner feelings and experiences. In effect, they (along with their counterparts in England, especially the Beatles) were making their private emotions public as a way of connecting to an American and ultimately a global audience hungry for musical reflections of their own individual and generational attitudes. This stress on the personal, on values that were internal rather than conventional or commercial, were the hallmarks of the war baby singers (as they were of the war baby directors and actors), and of the culture that was emerging in the 1950s and would dominate the movies, the music, the journalism, and the politics from the 1960s on.

Nonetheless, there were war baby singers who found in rock and roll an outlet for their inner turmoil. No one used rock more fervidly as a vehicle for personal expression than Janis Joplin. Joplin was born in 1943, and grew up in Port Arthur, Texas—a town she came to regard as a cultural desert. From her earliest years, Joplin was attracted to various forms of art and music. When she was six years old, her mother bought her a piano which Joplin quickly learned how to play. And whatever the drawbacks of Port Arthur, Joplin thought of her childhood as serene.

This tranquility vanished when Joplin reached adolescence in the 1950s. She started to gain weight and broke out with a severe case of acne that left scars on her face and her psyche for the rest of her life. In response, Joplin turned into a rebel with wild hair, shabby clothes, and a reputation for sexual promiscuity. She also developed a taste for jazz and the blues, as well as for alcohol. All of these traits left her estranged from her high school contemporaries in Port Arthur, and from her college classmates at Lamar Tech which she entered in 1960.

By 1962, Joplin had transferred to the University of Texas, largely because Austin was beginning to earn a reputation as a countercultural oasis, particularly for musicians. Joplin started singing at Threadgill's—now a restaurant but then a saloon that welcomed jazz, rock, folk, and country performers. At Threadgill's, and in a grubby neighborhood off campus filled with disciples of the Beat movement, Joplin felt at home. But the student body at the university was still ruled by fraternity types, football players, and Texas belles—none of whom Joplin, in the way she dressed and behaved, even vaguely resembled At one point, the school newspaper, the *Daily Texan*, nominated Joplin as one of the "ugliest men" on campus. So it was not surprising that in 1963, Joplin left Austin for the authentic Mecca of the counterculture, San Francisco.[13]

What Joplin found in San Francisco were would-be rock singers, most of them war babies, like Grace Slick (born in 1939) and Jerry Garcia. Both were insurgents, musically and personally. Garcia especially was a dissident as an adolescent. He smoked pot when he was fifteen, dropped out of high school after his junior year, joined the army but was dishonorably discharged, and became a fan of Beat novelists and poetry readings at San Francisco book stores like the legendary City Lights book shop opened by Lawrence Ferlinghetti.[14] Yet Garcia's deepest ambition was to be a rock and blues singer, an ambition he achieved by the 1960s.

But although they didn't know one another at the time, Joplin's closest comrade, musically and emotionally, was Jim Morrison. Like Faye Dunaway, Morrison was born in Florida, in his case in 1943. And also like Dunaway, Morrison had a tense relationship with his father, a career navy officer who fought in World War II and in the Korean War, and worked on the hydrogen bomb at Los Alamos. He gave his son the middle name of Douglas after his hero Douglas MacArthur. Morrison, however, was the antithesis of an obedient child or teenager. While his mother adored Frank Sinatra and the cast albums of *South Pacific* and *My Fair Lady*, Morrison became a devotee of rock and roll singers like Elvis Presley. More important, he loathed authority figures and being told how to behave. He was, like Joplin, an insubordinate adolescent whom his parents could never comprehend.

Morrison graduated from high school in 1961 and enrolled at Florida State. At the time, his real obsession, besides literature and music, was film. Eventually, he entered UCLA's film school where he hoped, at least for a while, to be a New Wave director like Truffaut or Godard. As it happened, one of his classmates was Francis Ford Coppola who was impressed not so much with Morrison's potential as a filmmaker as with his flair for disturbing poetry and songwriting.[15] Coppola went on to use one of Morrison's songs, "The End," in *Apocalypse Now* (1979) in the opening scene and during the killing of Kurtz (played by Marlon Brando). Indeed, Morrison's music and his sinister persona were ideal for the soundtrack of Coppola's cataclysmic portrait of the Vietnam War.

Besides their penchant for nonconformity in the 1950s and the ferocity of their music in the 1960s, Joplin and Morrison had one other fate, sadly, in common. Both flamed brightly, for a short time, in the musical universe of the late 1960s, and both died young soon after the decade came to a close. Their volatile temperaments, and their addictions to drugs and alcohol, made it impossible for them to sustain enduring careers. They were the war babies who were most notoriously the casualties of the generational and cultural insurrection of the 1950s and 1960s.

Yet not every war baby singer was damaged or spoiled by fame. Joan Baez, Judy Collins, Bob Dylan, Joni Mitchell, Carole King, and Simon and Garfunkel all enjoyed critical and commercial success during the 1960s and 1970s. But the most triumphant of the war baby singers, and certainly the one who achieved prominence at the earliest age was Barbra Streisand. Streisand was born in 1942 in Brooklyn, to quintessentially Jewish parents of Austrian descent. Streisand gave her first solo performance when she was seven, performed in nightclubs as a teenager, and appeared in summer stock and off Broadway in the late 1950s. By 1961, at the age of nineteen, she sang for the first time on national television, on the *Tonight Show*, hosted at the time by Jack Paar. Before long, Streisand would become a star on Broadway, on record albums, and in the movies. Though she never indulged in folk or rock music, she was one of the dominant stars of a generation that altered or reinterpreted the music Americans listened to and embraced. Along with the rest of the war baby singers and songwriters, Streisand helped create a revolution that remade American culture.

Politics in the 1950s and Early 1960s

Among the more durable clichés about postwar America is that young people in the 1950s were members of a "silent generation." The catchphrase was coined by *Time* magazine in a cover story in November 1951. *Time* announced in its omniscient manner that the current generation of high school and college students was politically passive, acquiescent, and conformist. This was, according to *Time*, a cohort that "does not issue manifestos, make speeches or carry posters" in vivid contrast to the radical students of the 1930s.

One problem with *Time*'s assertion was that it assumed political activism was the sole sign of an engaged generation. But the absence of 1930s-style political movements, particularly on the left, was not necessarily an indication of postwar conformity or apathy. On the contrary, the 1950s was a time in which a feeling of dissatisfaction with middle-class American values—as reflected in the decade's social criticism, its novels, its plays, the Beat movement, and the movies, as well as in the lives of war babies like Janis Joplin and Jim Morrison—was growing increasingly noticeable. Moreover, the interest of war babies like Joan Baez, Judy Collins, and Bob Dylan in folk music, with its own left-wing political implications, was another signal that the 1950s was not quiescent.

In any case, within three years *Time*'s characterization of a silent generation was obsolete. The most important event of the 1950s, an event that electrified an entire generation of African Americans and many whites as well, was the Supreme Court's decision in *Brown versus the Board of Education* in 1954, declaring segregation in the public schools to be unconstitutional. And if the doctrine of "separate but equal" as proclaimed in the Court's 1896 decision in *Plessy versus Ferguson* now no longer applied to schools, why was it not also unconstitutional to maintain segregation in all public accommodations: parks, water fountains, swimming pools, libraries, busses, railroads, movie theaters, and every other locale where people of all colors gathered?

For John Lewis, growing up in the 1940s and 1950s in the rigidly segregated South, the Supreme Court's decision transformed his world. School—even if it was segregated with second-hand books cast off by whites—had always represented his path out of poverty and a life as a sharecropper like his parents. Lewis loved hearing and reading about black pioneers like Booker T. Washington, George Washington Carver, and Joe Louis. Lewis couldn't enter the library in his hometown in Alabama because it was reserved for whites. But he could learn about black history from his teachers and from newspapers and magazines in his own school library.

He could also listen to preachers like Martin Luther King on the radio. Lewis first heard King's voice during the Montgomery bus boycott which King led in 1955. In the same year, Lewis learned about the mutilation and murder of Emmett Till, a fourteen-year-old black teenager from Chicago visiting his relatives in Mississippi. Lewis himself had traveled with his parents to Buffalo in 1951 to see family members who left the South. Lewis instantly sensed that the North was different from and more tolerant than Alabama, and over the next few years he became more and more embittered by the elaborate system of segregation in the South.

By the late 1950s, Lewis was turning into a civil rights activist, especially after the effort, requiring federal troops, to integrate Central High School in Little Rock in 1957. Lewis met Martin Luther King and Ralph Abernathy, the founders of the Southern Christian Leadership Conference, joined the NAACP, and determined that he wanted to be a preacher and protester like King. More significantly, Lewis was being trained in the tactics of non-violent civil disobedience.[16] He would soon emerge as a leader of the civil rights movement in the early 1960s.

Jesse Jackson followed a similar path. He was thirteen when the decision in *Brown versus the Board of Education* was handed down. Jackson was already an articulate student leader in his segregated high school in Greenville, South Carolina, and he organized a sit-in in front of Greenville's busses after the Montgomery bus boycott. Like Lewis, Jackson still couldn't enter the Greenville public library, and was arrested for trying to do so in 1960, the same year that four other black students in Greensboro, North Carolina staged a sit-in at a Woolworth's lunch counter and were refused service.[17] By the early 1960s, as marches, sit-ins, and freedom rides proliferated throughout the South, Jackson determined to become a Baptist minister and a civil rights organizer, emulating the leader he too most admired, Martin Luther King.

For Lewis and Jackson, the commitment to racial integration was both a social and a personal imperative. Like the rest of the war babies—whether they were involved in culture or in politics—Lewis and Jackson were dedicating themselves to remodeling America as well as their own lives.

White war babies were also affected by the civil rights movement in the 1950s and early 1960s. Richard Holbrooke, for example, attended Brown University and was editor of the school newspaper in 1961-1962. In that capacity, he invited Malcolm X to speak on campus at just the moment when Malcolm was emerging as a radical alternative to Martin Luther King.[18]

Other whites were becoming interested in politics in the 1950s, if not necessarily in civil rights. Barney Frank grew up in a family in Bayonne, New Jersey, that emphasized reading books and newspapers, and participating in political discussions around the dinner table. Frank himself was absorbed with politics from an early age. In grade school, he was elected president of the student council. In 1956, Frank rang doorbells soliciting votes for Adlai Stevenson in his second (losing) campaign against Dwight Eisenhower. At one point in the late 1950s, Frank's parents hosted a party for Eleanor Roosevelt. In 1957, Frank entered Harvard, majoring in government, and was continuously active in student politics. He went on to graduate school at Harvard, intending to earn a Ph.D. in government, a goal he never completed because he dropped out of school in the late 1960s to become a political aide for Kevin White, the mayor of Boston.

There was, of course, one area of Frank's life that remained secret. No one in high school or college knew he was gay. In the 1950s, to be openly gay and involved in politics was particularly hazardous since, in 1953 and 1954, President Eisenhower issued executive orders defining homosexuality as a potential security risk and therefore grounds for firing federal employees.[19] Essentially, Eisenhower's executive orders made being gay equivalent to being a Communist, both dangers to national security in Cold War America. So Frank had an excellent reason, as someone who wanted to pursue a political career, for concealing his sexual orientation.

While Frank was fascinated with politics from childhood, Mario Savio and Tom Hayden—both of whom became leading activists in the 1960s—remained relatively moderate in the 1950s. Yet there were hints of rebellion in each of their teenage years, a modest flame that ignited in the 1960s.

Savio's parents encouraged him to excel in school. But like Faye Dunaway and Jim Morrison, Savio had a thorny relationship with his father. After his father returned home from World War II, he was strict and domineering about the need for his family to be both faithful Catholics and consummate Americans. Savio tried, for a time, to live up to his father's expectations. He was, in high school and college, particularly drawn to science and philosophy. By 1960, Savio had overcome his stutter and spoke at his high school graduation, exhibiting an ability to hold an audience's attention that would magnify once he became the chief orator of the Berkeley free speech movement in 1964. Meanwhile, though, Savio (like Martin Scorsese) began questioning Catholic theology. Still, he stayed committed to Catholicism in the early 1960s as a device for achieving greater social justice.[20] Yet his tendency to revolt against his father's expectations made their relationship worse and virtually irreparable—another instance of the generational quarrels that first materialized in the 1950s.

For most of the 1950s, Tom Hayden was an apolitical Catholic, and a teenager with middle-class ambitions. But, as with Scorsese and Savio, Hayden eventually rejected the Catholic Church. When he was in high school, he edited the school newspaper but also published a satirical non-sanctioned paper based on *Mad Magazine*. In the late 1950s, Hayden's heroes were J.D. Salinger's Holden Caulfield, James Dean, and Jack Kerouac, and he hitchhiked throughout America (like Bob Dylan) after reading *On the Road* in 1957. Hayden then enrolled at the University of Michigan, edited the student newspaper, and started to recognize (as would Savio at Berkeley) the impersonal nature of the modern "multiversity." By the early 1960s, in part inspired by the election of John F. Kennedy, Hayden was turning increasingly to political activism, both on and off campus.[21]

Barney Frank, Richard Holbrooke, Mario Savio, and Tom Hayden all went to colleges or graduate schools (Harvard, Brown, Berkeley, Michigan) where politics, the civil rights movement, and nonconformist attitudes were familiar ingredients in student life, even in the 1950s. In South Dakota, where Tom Brokaw grew up, rebellion—either personal or political—was unknown. Being in the Boy Scouts was instead a central part of Brokaw's adolescence. There were few African Americans in South Dakota, and for Brokaw the struggles for integration in the South were remote. Brokaw, however, was aware of the mistreatment of Native Americans in South Dakota and elsewhere in the Northwest. So in this sense, he was concerned about "civil rights" for minorities in the postwar United States.

Nor was Brokaw just a typical inhabitant of rural America. During his teenage years, he traveled to Minneapolis and to New York (where he was a participant on a quiz show that later turned out to be rigged, like many of the television quiz shows of the late 1950s). During both trips, he was increasingly attracted to what it might be like to live full-time in a major metropolis.

He soon found out. After graduating from the University of South Dakota, Brokaw began to pursue a career in broadcasting. He started out as a student on local radio stations in Yankton and Rapid City, South Dakota, playing records and reporting on the 1956 elections. By the early 1960s Brokaw rapidly ascended to television stations in Sioux City, Omaha, and Atlanta, ultimately becoming the anchor of the 11:00 news program at the NBC affiliate in Los Angeles.[22] In these capacities, Brokaw now regularly covered political and international news, and was growing knowledgeable about the Kennedy Administration and the civil rights movement. Soon, he would become one of the principal television journalists in America.

Politics for the war babies in the 1950s and early 1960s was not only a matter of marching for integration, criticizing the bureaucratic structure of American universities, and experiencing the growing impact of televised journalism. The Cold War also intruded on sports. Ever since the first postwar Olympic games in London in 1948, the contest for gold medals between the United States and the Soviet Union (and later East Germany) symbolized whose civilization and ideology were superior. The Olympics became one more element in the global confrontation between the two superpowers that involved military might, economic growth, and cultural pre-eminence as well as athletic dominance.

Cassius Clay (as he was known throughout the 1950s and into the early 1960s) was not immune either to the civil rights movement or the Cold War. He was fourteen years old when Emmett Till was murdered, and this crime infuriated him as much as it did John Lewis and Jesse Jackson. But during his adolescence, Clay concentrated on boxing, though his performance both before a bout and in the ring reflected his roots in African American culture. He loved putting on a show, imitating the wrestlers he saw on television. Yet in Clay's case, the origins of his theatricality lay in the black oral tradition, in flinging insults at one's opponent, in rhymes designed to illuminate his own physical dexterity, and in the hyperbole of African American street language—a style he maintained all through his professional career.

In 1960, Clay won the gold medal as a light heavyweight boxer at the Olympic games in Rome. Instantly, he was celebrated as an icon of

American achievement, his race notwithstanding.[23] Yet his status as a superstar did not last long. Within a few years, Clay shocked his admirers by changing his name, and his religious and political identity. Nevertheless, like the other war babies he developed into a major figure in the upheavals of the 1960s that transformed America.

In the meantime, for all the cultural and political ferment of the 1950s, there was one feature of life in Cold War America that threatened to inhibit what people, the war babies included, could say and do. From the late 1940s through the 1950s, the menace of McCarthyism—of Senator Joseph McCarthy himself as well as the interrogations and blacklists inflicted by the House Un-American Activities Committee—seemed to impose a chill on the creativity of the arts, on popular culture, on the scope of social criticism, and on the quest for political alternatives to the apparent complacency of the middle class. For the war babies (and their parents) McCarthyism was a presence they could not ignore or elude. But in the end, McCarthy and HUAC did not prevent the war babies from changing their lives or their society.

CHAPTER 3

The Limits of McCarthyism

McCARTHYISM COINCIDED WITH the nastiest years of the Cold War. From the late 1940s through most of the 1950s, the hunt for "subversives" in American life was marked by the investigations of the House Un-American Activities Committee (HUAC), the loyalty oath program imposed by the Truman Administration, and the Attorney General's list of organizations presumably allied with the Communist Party. McCarthyism was exemplified as well by the trials of Alger Hiss and Julius and Ethel Rosenberg (with the latter trial ending in their conviction for transmitting secrets about the atomic bomb to their Soviet controllers and their executions); by the blacklists of actors, directors, and writers instituted by executives in the movie and television industries; and by the allegations by Joseph McCarthy himself that there were Communists or Communist sympathizers in the government, particularly in the State Department. The rationale for these actions was not only that the Soviet Union had in fact engaged in espionage with the assistance of American spies during the 1930s and World War II, but also that people allied with the Communist Party or its front groups were somehow responsible for the United States "losing" China, the division of Europe, and the deadlocked Cold War.[1]

It is commonly assumed that McCarthyism had a devastating effect on American culture in the postwar years. And there is no question that McCarthy's anti-Communist invective and investigations, as well as those of HUAC, destroyed people's careers in government, scientific laboratories, high schools and universities, and the entertainment world. As a result, it is reasonable to argue, as many historians have, that the early Cold War era was among the bleakest for American cultural and artistic inspiration in the twentieth century.

More significantly, the McCarthyite experience became the war babies' first instruction, mostly through television but sometimes in watching their parents' reactions, in how to behave under pressure— whether to cooperate or resist the investigations, the questions about what people did and who they knew, the invitation to inform on others to salvage one's own career. McCarthyism was therefore more than a political phenomenon. It posed a personal dilemma and raised the question of character, of innate decency (as the lawyer for the Army during the Army-McCarthy hearings, Joseph Welsh, accused McCarthy of lacking). The war babies carried the memory of Welsh's indictment and his lesson about private integrity into their adult lives.

Yet if one looks more closely at developments in American painting, architecture, literature, the theater, and social criticism, one is struck by just how extraordinary were the works of art, intellect, and entertainment produced during these years. Indeed, far from inhibiting the creativity of American culture, McCarthyism had almost no impact on the art or the ideas of the 1950s. Instead, America enjoyed a cultural renaissance comparable to, if not surpassing, the artistic innovations of the 1920s. And this was a renaissance that the war babies, as adolescents, all experienced.

Memories of the Inquisitions

For those war babies who were teenagers in the 1950s, the ominous images of Joseph McCarthy—in newspaper photographs and newsreels, and on television—were deeply imbedded in their consciousness and remembrances. Judy Collins recalled that her father hated McCarthy for ruining people's lives. Faye Dunaway learned that many of her professors at the Boston University School of Fine and Applied Arts had worked in Hollywood or on television shows, but had been blacklisted for refusing to answer HUAC's questions about whether they were members of the Communist Party. Nor were they willing to identify those they knew of having attended Party meetings.[2]

My own mother allowed me in the spring of 1954 to stay home from school so I could watch the Army-McCarthy hearings on television. She believed, correctly, that I would learn more from watching Senator McCarthy's brutal performance than from anything I might be taught in class. Barney Frank's parents felt the same way; he too remained home to watch the hearings.[3] The drama of the hearings, especially the confrontation between McCarthy and Joseph Welsh, was riveting. Nothing matched them in intensity until the Senate Watergate hearings, broadcast on television in 1973.

Yet no one among the war babies experienced the effects of McCarthyism more personally than Carl Bernstein. In 1989, Bernstein published a memoir called *Loyalties* about his parents' ties to the Communist Party and his own recollections of how much his entire family was hounded by the FBI in the 1950s. His parents were not thrilled that their son was delving into their political past, and his father refused to read the book. But they did answer his questions about what they had done and why.

Although Bernstein's parents had withdrawn from Communist activities and meetings in the late 1940s, they did not officially leave the Party because they felt their departure would have been disloyal. For this, they paid a heavy price. They were purged from the labor movement to which they had given most of their time and energies during the 1930s and the war years, and were ostracized by their former friends (those who were blacklisted in Hollywood also found their friends avoiding them in the years of their exile).

Nevertheless, Bernstein's parents continued to engage in left-wing politics, notably during the trial and imprisonment of Julius and Ethel Rosenberg. Bernstein recalled that the Rosenberg case was a constant topic of dinner-table conversation, and that his parents served on committees to exonerate the couple or at least have their death sentences commuted. On June 19, 1953, Bernstein and his parents spent the entire afternoon marching in front of the White House pleading for clemency. But nothing worked. On the night of June 19, at 8:00 p.m., the Rosenbergs were electrocuted (I recall that it got very quiet in my house when the news came over the radio that the Rosenbergs were dead). Bernstein himself cried hysterically at the death of the Rosenbergs. Yet he was also angry that his parents seemed to be risking their own lives; if the Rosenbergs could be jailed and executed, he feared, then so could his mother and father.

In fact, Bernstein's parents were under persistent surveillance by the FBI throughout the late 1940s and early 1950s. Two agents even showed up at Bernstein's Bar Mitzvah, though how his reading of the Torah could be regarded as dangerous was unknown both to Bernstein and the agents. In 1954, Bernstein's mother was summoned to testify before HUAC. She was an "unfriendly" witness, in the parlance of the time, because she declined to name the names of her former associates in the Communist Party. Bernstein's father explained to his son that one took the Fifth Amendment in order to protect one's friends, that this was the ultimate symbol of trustworthiness.

Eventually, in 1962 during the Cuban missile crisis, Bernstein was able to read the FBI files on his parents. He discovered that there was no information in the files that identified his parents as subversive or seditious to the United States. Clark Clifford, President Truman's closest adviser, later told Bernstein that Truman loathed Joseph McCarthy, and that Truman's loyalty oath program and Attorney General's list were just ways of neutralizing his political opponents on the right as well as justifying his anti-Communist foreign policy.

Still, Bernstein admitted in his book that he was exasperated at his parents for their commitment to a Communist movement that was dishonest, vicious, and (under Stalin) murderous. But at the end of his memoir, Bernstein reminded his readers that he had "tried to learn what happened in our family, and to set it down. In so doing," he confessed, "I may or may not have committed an act of disloyalty. My mother and father never did."[4]

Bernstein's memoir offered a harrowing portrait of what it was like to be the target of investigations and harassment in the Truman and Eisenhower years. So the break-ins and enemies list during Watergate seemed to Bernstein all-too-familiar. For Bernstein, the crimes of the Nixon Administration appeared to be a replay of the inquisitions during the McCarthy era, inquisitions that he had witnessed as an adolescent.

Yet for all the lives that HUAC and McCarthy wrecked, Mc-Carthyism itself barely impinged on the culture of the 1940s and 1950s. Painters, architects, novelists, playwrights, and social critics felt little constraint in their work. On the contrary, they contributed to a cultural and intellectual efflorescence that shaped the war babies' values and view of the world.

The Creativity of Postwar Culture

At the end of World War II, the United States was the strongest country, economically and militarily, on the planet. It had also become the home of Western culture. No longer was it obligatory, as it had been in the nineteenth century or the 1920s, for American scientists, artists, and writers to travel to Paris, London, Berlin, or Vienna to sit at the feet of their European masters, learning the latest developments in modern thought. Now, America was the center of science and scholarship, art and ideas.

Much of this transformation in the cultural balance of power between Europe and America was the result of one man: Adolf Hitler. During the 1930s and the early war years, thousands of refugees—many of them Jewish—fled Nazi Germany, Central Europe, and France for the United States. In most cases, in the face of the death camps, they were running for their lives. And though they had difficulty adapting to American customs, they usually created a new existence for themselves in America's universities, in the scientific laboratories (particularly at Los Alamos), in the art museums, as conductors of orchestras, and in Hollywood. They brought with them a modernist perspective that helped change American painting, architecture, literature, and the movies.[5]

McCarthyism had very little impact either on the refugees or on the native-born artists and intellectuals who dominated American culture after World War II. But the artistic and literary ferment that characterized American life in the late 1940s and 1950s did exert an enormous impact on the war babies. It was this cultural revolution with which they grew up, and that influenced their work once they became adults.

For any war baby interested in painting, like Joni Mitchell, Martin Scorsese, and Michael Cimino, the postwar years witnessed the coming of age of American artists, when the Abstract Expressionists dominated the modernist movement in painting throughout the world. There was no more magnetic figure among the Abstract Expressionists than Jackson Pollock, his works and his rebellious persona celebrated not only in global art exhibitions but in the pages of *Time* and *Life* to which the war babies' parents subscribed. Pollock and his colleagues were considered the new geniuses to which art aficionados paid homage. And art collectors began to pay large sums for the Abstract Expressionist paintings that could adorn the walls of their mansions and corporate headquarters.

When the Museum of Modern Art opened in New York in 1929, it devoted its exhibits over the next fifteen years to European painting: the Impressionists, the Cubists, the Surrealists, the artistic leaders of the first half of the twentieth century. Now, after the war, MoMA increasingly displayed the work of contemporary American artists, as did Frank Lloyd Wright's Guggenheim Museum when it opened in 1959.

By the time I entered college, at Rutgers in 1959, the Museum of Modern Art and the Guggenheim became for many war babies shrines of artistic worship to which they had to make a pilgrimage to discover the insurgency in American painting, sculpture, and design taking place all around them. Which explained why Robert De Niro's father started his career as an Abstract Expressionist, and why Joni Mitchell frequently created her own abstract record album covers in the 1960s and 1970s.

Similarly, modernist American architecture (though often the product of German refugees from the Bauhaus like Walter Gropius and Mies van der Rohe) altered the silhouettes of American metropolises in the 1950s from New York to Kansas City to Los Angeles. The ubiquitous "glass boxes" that Tom Wolfe later satirized in *From Bauhaus to Our House* were, at least for a time, the esthetic trademarks of American construction and urban planning, visible in all the cities in which the war babies lived. Moreover, none of these architects were affected by the anti-Communist hysteria of the McCarthyites.

Nor did America's new generation of novelists, with the exception of Norman Mailer (whose *The Deer Park* in 1955 dealt with the plight of a blacklisted Hollywood director), pay much attention to the political frenzies of the Cold War years. Saul Bellow, Bernard Malamud, John Updike, John Cheever, and Philip Roth all began writing during the 1940s and 1950s; their early novels and short stories were as inventive as the fiction of Hemingway, Fitzgerald, and Faulkner in the 1920s. And the post–World War II novelists were just as popular with the war babies as the writers of the 1920s had been with the expatriates and other young readers after World War I.

Indeed, nearly everyone I knew at Rutgers was reading Roth's *Goodbye, Columbus* in 1959 in part because the story took place in New Jersey and seemed to capture their own experience of growing up in the 1950s. But the most influential novels of the 1950s were J.D. Salinger's *The Catcher in the Rye* (1951) and Jack Kerouac's *On the Road* (1957). For Bob Dylan, *The Catcher in the Rye* and *On the Road*, along with Allen Ginsberg's 1956 poem *Howl*, were sacred texts, dramatizing how he wanted to live his life. Later, Ginsberg became a close friend of Dylan's. Jerry Garcia and Jim Morrison were equally enthralled with *On the Road*, and the Beat movement in general.[6]

What the novels of Mailer, Bellow, Malamud, Updike, Cheever, Roth, Salinger, and Kerouac all had in common was an obsession with self-definition. Saul Bellow's characters, for example—especially Augie

March—are perpetually pestered by family, relatives, friends, and aspiring mentors, all trying to mold his identity, telling him what they think he should do and feel. This social pressure, as portrayed in the novels, became a metaphor for the war babies' discontent with middle-class life in postwar America. Whatever else they wanted to be, they had (like Salinger's Holden Caulfield) a horror of being "phony."

In many ways, the works of America's playwrights were even more potent for the war babies than those of America's novelists. No period in the history of the American theater was as luminous as the one that saw the first productions of Tennessee Williams's *A Streetcar Named Desire*, Arthur Miller's *Death of a Salesman* (though Miller did confront the issue of McCarthyism in *The Crucible*), Eugene O'Neill's *The Iceman Cometh* and *Long Day's Journey Into Night* (both written in the 1930s or early 1940s but not staged until after the war), and Edward Albee's *Who's Afraid of Virginia Woolf?*

Francis Ford Coppola read *Streetcar* when he was fifteen; the play was instrumental in encouraging his interest both in the theater and film. I can vividly recall seeing *The Iceman Cometh* on public television in 1960 with Jason Robards and a very young Robert Redford. I also saw the original version of *Who's Afraid of Virginia Woolf?* on Broadway in 1962, as disturbing an experience in the theater as I was ever to have.

Apart from *The Crucible*, all of these plays were psychodramas, an illumination of how individuals and members of families act toward one another, love or fail to love, and mostly descend into despair. Despite the stereotypes of the 1950s, none of these plays were blissful portraits of family life but rather ones in which fathers (and mothers) never know best. Consequently, the novels and plays of the postwar era enhanced the idea for the war babies that America was a country full of private restlessness and dissatisfactions, emotions that turned into a mantra for them in the 1960s.

The works of social criticism in the 1950s had a similar impact on the war babies. We often think of the 1930s and the 1960s as decades in which America's intellectuals assaulted the reigning values of American capitalism. But neither decade scrutinized the complacency of the middle class, the tediousness of white- and blue-collar work, or the complexities of centralized power as did the books of the 1950s, most of them best-sellers. The 1950s was the decade which boasted the publication of David Riesman's *The Lonely Crowd* (1950), C. Wright Mills's *White Collar* (1951) and *The Power Elite* (1956), William Whyte's *The Organization Man* (1956), John Kenneth Galbraith's *The Affluent Society* (1958), and Paul Goodman's *Growing Up Absurd* (1960).

Many of the war babies avidly read all these books. Two of Jim Morrison's most cherished works were *The Lonely Crowd* and *The Power Elite*.[7] Tom Hayden was heavily influenced by *The Power Elite* whose ideas he incorporated into his "Port Huron Statement" in 1962, the manifesto that created the Students for a Democratic Society and helped launch the New Left. Indeed, the war babies encountered all of these books on their reading lists in college in the late 1950s and early 1960s; I can remember reading each one in various courses at Rutgers between 1959 and 1963.

None of the criticism in these books was restrained by McCarthyism. Neither, however, did they preach the virtues of revolution. Yet their indictments of contemporary America were frequently more scathing, and certainly more troubling, than the works of social criticism in what were allegedly angrier and more politically "radical" decades like the 1930s or the 1960s.

Their central themes were how to avoid "selling out," how to resist the conformist pressures of one's parents and friends, how to carve out space for an individual's own distinctive personality. As David Riesman observed in the preface to *The Lonely Crowd*, the central problem for Americans in the postwar years was "other people." This was a sentiment inconceivable in the 1930s or during World War II, where cooperating with other people was thought the only way of solving problems.

What these books suggested was that the war babies should want to be neither phonies nor "other-directed," or unconsciously wedded to the needs of whatever organizations (corporate, governmental, or military) for which they might later work. The books told us that we might not be insurrectionists, wild ones in black leather jackets (like Marlon Brandö), but that we could decide when to rebel against the suffocating conventionality of the men in grey flannel suits.[8] This was a message the war babies carried with them throughout their adult lives. As young impressionable readers, war babies like Martin Scorsese, Al Pacino, Joan Baez, Bob Dylan, Mario Savio, Carl Bernstein and others internalized the arguments of the writers of the 1950s, and their exposés of postwar American life, throughout the 1960s and beyond.

So America's artists and writers were hardly "silent" or fearful during the age of McCarthyism. Instead, they created a culture that was both unsettling and liberating for their war baby readers, a culture that shaped not only the war babies' adolescence but their adulthood as well.

Yet it was in the entertainment industries—those most vulnerable to McCarthyism and the blacklists—that the war babies discovered the new talent and new works of art that offered them the most challenging vision of America. In radio, television, and the movies, the war babies found a portrait of American life that was often darker even than what they encountered in the novels, plays, and works of social criticism of the 1950s. And the popular media of the postwar years became a yardstick not just for how the war babies interpreted their relationships with their friends, colleagues, and parents. The media—particularly the movies of the 1950s and early 1960s—also inspired their own films, music, and political activism as they entered their adult years.

CHAPTER 4

The War Babies and the Postwar Media

UNLIKE ANY OTHER GENERATION in twentieth century America, the war babies grew up with the three major forms of the modern mass media: network radio, television, and the movies. And all three influenced, though in different ways, how they understood and reacted to their world, even as adults.

The programs they listened to on the radio or watched on television, or the films they saw at the movie theaters or on late-night television channels, reverberated in their minds from childhood on. This was the culture that defined postwar America for them, affected their attitude toward their parents, and molded their perception of American values. The media—especially television and movies—gave them images of personal rebellion and insights that helped them to transform America from the 1960s to the present.

Nothing McCarthyism or HUAC tried to do could alter the media's critiques of postwar America. The careers of some actors, directors, and writers may have been devastated (although many of those who were blacklisted reappeared on television and, like Zero Mostel, in the movies of the 1960s and 1970s). But the overall impact of radio, television, and films became the permanent muse of the war babies as they began in the 1960s to create their own songs, movies, and political movements.

The Golden Age of Radio

At the end of his movie *Radio Days* (1987) Woody Allen—who was slightly older than the war babies—remarks, mournfully, "I've never forgotten... any of the voices we would hear on the radio. Though the truth is, with the passing of each [year], those voices do seem to grow dimmer and dimmer." Those of us a bit younger than Allen still remember listening to programs on network radio after World War II, before we started to sit hypnotized in the early 1950s in front of our first television sets.

The golden age of network radio was brief. It lasted for only twenty-five years, from the mid-1920s when NBC and CBS were launched, to the end of the 1940s when television supplanted radio as the principal form of household entertainment. Yet during the 1940s, when the war babies like me were children, radio was the chief transmitter of a world beyond our homes. And the voices that Woody Allen recalled have never really left our consciousness.

As a youngster, Judy Collins did her afternoon and evening chores accompanied by her favorite radio shows, especially *The Shadow* introduced by the chilling baritone of Orson Welles. While Joan Baez's mother cooked dinner, she and her daughter would listen to the adventures of *Sergeant Preston of the Yukon*. For Carole King at the age of five, radio was the vehicle that bound her family together, providing them all with a source of words, sounds, stories, and music. Moreover, radio gave King a series of aural cues long before she was exposed to the visual imagery conveyed by television. Bob Dylan had his own favorite radio shows as a child: *The Lone Ranger*, *Fibber McGee and Molly*, and *Dragnet*. In John Lewis's case, radio meant the *Grand Ole Opry*, a symbol of the universe transcending his circumscribed life as the child of tenant farmers. For Tom Brokaw, already a budding broadcast journalist, radio brought news of the outside world, particularly through the sonorous reports of Edward R. Murrow and Lowell Thomas.[1]

I myself found the radio comedians unforgettable. I couldn't wait to tune into Bob Hope, Jack Benny, Fred Allen, George Burns and

Gracie Allen. I can still hear in my mind the nasal voice of Fred Allen skewering the foibles of politicians, the Senator Claghorns who prefigured and deflated in advance the pomposities of Joe McCarthy. All of these programs and voices (as Woody Allen recognized) were staples of network radio, enjoyed by millions of Americans, as well as by the war babies across the land.

For a time, the radio set was the most important piece of furniture in America's living rooms. Families gathered around the radio, after dinner, to hear their favorite shows. In this fashion, network radio (like the New Deal and World War II) brought people together, parents and children alike, for news, information, and entertainment. Listening to the radio was a communal activity, as watching television (particularly if a family had multiple sets in different rooms) or going to the movies was not. Radio therefore was one reason why families in the 1940s still felt as if they were a cohesive unit, without the conflicts that would soon develop between parents and adolescents.

Of course, radio didn't vanish with the arrival of television. Instead, it became a local phenomenon, with individual stations playing popular music that war babies like Joan Baez, Judy Collins, Bob Dylan, and Simon and Garfunkel absorbed and internalized by themselves, in their bedrooms or in their cars, a private experience offering them a vision of the music they themselves would eventually compose and perform. But the sense of commonality that network radio bred did disappear, replaced by television shows (especially live dramas) that supplied a more disturbing version of family life and of the standards that reigned in Eisenhower's America.

Television in Postwar America

Within a six year period, from 1947 to 1953, television obliterated network radio. Never had there been such a sudden or sweeping revolution in the way Americans entertained themselves. By the early 1950s, most of the leading radio stars—like Bob Hope, Jack Benny, and Burns and

Allen—had switched their shows to television. At the same time, new television idols (formerly in vaudeville, nightclubs, or movies) emerged: Milton Berle, Sid Caesar, Lucille Ball, Jackie Gleason, Groucho Marx. In addition, television threatened the popularity of movies, and attendance at films steadily declined throughout the 1950s and 1960s. Traipsing to see a film, either at a downtown movie palace or at a neighborhood theater, was no longer a regular occurrence as it had been in the 1920s and 1930s, especially for adults. Why pay money to see some Western or biblical spectacle on a large screen when you could stay home and be spellbound for free?

Martin Scorsese's family was one of the first in Little Italy to buy a television set, in 1948, when he was six years old. Scorsese loved watching old movies on television, no matter how mutilated they were by relentless commercials and wretched sound. Barney Frank's parents were among the first on their block to purchase a set. Bob Dylan's family acquired a television in 1952, making them one of the earliest families in Hibbing, Minnesota to have a small blue light gleaming in their living room. As an adolescent, Dylan favored comedies and Westerns, notably *Gunsmoke*, with its hero Marshal Matt Dillon (James Arness), another inspiration for Dylan's changing his name from Zimmerman in the late 1950s. Dick Cheney's family owned one of the first television sets in their neighborhood; his sixth grade classmates crammed into his living room to watch President Eisenhower's inauguration in January 1953. Once Tom Brokaw's parents bought a television, he was drawn—prophetically for his adult career—to the *Today* show with Dave Garroway, to Walter Cronkite recreating events in American and world history on *You Are There*, and above all to the news on the *Huntley-Brinkley Report* which began broadcasting in 1956.[2]

John Lewis not only watched television, he appeared on it. In 1960, he was interviewed on an NBC documentary narrated by Chet Huntley on segregation in Nashville. In 1960 as well, television news covered sit-ins in Nashville in which Lewis participated. For the first time, Lewis recalled, Americans especially in the North glimpsed the anger and abhorrence of whites being pressured by the civil rights movement in the South.[3]

Faye Dunaway was captivated by every program she could find on television; she didn't care what she watched.[4] I did care. For me, television meant live plays, broadcast nearly every night of the week, most of them an hour long except for *Playhouse 90* which put on dramas for an hour-and-a-half between 1956 and 1960. Here, in these plays, you could see youthful actors learning their craft: James Dean, Paul Newman, Robert Redford, and the stunningly intense John Cassavetes. And young directors like Sidney Lumet, Arthur Penn, and John Frankenheimer who were experimenting with how to make a camera tell an intimate story of tension-filled families and haunted individuals, subjects they would enlarge upon when they became filmmakers.

The finest of the television plays ultimately became movies. These included *Marty* (which originally starred Rod Steiger), *12 Angry Men*, *Patterns* (about the ruthless competitiveness of American business), *The Miracle Worker*, *A Man is Ten Feet Tall* (a story of racial animosity and violence with a young Sidney Poitier), and *Requiem for a Heavyweight*, with its allusions to *On the Waterfront*, each a tale of a washed-up boxer seeking to preserve his dignity and self-esteem. In the movie version of *Requiem* in 1962, the punch-drunk boxer, called Mountain Rivera, is played by Anthony Quinn who fights one last bout with a man who outclasses him in speed and endurance. That man was played in the film by Cassius Clay under his original name at the time, and Clay looked as swift and handsome in the movie as he ever did in the boxing ring.

All of these television plays offered a gloomier view of America's values than HUAC, with its campaign to blacklist suspicious actors and playwrights, would have approved of. Indeed, HUAC might have tried to keep such dramas off the air entirely if the members of the committee had realized that viewers—particularly teenagers like me—were noticing in the plays the sordidness of postwar American life.

Somber dramas in the 1950s, however, always competed with the war babies' affection for comedy. Almost everyone in America, what-

ever their age, seems to have adored *I Love Lucy*. But my tastes ran to
more satirical fare. My grandmother purchased a television set before
my parents did. So I can remember our going over to her home on Saturday nights to watch *Your Show of Shows*, a ninety-minute assemblage
of comic skits broadcast between 1950 and 1954, starring Sid Caesar,
Imogene Coca, Carl Reiner, and Howard Morris. From 1954 to 1957, the
show changed into *Caesar's Hour*. I didn't know at the time that Caesar
was buttressed by some of the wittiest and most sardonic writers in the
industry: Neil Simon, Mel Brooks, Larry Gelbart (who created the television version of *MASH* in the 1970s and co-wrote the script for Dustin
Hoffman's movie *Tootsie* in 1982), and Woody Allen.

Jackie Gleason was another dazzling comedian who presided over
a variety show, featuring a sketch called "The Honeymooners," through
most of the 1950s. None of us realized that Gleason could also be a serious, even poignant, actor as he demonstrated playing Minnesota Fats
in *The Hustler* in 1961, and Mountain Rivera's manager in *Requiem for a
Heavyweight* in 1962.

Near the end of the 1950s and into the early 1960s, though, the
war babies' most cherished icons were the new generation of comedians
whom they first saw on the earliest versions of the *Tonight* show, hosted
first by Steve Allen and then by Jack Paar before Johnny Carson took
over the franchise in 1962. Here we caught our first sight of acerbic hu-
morists like Mort Sahl, Mike Nichols and Elaine May, Tom Lehrer,
Lenny Bruce, and soon Woody Allen. Long before Jon Stewart and Stephen Colbert, these comics were the war babies' reporters and tribunes,
lampooning the pretensions of the liberal, well-educated middle class.

Yet what really struck us was how personal (and improvisational)
the humor of these comedians was. Jack Benny, Bob Hope, and Sid
Caesar, however impeccable their timing, had a battalion of writers to
mold their show business characters and their public, even political,
comedy. Mort Sahl, with a newspaper under his arm, was telling us
what he himself, not his writers, thought of the news. As in his observation that if Unitarians were members of the Ku Klux Klan in the midst

of the civil rights movement, they would burn a question mark on your lawn. Mike Nichols and Elaine May mocked the behavior-patterns of modern romance, each of them imitating classic neurotics who didn't know whether they were in love until they consulted a shrink. Tom Lehrer sang about the ex-Nazi rocket scientist Wernher von Braun, now working for the Americans, who didn't care where the bombs landed once the rockets went up: "That's not my department," says the consummate nuclear bureaucrat. Woody Allen recalled his own days in college, where he cheated on his metaphysics exam by gazing into his classmate's soul. And Lenny Bruce was "spritzing" just like a traditional Catskills tummler, a descendant of Milton Berle but with his own derisive take (rather than an enormous joke file) on the foibles of his world and his audience.

The intimacy of this humor, the way it cut close to the bone of America's bourgeoisie, the comedians' private vision of an absurd universe, all influenced the war babies' own personal reactions to the country in which they were growing up. And the new comics had an effect not just on subsequent comedians, but on the actions and outlook of most of the war babies in the 1960s and beyond.

Mike Nichols, for example, had a profound impact in the late 1960s on the careers of both Paul Simon and Art Garfunkel. Yet no comedian was more charismatic for the war babies than Lenny Bruce. Bob Dylan encountered Bruce in Greenwich Village in the early 1960s, just as Dylan was starting to compose his own mordant songs about American life.[5]

Faye Dunaway's relationship with Bruce was even closer. She saw him perform in the Village in 1962, and was drawn to his rebelliousness and inner fury. Bruce's appeal was his willingness to challenge the status quo, to eviscerate the "establishment" in America, to utter the truth no matter what the consequences. For Dunaway, Bruce was as much a Method actor as a comic, his personality an indelible part of his routines. So, at the age of twenty-one, she entered into an affair with Bruce as he was nearing his forties. But this was an affair that was doomed from the beginning. In addition to his growing legal troubles on obscenity charges, Bruce was addicted to heroin. There was no way that Dunaway could save him from what seemed a preordained fate.[6] In 1966, Bruce died of an overdose of pills—in many ways, the first famous victim of the drug culture of the 1960s.

The idiosyncratic style of the new comedians did directly influence the humor of two war babies who became stars in their own right from the 1960s on: Garrison Keillor (born in Minnesota in 1942) and Lily Tomlin (born in Detroit in 1939). Like the comics of the late 1950s and early 1960s, Keillor and Tomlin relied on their own personalities rather than employing writers for their wit. Their material and characterizations were the product of their self-creation, the element that most marked the culture of the war babies and of America in the last half of the twentieth century.

Keillor, the descendant of Scottish immigrants, came from a family of talkers. Since his parents were members of a fundamentalist Christian sect that banned going to the movies or watching television, conversation was one of the few forms of entertainment for Keillor and his family. Keillor, however, also began writing at an early age, publishing a neighborhood newspaper when he was in the sixth grade. But throughout his adolescence and young adulthood, he was a bashful introvert, an observer of other people's behavior, though he was also endowed with a barbed sense of humor. And he listened to the radio, eventually patterning his own humor and narrative abilities after Arthur Godfrey and Fred Allen.

For Keillor, writing became both an outlet and an infatuation. When he graduated from high school, he enrolled in 1960 at the University of Minnesota where a number of novelists and critics taught during his time there: Saul Bellow, Robert Penn Warren, Allen Tate. Keillor worked on the university newspaper writing poems, short stories, and book reviews. He gravitated as well to the university's radio station, honing his skills as a commentator and storyteller, not to mention a disc jockey who first played for his local radio audience the Beatles' transformative album, *Sergeant Pepper's Lonely Hearts Club Band*, released in 1967. Here Keillor was commemorating, even if unconsciously, the transatlantic nature of the war babies' passions and music.

Once Keillor left the university, he dedicated himself to writing and radio. By 1970, he had become a regular contributor to *The New Yorker*. Yet it was radio at which Keillor truly excelled. Keillor's voice—with its smooth, soothing tones—was made for radio broadcasting. And it was on the radio that Keillor gained fame when he launched *A Prairie Home Companion*, first on Minnesota public radio in 1974, and then broadcast nationally starting in 1979.

Keillor's style—conveyed in yarns and commercials—was intimate, as if he were talking directly to a specific listener. His invention of "Lake Wobegon" with its rural characters combined the techniques of William Faulkner and Mark Twain, a mixture of myths, tall tales, and comic folklore that was purely fictional and yet seemed realistic to an audience that numbered four million people at the height of the program's popularity in America. Indeed so appealing was the show that the United States Information Agency broadcast the program to countries in Europe and Scandinavia.

Unlike Mort Sahl or Tom Lehrer, Keillor did not dissect politics or national events. He was never a satirist, simply a rustic humorist (or at least that was the mask he adopted for public consumption). While the show temporarily went off the air in 1987, various incarnations have resurfaced over the years.[7] And Keillor became as famous as a comedian, as droll and personal as any of his predecessors from the more urban Nichols and May to Woody Allen.

Like Garrison Keillor, Lily Tomlin from childhood on was an observer of other people's conduct, voices, and facial expressions. She was also exceptional at replicating their behavior. As a result, many of her comic portraits as an adult were based on the people she saw or knew growing up in Detroit.

In many ways, Tomlin was a self-taught Method actress who also happened to be a comedian. She began to appear in plays at Wayne State University before she dropped out after her junior year to pursue a professional acting career. Though she initially failed to attract attention or an agent in New York, she started to experiment with improvisations and invent her own characters when she went back to Detroit. Tomlin returned to New York in 1964, now equipped with an array of persons who were completely her own creation. In this sense, her comedy and acting performances exemplified the personal nature of the new humor and the new culture of the 1960s.

In 1969, Tomlin was recruited by the producer George Schlatter to join the cast of the hit television show on NBC, *Rowan and Martin's Laugh-In*. Tomlin became famous for her hilarious impersonations of fictional characters—especially "Ernestine," the telephone operator who conducted one-way conversations with renowned public figures like Henry Kissinger, Frank Sinatra, William F. Buckley, J. Edgar Hoover, Richard Nixon, and above all Gore Vidal, whose name she pronounced "Veedle." In fact, Lorne Michaels (another war baby, born in Toronto in 1944) was so impressed with Tomlin's comic personas and extemporaneous skills that he modeled a new program on her talents. The program, for which he was creator and executive producer, was called *Saturday Night Live*; it was launched in 1975, and has become a staple of modern political and social satire ever since.

Yet one more master of art and entertainment was equally awed with Tomlin's gifts. Robert Altman hired her for his epic movie *Nashville* (1975), one of the most memorable films of the Hollywood renaissance in the 1970s. Here, Tomlin proved—as Jackie Gleason had in *The Hustler* and *Requiem for a Heavyweight*—that she could be a compelling actress. She played Linnea Reese, the mother of two deaf children, a white singer in a black gospel choir, a lover (briefly) of a rock singer, and perhaps the one person in the movie who doesn't care about politics or stardom in the country music industry. For her superb performance— one that remained unforgettable despite the fact that there were twenty-three other characters in the film—Tomlin was nominated for an Oscar and won the prize for best supporting actress from the New York Film Critics association.[8]

Eventually, Tomlin and Garrison Keillor found themselves acting together. They were joined by Meryl Streep, Kevin Kline, Woody
Harrelson, John C. Reilly, and Tommy Lee Jones in Robert Altman's
last film, with a script written by Keillor, called appropriately *A Prairie
Home Companion* (2006). Tomlin plays Meryl Streep's dour, sarcastic
older sister, part of a singing duo that never quite makes it out of the
hinterlands. And the radio show itself is about to be canceled because
the audience has moved on. But the movie is a joyous celebration of the
talents of everyone involved—especially those of Altman, Keillor, and
Tomlin. And it reflected the personal, quirky genius of all three artists.

The programs on radio in the 1940s and on television in the 1950s—
the dramas as well as the comedies—certainly had an impact on the
demeanor and perspective of the war babies. Yet there is a reason why
we still recall a movie like *Nashville*, possibly more than any radio or
television show. No form of entertainment, in the 1950s or afterwards,
was as mesmerizing or as emotionally consequential for the war babies
as the movies—and as the unconventional actors who became America's
culture heroes in the postwar years.

"I Coulda Been a Contender"

For most adolescents and youthful adults in the 1950s and early 1960s,
dating normally meant going to a movie, and then maybe flirting afterwards at a drive-in hamburger joint. The war babies during these years
typically followed this pattern on Friday or Saturday nights.

Because such behavior seemed so prevalent among the young, one
of the myths embedded in the history of American films is that the 1950s
and early 1960s were a time of inane, big-budget movies intended only
to earn money and amuse the dwindling number of viewers—usually
teenagers—who could be seduced away from their television sets. In
addition, the specters of McCarthyism and the blacklists in Hollywood
purportedly frightened filmmakers into avoiding the major issues or
criticizing the dominant values of the era.

Thus, the movies of the postwar years were supposedly mindless and mediocre. And so it would not be until the late 1960s and 1970s that a new cohort of filmmakers, many of them war babies like Francis Ford Coppola and Martin Scorsese, began to make "serious" and personal works of art.

One might never know, then, that in the 1950s and early 1960s young audiences could see some of Alfred Hitchcock's and Billy Wilder's best films. Hitchcock's movies in particular upset the viewer's serenity about the ordinary experiences of daily life, whether it was taking a shower or seeing birds congregating on trees and telephone wires. Meanwhile, Wilder's movies, like *Sunset Boulevard*, specialized in the trepidations of film noir (as his work had done since the 1940s), and his prickly comedies (like *The Apartment* and *Some Like it Hot*) were hardly reminiscent of the good-natured humor one encountered on television situation comedies like *Leave it to Beaver* in the 1950s.

The war babies could also watch John Ford's *The Searchers* and *The Man Who Shot Liberty Valance*, movies in which John Wayne appeared less as an all-American hero than as something of a maniac. This was also the period of Elia Kazan's finest movies: his interpretation for the screen of *A Streetcar Named Desire*, as well as *Viva Zapata!*, *On the Waterfront*, *East of Eden* (all four of which made Marlon Brando and James Dean incarnations of untamed rebels), and *Splendor in the Grass* (Warren Beatty's first film).

Other movies from this era reinforced the biting point of view that characterized postwar entertainment. These films included Joseph Mankiewicz's *All About Eve* (the wittiest if also the most unsettling movie ever made about the theater or show business in general); Orson Welles's *Touch of Evil* (in which a crooked police captain frames suspects who are in fact guilty); John Huston's *The Misfits* (which proved that Marilyn Monroe, in her last film, could be a sensitive actress, not just a sex symbol); Robert Rossen's *The Hustler*; and Sidney Lumet's *The Pawnbroker* (in which Rod Steiger gave the performance of a lifetime as the impassive survivor of the concentration camps, haunted by the annihilation of his family but unable to articulate or transcend his hideous memories).

The Cold War was not spared from the criticisms or parodies in the period's movies. No one could continue to believe in the virtues of America's righteousness in its contest with the Communists after seeing John Frankenheimer's *The Manchurian Candidate*; Martin Ritt's adaptation of *The Spy Who Came in from the Cold*, John le Carré's portrait of what his main character, Alec Leamas (played in the movie by Richard Burton) calls the "seedy, squalid bastards" who, unlike the dashing James Bond, become spies in order to "brighten their rotten little lives"; and Stanley Kubrick's *Dr. Strangelove*, a black comedy that wholly dismantled the Cold War's mystique.

Most of these movies were inexpensive and shot in black-and-white. They may not have attracted the huge audience that flocked to a movie like *Ben-Hur* in 1959. But they did address the problems, especially the personal and psychological dilemmas of the young war babies—above all the ways the social system in which they were maturing was devoted to the incentives of greed or power, a society that drove human beings to manipulate and corrupt one another. The movies of the 1950s and early 1960s offered the war babies another variation on the theme of selling out—of compromising one's integrity in the interest of fame, conformity, and (as in the title of the 1957 film) the "sweet smell" of success.[9]

No movie better captured the underside of America's postwar self-satisfaction than *The Hustler* (1961)—one of the era's masterpieces. Here was a movie which took place in the grime and gloom of a city's back streets, alleys, bus stations, and pool halls. The film starred Paul Newman as Fast Eddie Felson, a pool-player with "talent" but no character; George C. Scott who delivered the iciest performance of his career as a pimp who profits off other people's skills; Piper Laurie as Fast Eddie's alcoholic lover; and Jackie Gleason as the peerless Minnesota Fats who always knows how to drink and still win.

This was a movie whose meaning my friends and I endlessly discussed. Ostensibly, *The Hustler* was about pool. But in large part the film didn't really focus on winning or losing. Like many other mid-century American films, *The Hustler* was preoccupied with how people use, deceive, betray, and destroy one another.

The obsessions in films such as these with the dangers that come from living by the ethic of success, and with the spiritual poverty that accompanies the acquisition of wealth, were commentaries on the presumed smugness of America in the 1950s. These were the genuine problems of an affluent society. And few among the career-minded organization men (or their wives and children) in the audience could feel free to pay to themselves the final, simple compliment that Fast Eddie and Minnesota Fats pay to each other: "You shoot a great game of pool." So it was hardly surprising that one of the most creative of the war babies, Martin Scorsese, returned to the squalid atmosphere and themes of *The Hustler* in his 1986 sequel, *The Color of Money*, starring Paul Newman, this time as an older, wiser Fast Eddie.

In fact, Scorsese was typical of those war babies who wanted to become directors or actors themselves. They all cherished the best, if also the most troubling, movies and the young often mutinous stars of the 1950s and early 1960s.

Scorsese himself saw his first movie when he was four years old (I saw my first film—John Ford's *Fort Apache* with John Wayne and Henry Fonda—when I was seven). In his early years, Scorsese cherished the Westerns of the 1940s and 1950s. His favorites were *Duel in the Sun*, Howard Hawks's *Red River* (a film in which John Wayne was no longer an archetypal hero but instead an obsessive who at times despises his adopted son, played by Montgomery Clift, for taking over a cattle drive), *High Noon*, and above all John Ford's *The Searchers* (featuring another John Wayne character consumed with wrath at and hatred of native Americans). Indeed many of the themes of *The Searchers* reappeared in one of Scorsese's most gripping films in the 1970s, *Taxi Driver*, where Robert De Niro portrays an urban and far more psychotic version of Wayne's Ethan Edwards.

As he entered his teens, Scorsese began to expand his cinematic

horizons. He saw *Citizen Kane* for the first time when he was an adolescent and after that on dozens of occasions. *Citizen Kane* (and Orson
Welles) made Scorsese aware of what a director could accomplish not
just as an entertainer but as an artist. Scorsese also became addicted to
film noir, particularly Billy Wilder's *Sunset Boulevard*, as well as to the
movies of Alfred Hitchcock (with whom Scorsese shared a sense not
only of the existence of evil in ordinary situations, but also of Catholic
guilt).[10]

Michael Cimino was also influenced by John Ford along with
Luchino Visconti, Akira Kurosawa, and Clint Eastwood. As it happened, Cimino directed and wrote the screenplay for his first film, *Thunderbolt and Lightfoot*, in 1974, a movie that starred Eastwood and was the
only picture Cimino made in the 1970s until his masterwork in 1978, *The
Deer Hunter*.

Other war babies had their own treasured movies or actors. Faye
Dunaway was awestruck by George C. Scott's performances in *The Hus-
tler* and *Dr. Strangelove* (although Scott himself wound up loathing
Stanley Kubrick because the director used only those takes in which
Scott was performing as clownishly and as outrageously as possible).
Paul Simon originally started writing songs under the pseudonym of
Paul Kane in an homage to *Citizen Kane*, the film he most venerated as
a teenager.[11]

Yet it wasn't simply movies that fascinated the war babies. It was
also the new generation of Method actors—like Montgomery Clift,
Marlon Brando, James Dean, and Warren Beatty—who served as role
models for the war babies as they moved through their adolescence and
approached adulthood.

Most of the films in the 1950s and early 1960s that the war babies
revered—like *On the Waterfront*, *Rebel Without a Cause*, *East of Eden*,
and *Splendor in the Grass*—starred Brando, Dean, or Beatty. They also
reinforced the war babies' sense that their own families were dysfunctional, that parents (especially fathers) were ineffectual, and that authority figures of all sorts were not to be trusted. These feelings would later

be confirmed by the mendacity of those in power during the Vietnam War and Watergate.

Despite the influence of the war babies' mothers during World War II, many American movies in the 1950s focused on the failure of parents, older siblings, and anyone with political or cultural clout to comprehend the young. Unlike the situation comedies on television (with the conspicuous exception of Jackie Gleason's *The Honeymooners*), Hollywood rarely exalted family life. Rather, the movies lamented the absence of strong fathers and empathetic mothers (as in *Rebel Without a Cause* or *Splendor in the Grass*), parents who might have provided some credible moral guidance to their offspring. In effect, the parents in these films are reminiscent of all the adults in J.D. Salinger's *The Catcher in the Rye*. The adults in that novel and in many movies of the 1950s are banal, hypocritical, and oblivious to their children's needs.

This conflict between the generations was reinforced for the war babies by the emergence of new, eccentric movie stars whose screen personalities (as instilled by the techniques of the Method) were often nonverbal but highly emotional, as if the actors were thinking their own private thoughts, gazing into their own psyches, searching for a more personally evocative line than any screenwriter could invent. Moreover, these were actors who personified the insurgencies in the 1940s and 1950s of the Abstract Expressionists, the Beats, the African American jazz musicians, and the rock and roll singers, all of whom seemed to the war babies to be antidotes to the complacency of the postwar years.

None of the new actors was more magnetic, or better captured the personal dilemmas of the war babies, than Marlon Brando. Martin Scorsese saw *On the Waterfront* twenty times. When Brando appeared on the screen, Scorsese's whole idea of acting changed (which is partly why Scorsese used a Method actor like Robert De Niro—who at his best was so reminiscent of Brando—in many of his own films).

For Faye Dunaway, Brando was a genius as an actor because he never pretended to play a role. Instead, he was able to project the inner truth and intensity of the character he was embodying. Throughout

Dunaway's career, she yearned to act with Brando. She almost got her wish when she was considered for Arthur Penn's film, *The Chase* (1966), but lost the part to Jane Fonda. Ultimately, Dunaway did co-star with Brando (and Johnny Depp) in *Don Juan DeMarco* in 1994.

As a young girl and then a woman in the 1950s and early 1960s, Joan Baez fantasized about having an affair with Brando. Finally, she met him in the late 1960s and again in the 1980s when he had grown older, paler, and heavier. Yet to Baez, Brando was still sexually alluring, still "tough and tender" at the same time. Brando was in her eyes like an elderly but majestic lion, king of the acting jungle, as he proved in the early 1970s when he played Don Vito Corleone in Francis Ford Coppola's *The Godfather: Part I*.[12]

Brando's characters, even when he was younger, were never adolescent. But they were just as defiant and as tongue-tied, and had the same difficulty navigating the complexities of maturity as the war babies in the 1950s. "What are are you rebelling against, Johnny?" a waitress famously asks Brando in *The Wild One* (1953). "Whaddya got?" Brando replies. Brando's shredded t-shirt in *A Street Car Named Desire* and his pose in a motorcycle cap and black leather jacket in *The Wild One* (represented in a poster that decorated the bedroom walls of many war babies) symbolized the general, if incoherent, alienation felt by a large number of young moviegoers in the 1950s. Indeed, there always seemed to be a "Johnny" slouching in the back of their high school classrooms (as there was in mine), with slicked-back hair and a smirk on his face, sneering at the "good" students in the front of the room who always raised their hands to answer the teacher's questions.

Even when he played roles rooted in historical periods or concrete social settings (as in *Viva Zapata!* or *On the Waterfront*), Brando's singular magic lay in the loneliness and estrangement he portrayed beyond the special situations in these movies. Brando raised the image of the outsider to the level of myth, transcending time and place. This dramatization of marginal figures was replicated by the war babies in their own films in the late 1960s and 1970s: Faye Dunaway in *Bonnie and Clyde*;

Robert De Niro in Martin Scorsese's *Mean Streets, Taxi Driver*, and *Raging Bull*; Al Pacino in Sidney Lumet's *Dog Day Afternoon*.

Brando as an actor, first on stage and then in the movies, was initially dependent on the direction of Elia Kazan. Although he appeared before HUAC in 1952, naming his fellow-Communists in the Group Theater, Kazan was one of the preeminent filmmakers of the 1950s. So despite the controversy that remained about Kazan in Hollywood because of his HUAC testimony, his artistic impact was so immense that two war babies—Martin Scorsese and Robert De Niro—jointly introduced him at the Oscar ceremonies in 1999 to receive a lifetime achievement award.

In addition, Kazan was the director who most acutely explored for the war babies the generational tensions in American society. In Kazan's world, you cannot have faith in your elders because (like Andy Griffith's hillbilly demagogue in *A Face in the Crowd* or both sets of parents who try to control the lives of the young characters played by Warren Beatty and Natalie Wood in *Splendor in the Grass*) they will always fail in their obligations to you. In *On the Waterfront*, Terry Malloy (as played by Brando) is a more embittered version of the 1950s juvenile: enraged, instinctive, uncomfortable with words, and let down by the adults in his milieu—the crooked labor leader, John Friendly (Lee J. Cobb) and especially his older brother (Rod Steiger).

"You was my brother, Charlie," Brando reminds Steiger in *On the Waterfront*'s legendary taxicab scene, "you shoulda looked out for me a little bit. You shoulda taken care of me just a little bit so I wouldn't have to take them dives for the short-end money." When Steiger replies that the mob had some bets down for him (to lose), Brando responds with a wail that could have summed up the frustration of every adolescent in the 1950s confronted with a baffled adult: "You don't understand." And then Brando utters some of the most memorable lines in the history of American movies, lines every war baby could repeat: "I coulda had class. I coulda been a contender. I coulda been somebody, instead of a bum, which is what I am, let's face it." At that moment, we are at the core of the longing, among the war babies, not just for success but for self-respect and personal integrity. In this scene alone, Brando (though older than the war babies) became their spokesman.

Brando's characters in the 1950s and early 1960s are often punished for being rebels and outcasts. They get beaten up in *On the Waterfront* or killed in *Viva Zapata!* and *The Fugitive Kind*. For lots of war babies, James Dean was easier, though no less disquieting, to identify with largely because he did play teenagers or youthful adults in movies like *Rebel Without a Cause* and *East of Eden*.

Dean, for instance, served as something of a deity for the young Bob Dylan. Dylan saw *Rebel Without a Cause* four times, cut out and framed photographs of Dean to adorn his bedroom, and bought a red jacket just like the one Dean wore in the film. Dean's embittered façade combined with his delicate sensitivity suggested to Dylan an aura of alienation from and antipathy toward adult society that Dylan then incorporated into his songs in the 1960s and 1970s.

Dean also supplied Tom Hayden with an image of clandestine defiance which Hayden translated in the 1960s into a political as well as personal philosophy. *Rebel Without a Cause* inspired Jim Morrison to make movies of his own, although his jagged life as a musician and performer more accurately mirrored the turbulence of Dean's life offscreen. Even Tom Brokaw, though not himself a dissident, was nonetheless intrigued by Dean's murky, inarticulate passion, as if Dean was an individual never at ease in his surroundings or with his family. And for Martin Scorsese, *East of Eden* appeared to depict the strains between his father and Scorsese's older brother, a family clash that Scorsese reproduced in *Raging Bull* and *Casino* in the characters played in both movies by Robert De Niro and Joe Pesci (another war baby, born in 1943).[13]

At the core of Dean's movies was precisely this struggle between fathers and sons, or between older and younger siblings. The characters Dean created in two of his three movies (Jim Stark in *Rebel Without a Cause* and Cal Trask in *East of Eden*) suffer incessantly from a lack of parental insight or love, or from the antagonism between "good" and "bad" brothers. Their problems, unlike Brando's, stem from inept families and from the moody neurosis that comes from growing up in a home where no one appreciates anyone else. Mothers are absent and fathers (as in *East of Eden*) are unapproachable. One had the feeling that if only the parents in Dean's films displayed some sympathy and affection Dean's torments would be eased. The same dilemma was central for the characters played by Warren Beatty and Natalie Wood in *Splendor in the Grass*. Nevertheless, Dean especially was a cultural hero for the war babies in the 1950s because of his aching, trembling portraits of middle-class delinquents craving some form of compassion in a nation of inflexible law-abiding conformists.

"What we have here is… failure to communicate." This immortal line, delivered by the great character actor Strother Martin, playing the captain of a chain gang in *Cool Hand Luke* (1967), seemed to capture the political and social discord of the 1960s. But the line was equally applicable to the generational quarrels of the 1950s, certainly as explored in American movies.

Generational conflict was at the heart of the 1960s. But the deterioration of the relationships and trust between parents and teenagers began in the 1950s. If anything, the films of the 1950s—like the novels and plays of the early Cold War years—foreshadowed the breakdown in communication between parents and children, and between the government and its citizens. It was this disintegration that the war babies experienced firsthand in the 1950s, and that inflamed them while it tore America apart during the war in Vietnam and crisis of Watergate.

But the pain of these ruptures also had positive consequences—ones that were both nerve-racking and exhilarating. The familial and psychological turmoil that originated in the 1950s led to a new music, new types of movies, a new more investigative journalism, and a new more individualistic and combative political style that marked American life from the 1960s until the present. And it was the war babies, having lived through the anxieties of the postwar era, who more than anyone else reshaped and personalized the country's culture and politics over the past fifty years.

CHAPTER 5

The Music of the War Babies

ONE OF THE FABLES OF THE 1960s and early 1970s is that these years revived the left-wing political and ideological activism of the 1930s. And certainly the civil rights movement and the opposition to the war in Vietnam in the 1960s seemed reminiscent of the Old Left's efforts during the Depression to renovate the American economy and halt the ominous spread of fascism in Europe.

Yet for all the publicity surrounding the rise of the New Left and the counterculture, and the demonstrations against racial segregation and the slaughter in Vietnam, the years between 1960 and 1975 were marked far more by a preoccupation with personal liberation than with political change. This search for self-realization, along with the effort to deal with private tensions and pain, was echoed in the music composed and performed by the war babies in the 1960s and 1970s. Theirs was a music that resonated with an audience made up largely of baby boomers who heard their own troubled lives being depicted in the songs of Joan Baez, Bob Dylan, Paul Simon and Art Garfunkel, Judy Collins, Joni Mitchell, Carole King, the Grateful Dead and the Jefferson Airplane, Jim Morrison, and Janis Joplin, as well as from across the Atlantic in the albums of the Beatles and the Rolling Stones. All of these artists were responsible for the new sounds and lyrics of the generation born during World War II and growing up in the 1950s.

What was remarkable about the new music was how much it differed in form and intention from the classic American songbook of the 1920s and 1930s. The tunes written by the war babies were more complicated and their lyrics were often more opaque than the songs of George and Ira Gershwin, Irving Berlin, Cole Porter, Richard Rodgers and Lorenz Hart, and Harold Arlen. Indeed, only one war baby—Barbra Streisand—continued performing the types of songs the earlier generation had created. For the rest of the war baby singer/composers, the point was to "modernize" American music: literally to adopt the techniques of modernism in their works. Thus, their songs were more dissonant and less melodious than those of their forbears, their rhythms more intricate, and their lyrics more discordant and harder to decipher. It was almost as if the war baby songwriters in New York, San Francisco, and Nashville were replicating the artistic experimentation in painting, architecture, literature, and avant-garde music that flourished in Paris and Berlin in the 1920s.

But unlike their modernist predecessors in music, composers like Igor Stravinsky and Arnold Schoenberg, the war babies were able to connect intimately with a mass audience. Their songs touched the hearts of the baby boomers who listened and danced to the music of their elders born between 1939 and 1945. And the war babies' music gave meaning to the lives of those younger than them who were trying to comprehend, personally, the upheavals of the 1960s. So in effect the war babies revolutionized American music (in the same way that the war baby filmmakers of the late 1960s and 1970s transformed the American cinema). This artistic insurgency was central to what the war babies contributed to American culture, not only in the 1960s and 1970s, but for the remainder of the twentieth century.

The Musical Revolt of the 1960s

The first musical star of the 1960s was Joan Baez. Baez was the war baby singer who seemed least afflicted by inner demons. And therefore least dependent on those ubiquitous anodynes of the 1960s, drugs and alcohol, that enabled other artists both to perform on stage and to try to cope, at times unsuccessfully, with the turmoil of their private lives.

By the time she was eighteen years old, Baez was performing before increasingly larger audiences, a benefit not only of her mounting status in the Cambridge folk club milieu in which she began but also of her debut at the Newport Folk Festival in 1959. Her mezzo-soprano voice and her intense approach to the songs she sang had a purity of tone that other singers could not equal. Before an audience, Baez seemed regal, ethereal, and mysterious, images that other singers of her own and previous generations rarely matched (it's hard to think of Frank Sinatra on stage or in his movies as delicate or enigmatic—the way many people perceived Baez).

Baez was soon giving concerts in New York and at the Hollywood Bowl. At the same time she moved to Carmel, California which became her permanent home. Ironically, she would find herself a neighbor of Clint Eastwood's, who represented in the 1970s the very violence and right-wing outlook that Baez detested, though eventually Eastwood turned into as brilliant a filmmaker as Baez was a singer. Baez also released her first two albums, each one a commercial triumph. Her repertoire mostly reflected the folk music of the 1950s and early 1960s, although she was never as politically engaged as that troubadour of the Old Left, Pete Seeger, or as Bob Dylan was assumed to be at the beginning of his career.

By 1962, a painting (largely a cartoon) of Baez was featured on the cover of *Time* magazine. Despite its irreverent prose, the article acknowledged that Baez had emerged as the queen of the folk movement and a heroine of the incipient counterculture. The recognition of Baez's fame made it easier for other women singers of the 1960s to become celebrities. But Baez exuded a beauty and a sexuality very different from the movie stars of the 1950s like Marilyn Monroe, Ava Gardner, and Elizabeth Taylor.[1] Baez—slender, serious, almost gloomy in her performances—exhibited an aloofness with even an aura of menace that made her seem more like the tortured heroines of film noir in the 1940s.

Despite her initial reputation as a folk singer and political protest-er, Baez was never an ideologue. And she carefully picked the causes in which she became involved. She sang and led a march for the Free Speech movement at Berkeley in 1964. After a lengthy discussion with Martin Luther King in 1965, Baez became even more committed than she had been in the 1950s not only to the civil rights movement but to the tactics and philosophy of non-violence. She publicized her opposition to the Vietnam War in interviews with newspaper and magazine reporters. She dutifully visited Hanoi in 1972, just as the Nixon Administration was carpet bombing the country to get the Communists back to the bargaining table. In addition, Baez organized Amnesty International on the West Coast, refused to sing in Spain until after Francisco Franco's death in 1975, and was banned from singing in Chile because of her crit-icisms of the CIA's role in removing Salvador Allende from power in 1973. Yet five years after the end of the Vietnam War, Baez tried to gath-er support for the victims of the Communist regime in South Vietnam. She gave concerts to raise money for the Vietnamese boat people and for the refugees from the genocide in Cambodia. At one point, Baez com-posed an open letter to the Vietnamese Communists criticizing them for persecuting the South Vietnamese and filling the jails with political prisoners. The letter was signed by, among others, Cesar Chavez, Allen Ginsberg, E. L. Doctorow, Mike Nichols, William Styron, and Lily Tomlin (but conspicuously not by Jane Fonda). Not surprisingly, the letter enraged the left in America (in the same way that Michael Cimi-no's *The Deer Hunter*, released in 1978, was denounced by the left for its antagonistic portrait of the Vietnamese, north and south).

In the meantime, by the 1970s and 1980s, Baez had ceased to be celebrated as a folksinger, nor was she any longer as fashionable as she had been in the early 1960s. Still, at *Newsweek*'s 50th anniversary party in 1983, Baez was seated at the head table across from Mary McCarthy—another artist who refused to succumb to the dogmas of her times.[2] Fi-nally, though Baez had never openly supported a political candidate, she did endorse Barack Obama for President in 2008. But her trajectory had become increasingly apolitical; the songs she now sang were personal rather than expressions of social fury.

Baez's nearest counterpart among the women folk singers of her age was Judy Collins. At least, like Baez, Collins started out as a folk singer before graduating to more multifaceted and contemporary songs.

After Collins started singing professionally in Colorado, she became increasingly well known. At the dawn of the 1960s, she moved to Chicago and then to New York, becoming a trendsetter in folk music. Performing at Gerde's Folk City in Greenwich Village, the dominant venue for the new music, Collins met Baez and Bob Dylan, both of whom impressed her with their talent and originality. By 1961, Collins recorded her first album, followed by two other albums, all of them featuring her renditions of folk music in a voice that was almost as pure and lilting as Baez's. Eventually, in the mid-1960s, Collins was giving concerts all over New York, especially at Carnegie Hall in 1965.

She was also starting to participate in the political movements of the 1960s, motivated particularly by her antipathy to the Vietnam War and her involvement in the Civil Rights movement. In 1964, like so many other war babies, she journeyed to Mississippi to help register black voters.

But Collins's most important battles were personal. She was constantly burdened by depression, and she resorted to liquor for comfort to the point where she was an alcoholic until the late 1970s. There were moments when Collins came as close to the brink of self-destruction as war baby singers like Janis Joplin and Jim Morrison. Yet for her fans, she remained through much of the 1960s a folk singer redolent of innocence and serenity, encircled by a field with wildflowers in her hair.[3]

Joan Baez and Judy Collins were the female architects of the music of the 1960s. With the possible exception of Barbra Streisand, however, no war baby singer—male or female—was more ambitious and none was more unpredictable than Bob Dylan. Over the decades, Dylan composed 600 songs, many of them exhibiting different musical conventions and tastes. He could not be defined as an artist by any single adjective, and his audience had to continually adjust to the variations he incorporated into his concerts and albums. On the one hand, Dylan could appear artless and even childlike (unlike Baez, Collins, and particularly Streisand). On the other hand, Dylan was crafty and narcissistic in pursuing his career. He started out emulating Woody Guthrie, and ended up like a character in a Stephen Sondheim musical.

In the early 1960s, Dylan was admired as a folk singer in the tradition of Woody Guthrie and Pete Seeger. His songs seemed not just topical but full of anger at the state of American society. His initial compositions—"Blowin' in the Wind," "A Hard Rain's A-Gonna Fall," "Masters of War," "With God on Our Side," "The Times They Are A-Changin'," "Only a Pawn in Their Game"—became political anthems, an indispensable part of the resurrection of radicalism in the 1960s. The force of these songs was amplified by Dylan's initiation at the Newport Folk Festival in 1963, with the audience applauding him as a prophet and polemicist—but also as a throwback to those rebels of the 1950s, Marlon Brando and James Dean. Moreover, Dylan confirmed his leftist credentials by withdrawing from the *Ed Sullivan Show* when the producers would not allow him to perform a satirical song about the John Birch Society.[4]

As if to corroborate his activist credentials, Dylan and Joan Baez became lovers in 1963. Baez served not merely as Dylan's consort, but as his sponsor, singing his songs, inviting him on stage to perform with her, helping to heighten Dylan's stature as the king of the protest movement to her queen. One could imagine that Baez and Dylan were like Katharine Hepburn and Spencer Tracy, each bringing out in the other a sensuality and humor that neither possessed alone. So it was appropriate that they both sang at the civil rights movement's March on Washington in August 1963.[5]

Nevertheless, for all his early success and his image as a musical insurrectionist, Dylan soon abandoned the role of political leader. In reality, he had never yearned to be a spokesman for a cause, any cause. Indeed, he often thought of himself as a writer rather than as a folk or any other kind of singer. Sometimes he saw himself as a successor to the Beat poets of the 1950s. It was no surprise that Allen Ginsberg and Dylan became close friends in the 1960s. And as a writer, like all writers, Dylan's basic preoccupations were personal.

Dylan had been upset when in 1962 he first saw Elia Kazan's 1957 movie *A Face in the Crowd*, the tale of a rural singer and folksy commentator (played by Andy Griffith) who turns into a treacherous demagogue. The last sort of creature Dylan wanted to be was another Lonesome Rhodes, Griffith's character in the film. Dylan's aversion to politics was intensified by the assassination of John F. Kennedy in November 1963, instilling a fear in Dylan that he might himself—as a celebrity—be killed. Dylan carried this terror with him for the rest of his career—a dread exacerbated by the murder in 1980 of the former Beatle with whom Dylan most identified, John Lennon.

So by the mid-1960s, Dylan had deserted both folk music and the political left. From this point on, he seldom included references to current events in his songs. If anything, his lyrics became more private and pensive, and often more obscure as well. Nor did he appear at protest marches after the massive civil rights demonstration in Washington in 1963.[6]

Where Woody Guthrie, Pete Seeger, and Joan Baez had once been models for Dylan, he now was deeply influenced by his British contemporaries, the Beatles. The impact on both sides of the Atlantic was mutual. Dylan and the Beatles (along with the Rolling Stones) inspired one another to experiment with more intricate rhythms and more poetic and introspective lyrics. Their musical rapport was an example of how much the music of the British and American war babies developed into a global trend by the 1960s.

Between 1964 and 1966, Dylan released four albums that signaled his break with the folk and political past: *Another Side of Bob Dylan*, *Bringing It All Back Home* (which contained "Subterranean Homesick Blues," "Mr. Tambourine Man," and "It's All Over Now, Baby Blue"), *Highway 61 Revisited* (with one of Dylan's biggest hits, "Like a Rolling

Stone"), and *Blonde on Blonde*. Most of the songs on these albums confronted the problems of love, loss, and private freedom.

The reaction of the audience and his fellow singers to Dylan's musical transformation was not entirely gracious. When Dylan showed up at the 1965 Newport Folk Festival with a band and an electronic guitar, many in the audience booed. Pete Seeger was infuriated at what he considered Dylan's betrayal of the authentic folk tradition. Joan Baez was dismayed by the change in Dylan's style and songs, but their love affair had already ended when Dylan married in 1965. On the other hand, Dylan was himself eradicating his ties to old friends and colleagues, and attracting new enthusiasts like Ginsberg, Marlon Brando, and Andy Warhol.[7]

In 1967, Dylan was injured in a motorcycle accident, an event eerily reminiscent of James Dean's death in a car crash in 1955. From this point on, Dylan grew more secluded but he continued to innovate, particularly with country music in *John Wesley Harding* in 1967 and *Nashville Skyline* in 1969 (an album that included "Lay Lady Lay," originally meant to be the theme song for the Dustin Hoffman-Jon Voight movie *Midnight Cowboy* though Dylan did not complete the song in time to be used in the film). He also grew increasingly religious, at one point converting from Judaism (which he had never bothered to practice) to Christianity.

Dylan was conspicuously absent from the Woodstock festival in 1969. But in 1975, he did tour the country with what was called the Rolling Thunder Revue, a peripatetic concert that included Joan Baez, Joni Mitchell, and Ronee Blakely (who starred as a doomed country singer in Robert Altman's *Nashville*). Nevertheless, Dylan was losing his personal and musical magnetism to a new singer, Bruce Springsteen. By the 1990s, as he entered his fifties, Dylan's album sales were declining and he was no longer able to pack arenas with his concerts. He was becoming progressively more peculiar and severed from the stardom he had enjoyed in the 1960s and 1970s. But like an aging Hollywood director or actor, Dylan began to receive lifetime achievement awards: he was installed in the Rock and Roll Hall of Fame in 1988; and he received the Kennedy Center Medal in 1997 and the Medal of Freedom in 2012. Meanwhile, Dylan's war baby colleague, Martin Scorsese, directed a television documentary of Dylan's musical evolution from 1961 to 1966, called *No Direction Home*, which was broadcast in Britain and America in 2005.[8]

For all his eccentricities, and the efforts by multiple critics to decode his increasingly supernatural lyrics, Dylan was no doubt the premier war baby songwriter of the 1960s and 1970s. He was at the forefront of the metamorphosis of modern American popular music. And his legacy would continue to influence musicians into the twenty-first century.

Dylan's only real rival in the United States, among the male war baby singers and composers, was Paul Simon. And Simon, no slouch when it came to competitiveness, always compared himself to Dylan as well as to the Beatles, at least as far as who was the most successful and inventive of the singers of the 1960s and 1970s. Simon's sense of rivalry was enhanced by the fact that, though he and Art Garfunkel survived only five years as a duo, their albums and soundtrack for Mike Nichols's *The Graduate* (1967) became symbols for an entire generation of baby boomers who were their principal audience.

Like both the later Dylan and the Beatles, Simon never yearned to be a political composer. He and Garfunkel were much more insistent on a quest for musical perfection, on the rhythmic cadence of their songs and the harmonic merger of their voices, and on the intellectual and poetic density of Simon's lyrics. Indeed, Simon (along with Joni Mitchell) was emblematic of how little the songwriters of the 1960s and 1970s engaged in either topical or protest music—despite the reputation of these years as an era of ideological fervor.

In 1964, Simon wrote one of his most memorable and haunting songs, "The Sound of Silence," which originally appeared on Simon and Garfunkel's first album. It is now nearly impossible to hear "The Sound of Silence" without visualizing Dustin Hoffman riding a people-mover upon his arrival at the Los Angeles airport at the beginning of *The Graduate*. But the song, like the movie, captured the aura of solitude and estrangement that permeated almost all of Simon's music.

From that point on, Simon produced some of the loveliest (and also some of the most satirical) songs of the 1960s: "Parsley, Sage, Rosemary, and Thyme," "Homeward Bound," "Feelin' Groovy," "The Dangling Conversation," "Bridge Over Troubled Water." And then, of course, there was "Mrs. Robinson."

Mike Nichols, already a fan of Simon and Garfunkel's music, invited them to provide the score for *The Graduate*. Nichols felt an emotional connection with Simon's music since both were Jewish, children of Eastern European immigrants, and personally awkward (unlike Robert Redford who desperately wanted to play the role of Benjamin Braddock until Nichols asked Redford if he had ever been turned down by a girl, and Redford had no clue that Nichols meant Benjamin was supposed to be something of inept schmuck around women—the last quality Redford could ever have personified). If anything, Simon also resembled— both physically and psychologically—the young Dustin Hoffman, the perfect Benjamin.

At one point during the filming of the movie, Simon informed Nichols that he was working on a song to be called "Mrs. Roosevelt," but that the title could easily be changed to "Mrs. Robinson." Nichols was flabbergasted that Simon was imagining such a song, but hadn't told Nichols about it. In either case, "Mrs. Robinson" was a song that could have only been written by a war baby. No baby boomer would have been old enough to have seen (as Simon had) Joe DiMaggio play for the New York Yankees. Nor would a baby boomer have composed the song's most famous line—"Where have you gone Joe DiMaggio"—or understood DiMaggio's metaphorical significance for a "lonely" America. (Actually, DiMaggio—an extraordinary baseball player but not too well acquainted with metaphors—didn't understand the meaning of the lyric either since he was still here, as he told Simon; he hadn't gone anywhere. Meanwhile DiMaggio's successor in center field for the New York Yankees, Mickey Mantle, was annoyed that Simon hadn't referred to him instead of Joltin' Joe. So Simon had to explain to both of them what the line meant).[9]

"Mrs. Robinson" was unfinished by the time the movie was shot, so we only hear a few chords and lines from the song. But when the completed song was released in 1968, it became not just one of the most legendary works of the 1960s but of the twentieth century. The score of *The Graduate*, as well as Simon and Garfunkel's final joint album, *Bookends* (1968), secured their stature as among the most crucial singers of the decade, and of the music that was truly the successor to the Great American Songbook of the 1920s and 1930s.

Yet at the summit of their fame, Simon and Garfunkel broke up. Mike Nichols was encouraging Garfunkel to pursue an acting career, and cast him in two of his next movies: *Catch-22* (1970) and *Carnal Knowledge* (1971). While neither film was a hit, they gave Garfunkel the chance to establish his own identity distinct from his connection with Simon. Meanwhile Simon was becoming increasingly envious of the way Garfunkel's voice dominated their songs. Moreover, Simon's taste in music was growing more eclectic while Garfunkel still preferred the lush qualities that had distinguished many of their songs in the 1960s. But most important, the two singers were simply growing weary of performing together.

So Simon set out in the 1970s to become a solo artist with a different sound that reflected his own evolving musical personality. Additionally, he hoped his new music might equal the compositions and status of George Gershwin and the Leonard Bernstein of *West Side Story*. Although their fans were stunned when Simon and Garfunkel ended their partnership, George Harrison (who knew a thing or two about the disintegration of a musical group) encouraged Simon in his goal to pursue his own separate career.

Nonetheless, their divorce was cordial. Simon and Garfunkel remained friends, and they often reunited for concerts—the most celebrated of which was their joint performance in Central Park in 1981 which attracted half a million people, all of them enthusiastic for all the old songs of their own youthful years. The concert was edited for HBO by Lorne Michaels, a war baby and friend of Simon's who had often invited him to host *Saturday Night Live*.[10] The duo also embarked on several world tours. But like the Beatles, they never reunited on a permanent basis. From the 1970s on, Simon appeared on stage and on records with a band and sometimes backup singers, but starring alone.

Joan Baez, Judy Collins, Bob Dylan, Simon and Garfunkel, and eventually Joni Mitchell were the foremost and most influential American singers and composers of the 1960s and 1970s. All of them war babies, they were the leaders in changing and modernizing America's music.

But other singers also contributed to the musical revolution during this time. Carole King, for example, was deeply affected (like all of her peers) by the ingenious lyrics and novel arrangements of the Beatles—innovations which she tried to incorporate into the songs she herself composed and performed. Similarly, Grace Slick of the Jefferson Airplane (later Starship) was inspired by the Beatles and even more by the Rolling Stones, as well as by the ground-breaking jazz of Miles Davis and John Coltrane. Moreover, Slick, living in San Francisco in the late 1960s with many of the other new and experimental bands like Jerry Garcia's the Grateful Dead, felt as if she were an American expatriate in Paris in the 1920s.[11] And it's probably true that musicians like Bob Dylan, Paul Simon, and Joni Mitchell—had they lived in the 1920s—might well have become novelists and poets in the tradition of Ernest Hemingway, William Faulkner, F. Scott Fitzgerald, and Hart Crane. Woody Allen in *Midnight in Paris* (2011) was not the only artist to notice the potential creative parallels between the 1920s and late-twentieth century America.

The music of the 1960s reached its apogee in three renowned festivals—two of them triumphs, but the third a catastrophe. In 1967, the Monterey Pop festival was held in California, lasting for three days. The festival featured the music of Simon and Garfunkel, the Jefferson Airplane, the Grateful Dead, Janis Joplin, and Jimi Hendrix—another war baby born in 1942—among other soloists and groups.

Monterey was surpassed in legend by Woodstock, held in upstate

New York in 1969, and attended by 500,000 people. Many of the same bands and groups performed at Woodstock, in addition to Joan Baez and Crosby, Stills, and Nash (all three of them born between 1941 and 1945). Woodstock rapidly became symbolic of the 1960s. And no one felt its cultural tremor more than Martin Scorsese who worked as an editor on the film of the festival that was released in 1970. For Scorsese, then just starting to make his own movies that would help renovate the American cinema of the 1970s, Woodstock was the emblem of a cultural reformation in the United States.

The third festival was held at Altamont in California, also in 1969, this concert starring the Rolling Stones along with (at least in its intent) the Grateful Dead and the Jefferson Airplane. But the Hell's Angels, inexplicably hired to provide "security" by the Rolling Stones, managed to beat and stab one of the young men in the audience to death.[12]

In the aftermath of the violence and chaos, many groups declined to perform and the festival collapsed—along with the idealism of the 1960s. And the festival was followed over the next several years by several more tragedies, especially to those artists who had come to embody the musical upheavals of the decade. A substantial number of the war baby singers continued to write and perform from the 1970s on. Yet the decade that had come to epitomize for so many the creative possibilities of America in the 1960s had unhappily vanished.

The Deaths and Death of the 1960s

For many baby boomers who lived through these years, the 1960s and early 1970s has acquired—in memory and myth—the aura of liberation, when everything was possible and all sorts of behavior were permitted. Yet in reality, this era was full of its share of personal calamities, particularly among musicians. Since everyone was allegedly "free" to do or try whatever they wanted, it is no shock that some people destroyed themselves. The culprit, in most cases, was drugs and alcohol.

Jerry Garcia of the Grateful Dead was initially motivated in his own career both by Joan Baez (since they each shared a Hispanic background) and the Beatles. He also became a disciple of Ken Kesey, the author of *One Flew Over the Cuckoo's Nest* (1962) and himself a devotee of modern jazz, the French New Wave movies, Lenny Bruce, and the new hallucinatory drug, LSD. In 1964, Garcia accompanied Kesey on his "Merry Prankster" Volkswagen bus tour of America, a journey drenched not only in the glorification of personal nonconformity but also of psychedelic drugs.

Like Bob Dylan and Paul Simon, Garcia was uninterested in political movements. But by the late 1960s, Garcia's band was achieving fame throughout the country. For a moment, it seemed as if Garcia and the Grateful Dead might become the heirs of the Beatles, the Rolling Stones, Dylan, and Simon and Garfunkel. Yet this apotheosis never happened. For all the publicity surrounding the Grateful Dead and Garcia himself, the musicians did not have the innate talent of their famous contemporaries. Instead, Garcia—who was afflicted with asthma—managed to survive until 1995 when he died at the age of fifty-three of a heart attack at a drug rehabilitation center.[13]

War baby singers like Jim Morrison and Janis Joplin were not so "fortunate" as to live relatively lengthy, if tortured, lives. Morrison, like Garcia, was influenced by Joan Baez, and he was—also like Garcia—apolitical. He and his band, The Doors, released their first albums in the late 1960s, featuring songs like "Break on Through," "Light My Fire," and "The End." These albums merged rock, jazz, and music that sounded as if it could have been composed by Bertolt Brecht and Kurt Weill. Moreover, Morrison cultivated publicity from newspapers and magazines, implying to interviewers that he was a symbolic reincarnation of James Dean.

By 1969, Morrison and The Doors were celebrities as well as artists. Nevertheless, Morrison was showing signs—which he had displayed since his wartime and postwar childhood—of rage and discontent, even despite his fame. His conduct, on and off stage, grew increasingly outrageous and volatile, behavior fueled by liquor and drugs.

Finally, at the beginning of the 1970s, Morrison fled to Paris. But Paris was no longer the artistic capital of the world, as it had been for so many American exiles and outcasts from other countries in the 1920s. Paris offered Morrison neither stimulation nor solace. Instead the city was where he collapsed and died in 1971 of mysterious causes, possibly of a heart attack though heroin may also have been involved. Morrison was at the time of his death all of twenty-seven years old—the same age as Jimi Hendrix who likely died of an overdose of barbiturates a year earlier.[14] Morrison's grave in Paris soon became a shrine for war babies and baby boomers alike, a memorial as much to the 1960s as to the singer himself.

Morrison was undoubtedly disturbed throughout his brief life. No war baby singer of the 1960s, however, endured a more tormented existence than Janis Joplin. Joplin had always esteemed black women vocalists like Bessie Smith, Odetta, and Tina Turner (but not necessarily Billie Holiday whose quiet sorrow did not fit Joplin's musical tastes or personality). And like Elvis Presley, another of Joplin's idols, Joplin merged the blues performed both by black and white singers. But Joplin's style was more explosive than any of these forbears. Often on stage, she shrieked and moaned, assaulting her audience with her own feelings that she was both ugly and unloved. The effect was one of extreme self-absorption, as if only attention and appreciation could assuage Joplin's innate sense of alienation, largely from herself.

Like so many other adherents of the counterculture in the 1960s, Joplin experimented incessantly with drugs and drink—in the forlorn hope that these would make her a better singer if not a better person. For a while, the narcotics seemed to work: the media praised her defiance, impulsiveness, and candor. In 1969, Joplin was pictured on the cover of *Newsweek* and also written about in *Time* as the quintessence of blues and rock in the 1960s. *Rolling Stone*, the new magazine that was reporting on the music of the 1960s, called her the "Judy Garland of Rock and Roll"—an uncanny observation since Garland shared many of the same personal agonies as Joplin.

Joplin rarely wrote her own songs. Her biggest hit was her version of Kris Kristofferson's "Me and Bobby McGee." Yet however triumphant Joplin became in the late 1960s, she was never able to surmount the feeling that she was worthless. And like many stars, not just in music, she worried about what she feared was her inevitable loss of fame and wealth.

What Joplin, like Morrison, desperately needed was psychological intervention. But given the motto in the 1960s of everyone "doing their own thing," none of Joplin's friends tried to intercede. By the end of the decade, Joplin had overdosed on drugs six times, and was exhibiting traits of being suicidal. The inevitable end came in 1970 when Joplin overdosed on heroin, intensified by great quantities of alcohol. She too, like Morrison and Hendrix, was only twenty-seven.[15]

The saga of Hendrix, Morrison, and Joplin—their addictions and self-destructiveness—was a cheerless commentary on the end of the 1960s. For them, personal and artistic freedom had meant obliteration. Meanwhile, the 1960s itself was coming to a close with the election of Richard Nixon in 1968, the racial upheavals in many of America's major cities, and the persistence of the Vietnam War for another seven years. These disasters were duplicated overseas with the failure of the student and worker uprising in France in 1968, the Red Army tanks rumbling into Prague to crush an effort to reform Czechoslovak Communism, the human wreckage in China as a result of the "cultural revolution," and the violence against students in Mexico and Brazil.

Still, the art of the 1960s, as invented by the war babies, endured and expanded in originality into the 1970s and beyond. Whatever the shattering effect of the 1960s on the lives of certain musicians, the music itself (along with the movies) entered a phase as dazzling as any of the literature produced in the 1920s. And this brilliance too was the creation of the war baby generation.

The Global Impact of the War Babies' Music

Ever since the 1920s and 1930s, especially with jazz and the serious compositions of George Gershwin—notably *Rhapsody in Blue, Concerto in F, An American in Paris*, and *Porgy and Bess*—American music had always electrified international audiences. This global popularity continued from the 1960s on with the songs of the war babies. For most of the 1960s, there had been a reciprocal influence between Britain and America, as the music of Beatles and the Rolling Stones affected and were in turn altered by the works of Bob Dylan and Paul Simon. If anything, even with the break-up of the Beatles in the late 1960s, American singers and songwriters continued to be shaped by John Lennon as well as by other foreign composers. And the audiences for American music were consistently transnational as Dylan, Simon and Garfunkel, Joan Baez, Judy Collins, and Carole King embarked on concert tours of Europe, Asia, and Latin America.

Perhaps the best-known war baby star, and certainly the most multi-talented, was Barbra Streisand. From the moment she appeared on Broadway in 1964 as Fanny Brice in *Funny Girl*, and then in the movie version in 1968, Streisand accumulated Oscars and Emmys as well as making albums that sold all over the planet. Unlike the other war baby singers, Streisand depended on updated interpretations of the American standards and songs for her movies rather than trying to invent a new kind of music. She was particularly reliant on the songs of the composer Marvin Hamlisch—another war baby, born in 1944—whose aria for her, "The Way We Were," the title song for her 1973 movie with Robert Redford, became a signature for the ample range of her voice and her ability to make lyrics simultaneously romantic and heartbreaking. Hamlisch himself went on to win an Oscar for the score of *The Sting* in 1973 and to compose the music for the most spectacularly successful Broadway musical of the 1970s, *A Chorus Line* in 1975. Though as her career progressed Streisand rarely gave live concerts, she did appear in 2007 before enthusiastic audiences in Zurich, Paris, Berlin, and Britain.

By the late 1960s, Judy Collins began to depart from her image and

repertoire as a folk singer, adapting contemporary songs from composers in Europe and Canada. Her albums started to include more theat-
rical works by Kurt Weill, Aaron Copland's rendition of the Quaker
hymn "Simple Gifts" from his ballet *Appalachian Spring*, the Belgian
songwriter Jacques Brel, and Joni Mitchell (especially an elegiac rendition of "Both Sides Now" which was Collins's first hit single). She
also recorded a poignant version of Stephen Sondheim's "Send in the
Clowns"—an interpretation equaled only by a melancholy recording of
the song by Frank Sinatra.

But Collins's favorite composer was the Canadian songwriter
Leonard Cohen. She popularized on her albums as probably no oth-
er American singer could have Cohen's "Dress Rehearsal Rag," "Hey,
That's No Way to Say Goodbye," "Suzanne," and "Sisters of Mercy."
(Robert Altman was similarly entranced, or in his case possibly amused,
by Cohen's music. In his great revisionist Western in 1971, *McCabe and
Mrs. Miller*, Altman used Cohen's songs for the soundtrack, including
"Sisters of Mercy" accompanying a group of prostitutes as they arrive
in a wagon to take up residence in Warren Beatty's ramshackle whore-
house). More seriously, Collins at last gave up drinking in 1978, thereby
preserving her voice and career.[16]

Although Joni Mitchell was originally Canadian, she had moved
to the United States in 1965, after which she became both an American
and cosmopolitan singer/songwriter. Mitchell, like almost all of the war
baby singers, was not a political artist. Her most famous songs—like
"Chelsea Morning," "The Circle Game," and "Both Sides Now"—and
her albums like *Blue* in 1971 and *Court and Spark* in 1974—were personal
and intimate expressions of her varying moods and failed love affairs.
Her lyrics were composites of unrequited romantic attachments, puzzle-
ment, cynicism, and disillusion. By the 1970s, Mitchell (alone among
her war baby cohorts) was also evolving into a jazz singer, working with
musicians like Herbie Hancock and Charles Mingus. Yet like her contemporaries, she too performed on a world stage, touring Japan, Austra-
lia, Ireland, Britain, France, Germany, and Italy in 1983, and singing at

a concert to celebrate the fall of the Berlin Wall in 1990.

No war baby songwriter, however, was more global in his tastes and aspirations by the 1970s than Paul Simon. Like Judy Collins's song selections and Joni Mitchell's compositions, Simon's solo work grew more elaborate than it had been in the 1960s. And often wittier. This was especially true of the lyrics for his hugely successful album in 1975, *Still Crazy After All These Years*. The title song contains a line that could have applied to most of the war baby singers who, like Bob Dylan, preferred their own company to those of their fans or mass movements: "I'm not the kind of man who tends to socialize." The line certainly applied to me; as an only child, I was told by a teacher in grade school that I was "unsatisfactory" in "getting along with others"—an observation that has endured throughout my life, which is likely why I chose the solitary pursuit of being a writer. Additionally, *Still Crazy After All These Years* includes one of the most sardonic songs of the 1970s, one comparable to the acerbic lyrics of Lorenz Hart: "50 Ways to Leave Your Lover."

In 1975 as well, Simon first appeared on *Saturday Night Live*. Two years later, Simon turned up as a parody of himself in Woody Allen's *Annie Hall*. Simon played Tony Lacey, a star singer but a short ingratiating nebbish surrounded by impossibly tall shiksas. Lacey ultimately persuades Annie (Diane Keaton) to move in with him in California and pursue her own singing career, while her former lover Alvy Singer (Allen) thinks of California as a place where in restaurants you can only order mashed yeast. In reality, the public personalities of Simon and Allen were similar (not to mention their scrawny physiques) and they became good friends.

Eventually, Simon started to incorporate foreign music into his songs. He traveled to South Africa in the 1980s (despite the opposition of his peers who loathed apartheid), and returned to America to make *Graceland* in 1986. In 1990, Simon released *The Rhythm of the Saints* which was shaped not only by South African but also by Brazilian musical traditions.

Simon and Garfunkel were inducted into the Rock and Roll Hall of Fame in 1990, as was Simon as a solo performer in 2001. Meanwhile, Simon toured in 1999 with his long-time competitor, Bob Dylan. Above all, in 2007, at the age of sixty-five, Simon received the first George Gershwin Prize for Popular Song—an honor that confirmed Simon's distinction as among the most creative of American composers since the golden age of music in the 1920s and 1930s.[17]

Simon's music, perhaps more than anyone else's of his generation, has lasted and had an indelible impact both on other war babies and their baby boom successors. Nowhere was this more evident than on September 11, 2011, at the tenth anniversary of the destruction of the Twin Towers in lower Manhattan. The memorial was replete with speeches and the ritual reading of the names of the dead. But by far the most moving moment of the commemoration occurred when Simon emerged before the microphones to sing a mournful version of "The Sound of Silence." The television cameras covering the event switched back and forth between Simon and the people in the crowd who were crying, hugging one another, and singing the lyrics along with him—as if everyone there, whatever their age, knew the song and recognized what it had meant in their lives for the past fifty years.

"The Sound of Silence" was a superlative if painful choice for the occasion. And it summed up the cataclysms the war babies had lived through from their childhood through their turbulent postwar adolescence to the power of their work as a commentary on the changes, noble and horrific, that America had experienced over the past half century. The war babies' music provided the soundtrack for all of our lives, and for the uncertain, apprehensive country America had become at the dawn of the twenty-first century.

CHAPTER 6

The Revolution in Movies

FOR FIFTY YEARS, from the second decade of the twentieth century until the 1960s, the major Hollywood studios had reigned over the movie industry in America. MGM, Paramount, Twentieth Century-Fox, Warner Brothers, Columbia, and Universal controlled every aspect of filmmaking from the production and distribution of movies to long-term contracts that bound directors, actors, and technicians to a particular studio. The studio system was extraordinarily successful not only in making money but in turning out some of the most entertaining and artistic movies in the history of any country's motion pictures.

In 1946, Hollywood enjoyed one of its most profitable years. American films grossed $1.7 billion domestically, collecting ninety cents of every dollar Americans spent on entertainment. Nearly 100 million people went to the movies each week. Movie-going was a habit, as it had been since the 1920s. And Hollywood films were designed to appeal to entire families, not just segments of the audience.

But from 1947 on, attendance at movies steadily declined. Hollywood found itself competing for the attention of millions of people who were moving to the suburbs, and finding other forms of amusement—especially television—to occupy their leisure time and dollars. In addition, the movie audience was fragmenting by the 1950s; those who still went to films were increasingly younger and more attracted to the gritty realities, sexual and otherwise, that they could see in foreign movies.

Moreover, the men who had constructed the studio system—moguls like Louis B. Mayer at MGM, Jack Warner at Warner Brothers, Harry Cohn at Columbia—were either forced out (as in the case of Mayer) or they retired or died. Many of the studios by the 1960s were being absorbed by conglomerates run by executives who knew little about filmmaking except what it could contribute to the corporate bottom line. At the same time, the idols who had graced the moguls' movies were dying as well: Humphrey Bogart in 1957, Errol Flynn in 1959, Clark Gable in 1960, Gary Cooper in 1961, Marilyn Monroe in 1962.

None of this meant that Hollywood did not continue to release superb films in the 1950s and early 1960s. John Ford and Alfred Hitchcock were still in their prime, and their work was supplemented by directors like Elia Kazan, Stanley Kubrick, and Sidney Lumet. And new stars were emerging—Marlon Brando, James Dean, Paul Newman—who illuminated the passions of a younger audience.

Yet by the 1960s, the bosses who now ran the studios were clueless about what kinds of films might appeal to youthful moviegoers. Their bewilderment, however, offered precisely the opportunity for a new band of directors and actors—most of them born during World War II—to start making personal, idiosyncratic movies influenced by the giants of both foreign and American filmmaking. Beginning with *Bonnie and Clyde* and *The Graduate* in 1967, *Easy Rider* in 1969, and *The Last Picture Show* in 1971—followed by *The Godfather: Parts I and II, Chinatown, Dog Day Afternoon, Taxi Driver, Raging Bull, The Deer Hunter*, and *Apocalypse Now*, among many others—Hollywood movies once again became essential to anyone anywhere who cared about the cinema. These were the films that people argued about and remembered, that spoke directly to their social concerns and private predicaments.

The renaissance in American filmmaking coincided with the political and cultural upheavals of the late 1960s and 1970s, above all with the corruption of power emanating from Watergate and the catastrophe of the Vietnam War. While the movies did not always deal directly with such issues, the characters in these films often seemed ambivalent and morose, and the movies themselves were ambiguous and confusing, as if they were commenting on a country whose people could no longer agree on a definition of the good life. This polarization, this perplexity, would persist in American movies from the 1970s until today.

As Martin Scorsese recalled, the movies of the late 1960s and 1970s (and beyond) were created by a generation of "outsiders."[1] This was a generation of war babies who discovered, at least for a time, that they could make any sort of movie they wanted in any way they liked. Hence, Peter Bogdanovich (born in 1939) and Peter Fonda (born in 1940) shaped *The Last Picture Show* and *Easy Rider* according to their own tastes and obsessions. And the directors could cast in their movies war baby actors who were initially unknown but immensely talented—actors like Faye Dunaway, Al Pacino, Robert De Niro, Jill Clayburgh, Harrison Ford, Harvey Keitel, Christopher Walken, and Joe Pesci.

All of these directors and actors were responsible for a revolution in American filmmaking, and in a larger sense American culture. Like the war baby singer-composers (and at the same time the war baby politicians and social activists, athletes, and journalists), they helped change America. And at least insofar as the movies are concerned, we have been living with the legacy of their films ever since.

The New Auteurs

One of the consequences of the collapse of the old studio system and the shift in audience tastes was that producers in the late 1960s and 1970s were willing, almost out of desperation, to entrust their movies to directors who had little or no experience making films. The new studio heads took chances on people their predecessors would have thrown out of their offices.

Thus Peter Bogdanovich, a New Yorker, had spent most of his early career as a film critic. He had directed only one movie, *Targets* in 1968, before he was hired (despite the fact that he had never been to Texas) to make the movie version of Larry McMurtry's novel, *The Last Picture*

Show. Yet Bogdanovich captured the drab, dusty landscape of rural Texas in which the characters can do little more than roam, without purpose or point, through the empty streets, their barren lives underlined by the gloominess of the country music on the soundtrack.

Similarly, no film was less planned, with episodes that were more impromptu, than *Easy Rider. Easy Rider* could never have been made in any other era. What reputable studio in the 1950s would have given half a million dollars to a madman like Dennis Hopper (who had never directed a film) and the equally eccentric Peter Fonda to shoot a movie that had no script, about characters called Captain America and Billy the Kid who score a drug deal and hop on motorcycles heading for Mardi Gras in New Orleans, picking up an alcoholic lawyer along the way, played by a marginal actor named Jack Nicholson? And with all of their adventures accentuated by the hallucinogenic sounds of Steppenwolf, the Byrds, and Jimi Hendrix until all the main characters are slaughtered by rednecks? No wonder older people in America, raised on comedies and romances when they went to the picture show, shunned the grim, experimental movies Hollywood was now presenting.

So given the disarray of the movie industry, it made a weird kind of sense for Paramount—which had purchased the rights to Mario Puzo's best-selling 1969 novel *The Godfather*—to select Francis Ford Coppola to direct the film version. Coppola had won an Oscar in 1970 for the screenplay for *Patton.* But he had previously directed only four movies, all of which were critical and commercial failures. By 1969, Coppola had founded his own studio, American Zoetrope, along with his friend and protégé George Lucas. Coppola's intention—like most of the young American auteurs—was to make artistic films, not blockbusters. Still, he needed the money and the screen credit, both of which Paramount was offering.

Nonetheless, the marriage between Paramount and Coppola was tumultuous. The studio, having invested a bundle of money in the film, wanted a big-budget spectacle with major stars, not another cult movie for the art-house crowd.

Coppola initially caused Paramount apoplexy when he insisted that Marlon Brando play the role of Don Vito Corleone. By the early 1970s, Brando carried with him the baggage of box office flops and a reputation for causing trouble on the set. Coppola then filled most of the cast with actors who were virtually unknown.

For the role of Michael Corleone, Coppola debated between two young actors, Al Pacino and Robert De Niro, before settling on Pacino. He chose Robert Duvall, hardly a familiar name at the time, to play Tom Hagen, the family consigliore. For the role of Kay Adams, Michael's American wife, Coppola selected Diane Keaton who was just beginning to earn a reputation in Woody Allen's films. Talia Shire, Coppola's sister, played Connie, the Corleone's insubordinate daughter. And in what may have been his most clever casting decision, Coppola picked John Cazale to play Fredo, the Corleone's middle, incompetent son (Cazale appeared in only five movies in the 1970s before his death from bone cancer in 1978. But the movies—*The Godfather: Parts I and II*, Coppola's *The Conversation*, *Dog Day Afternoon*, and *The Deer Hunter* were among the finest films of the decade, all of which benefited from Cazale's stunning performances).

So controversial were Coppola's casting and direction that during the course of filming, Paramount nearly fired him (possibly to be replaced by Elia Kazan). But Brando threatened to leave the picture if the studio sacked Coppola, and so (with a lot of the movie already shot) he remained as the mastermind of the movie.

Coppola, like Martin Scorsese, was eager to explore his Italian heritage, and he was fascinated with the historic connections between the Catholic Church and organized crime.[2] As a result, Coppola turned *The Godfather* and its sequel in 1974, *The Godfather: Part II*, into an epic not merely about the Mafia but about the breakdown of Italian family life amid the consolidation of capitalism in the twentieth century. Both films featured shadowy rooms where men softly plotted massacres (in *The Godfather: Part II* when Tom Hagen tells Michael he doesn't have to kill everyone, Michael replies "I don't feel I have to wipe everybody out,

Tom. Just my enemies"). These scenes alternated with sunlit exteriors, especially at moments of weddings and Sicilian festivals. In effect, both *Godfathers* resembled Italian operas with actors delivering arias on their familial obligations and adherence to criminal codes, all underscored by the haunting music of Nino Rota who had collaborated for two decades with Federico Fellini.

Yet Coppola was recounting a cheerless American tale as well. The saga of the Corleones is a commentary on the disappearance of an older, more intimate society and the rise of an impersonal corporate-style capitalism, packed with lawyers and accountants arguing about (in this case murderous) mergers and acquisitions. Robert De Niro, cast in *The Godfather: Part II* as the young Vito Corleone just starting out in America in the early twentieth century, is depicted as an Italian Robin Hood acting on behalf of his neighbors and friends victimized by primitive mobsters. By the 1950s and 1960s, his son Michael has evolved into a modern and rational businessman, coldly eliminating competitors.

Ultimately the Corleone family itself—which is the bond that holds all the characters together when most other American films from the 1950s on were portraying the absence of communication between parents and children—crumbles in *The Godfather: Part II*. Michael throws his wife (Dianne Keaton) out of the house because she has aborted his next son. And he has his brother Fredo executed because Fredo betrayed the family to Michael's opponents. At the end of the second film, all we see is the death of the immigrant (and American) dream, Michael sitting alone in a chair, his foes purged, the camera closing in on his lifeless eyes.

Coppola managed in both movies to fuse art and commercial success. Each film won the Oscar for best picture (though Coppola lost the best director Oscar for *The Godfather: Part I* to Bob Fosse for his direction of *Cabaret*). Coppola did receive an Oscar for best director for *The Godfather: Part II*, which was perhaps the only sequel in the history of American movies that was superior to its original incarnation. Marlon Brando won an Oscar for best actor for his performance in *The Godfather: Part I*, his second Oscar since *On the Waterfront*. Robert De Niro earned his first Oscar, this one for best supporting actor in *The Godfa-ther: Part II*. The first film made more money, $150 million worldwide, than either *Gone with the Wind* or *The Sound of Music*. Together, both *Godfathers* became among the most memorable of all American movies, not just in the 1970s but in the history of the global cinema. As impor-tant, Coppola—like most war babies—had transformed two blockbust-ers into an expression of his own private concerns.

In between the two *Godfathers*, Coppola made an even more per-sonal movie, *The Conversation*. The film was Coppola's entry in a series of paranoid thrillers released in the mid-1970s, movies which included *The Parallax View* (1974), *Chinatown* (also 1974), *Three Days of the Condor* (1975), and *All the President's Men* (1976). Each of these movies reflected the mood of the country during Vietnam and Watergate, the sense that the government lied, that institutions were corrupt, and that there were conspiracies proliferating in the highest echelons of American power.

The Conversation won the Palme d'Or for best picture at the Cannes film festival in 1974. But it is a bleak movie. Gene Hackman plays Harry Caul, a surveillance expert hired by a sinister and omnipotent corpora-tion, who compulsively replays a tape about a murder plot yet utterly misunderstands who's scheming to kill whom. When Harry finally de-ciphers the real plot, the revelation does him no good. At the end of the film, he discovers that his own apartment has been bugged. After ripping up the walls and the furniture in a futile effort to find the hidden microphone, Harry winds up sitting in the wreckage of his apartment, playing a mournful saxophone, isolated (not unlike Michael Corleone at the end of *The Godfather: Part II*) and conquered by the faceless forces he can't identify or expose.

The Conversation had one crucial element in common with *The Parallax View*, *Chinatown*, and *Three Days of the Condor*. Even when the protagonists (they are hardly "heroes") in these films unravel the source of treachery, they are unable to prevent the crime or crush the conspiracy. The one notable exception to these tales of defeat is *All the President's Men*. But here as well, Bob Woodward and Carl Bernstein (as played by Robert Redford and Dustin Hoffman) spend most of the movie gathering information, unsure of where the evidence leads or how high up in government the conspiracy ascends, before we finally watch on television as—one by one—Richard Nixon's men are convicted and jailed, and Nixon himself resigns the Presidency.

Francis Ford Coppola had made three brilliant movies that displayed his own inner disenchantment with the course of American life in the 1970s. But not until late in the decade did he confront the worst American debacle of all, the war in Vietnam.

During World War II, Hollywood had made dozens of films about the war in Europe and the Pacific. The most illustrious of these was *Casablanca*, released in 1942—though the movie was as much about refugees fleeing from Nazism as it was about the military conflagration in Europe. In the early 1950s, the studios had also turned out a number of films about the Korean War. But with the exception of *The Green Berets*, starring John Wayne in 1968, Hollywood had meticulously avoided the subject of Vietnam as too controversial for American or global audiences.

This did not mean that Vietnam was utterly ignored. The war hovered in the background of many American movies and television shows in the 1970s. Robert Altman's *MASH*, released in 1970, was ostensibly about the Korean War. But the sardonic attitudes of the characters—both in the movie and the television series that followed—toward the futility of the war, and the ubiquitous helicopters transporting the wounded from the battlefields were unmistakably metaphors for Vietnam. Later, in Martin Scorsese's *Taxi Driver* (1976), we are told that Travis Bickle's pathology is caused, at least in part, by his experiences as a veteran in Vietnam.

Yet it was not until the Vietnam War ended in 1975, with the evacuation of the last American troops from the rooftops of the United States embassy in Saigon, that Hollywood began to candidly confront the war. In 1976, Francis Ford Coppola and his crew traveled to the Philippines to make a movie about the war, based on Joseph Conrad's *Heart of Darkness*.

For Coppola, everything about the war was insane, and no one—from Washington to Saigon—was in control. This chaos extended to the making of the movie itself. The weather in the Philippines was atrocious; at one point, a typhoon demolished the sets. Coppola originally chose Harvey Keitel to play Captain Willard, then replaced him after two weeks with Martin Sheen, another World War II baby, born in 1940. Sheen promptly had a heart attack. Marlon Brando, slated to play the crazed Colonel Kurtz, showed up vastly overweight, without having read either Conrad's novella or the screenplay. Dennis Hopper as a drugged-out photojournalist looked and sounded as if he had just walked off the set of *Easy Rider*. The movie took sixteen months to shoot, and it wasn't edited or released until 1979. Yet despite all this bedlam, Coppola managed to make a great movie—*Apocalypse Now*—and one that was a personal testament to his own feelings about the madness of Vietnam.

Captain Willard's assignment is to journey upriver into Cambodia, locate Colonel Kurtz who has allegedly gone berserk, and "terminate" him "with extreme prejudice." Along the way, everything and everyone Willard encounters is surreal. No one seems more barmy than Robert Duvall's Colonel Kilgore (the name is appropriate) who appeared to be channeling Coppola's own portrait of a fanatical General Patton. Kilgore is a deranged military officer who obliterates Vietnamese villages from helicopter gunships blaring Wagner ("My boys love it"). And he adores "the smell of napalm in the morning" because it smells like "victory." Meanwhile, as Willard's trip progresses, American outposts are soaked in thunderstorms, skirmishes with the enemy occur in a supernatural nighttime glow, Playboy Playmates emerge out of nowhere to entertain the besotted troops, and innocent Vietnamese in sampans are blown away.

As Coppola recognized, we are waiting throughout the movie for the discovery of Kurtz because he will be played by Marlon Brando. When the film came out, critics derided Brando's performance for being unintelligible and incoherent. But Brando, with his half-swallowed words, gives Kurtz a subtlety as well as a maniacal majesty that dominates the final segment of the film. We strain to listen to him, just as we struggled to hear the Godfather's hoarse voice. In each instance, this is the hushed voice of power.

Willard ultimately slays Kurtz. But the last words on the soundtrack are Brando's. Echoing the close of Conrad's novella, Brando whispers "The horror . . . the horror." Brando's final mutterings summarize the senseless carnage in Vietnam. Coppola—the most prominent American director of the 1970s—had offered an unforgettable portrait of the war's lunacy. For all of the anarchic tribulations Coppola suffered in making the film, *Apocalypse Now* won the Palme d'Or for the year's best picture at Cannes in 1979. And it has remained one of the most disturbing movies ever made about modern warfare, particularly American wars in countries we know nothing about like Iraq and Afghanistan.

Yet the ghastliness of Vietnam had been presented even more frighteningly in a movie released a year before *Apocalypse Now*. Until 1978, few people in Hollywood or anywhere else had heard of Michael Cimino, another child of World War II. Cimino never started out to be a filmmaker. He graduated from Yale in the early 1960s with a degree as a Master of Fine Arts in painting. After Yale, Cimino moved to Manhattan where he began to direct television commercials for Kool cigarettes, Eastman Kodak, United Airlines, and Pepsi-Cola. Eventually, in 1971, he traveled to Hollywood in the hope of becoming a screenwriter. He managed to direct his first movie in 1974, an offbeat film starring Clint Eastwood, called *Thunderbolt and Lightfoot*.

Yet like so many of his war baby peers, Cimino finally got the chance to direct a major movie, this one about the inferno in Vietnam. The movie, called *The Deer Hunter*, starred Robert De Niro, Christopher Walken (who won an Oscar for best supporting actor, and whose later reputation as one of America's most eccentric actors is belied in this movie by his exquisitely sensitive performance), Meryl Streep, and John Cazale. For Cimino to make his second movie, with actors of this magnitude, was conceivable only in the 1970s.

The film, however, was not just about the war. Instead, *The Deer*

Hunter focused in an intensely personal way on the lives and tragedies of three soldiers and the friends they'd left behind in a steel-manufacturing town in western Pennsylvania. In fact, the first hour of the movie had little to do with Vietnam. It is rather a scrupulous and joyous portrayal of working-class life of the kind viewers rarely saw in an American film. Amid the rituals and wedding festivities in a Ukrainian community, what we glimpse is the camaraderie among the townspeople, their lives in taverns and bowling alleys, and the holy grail of the deer hunt—especially the necessity, as De Niro's character Michael insists, of killing a deer with "one shot" to the head.

The metaphor of one shot prefigures the most traumatic scenes in the movie. Three of the friends who go off to the war are catapulted from the comforts and ceremonies of their community into a harrowing land-scape of violence and sadism. They are captured by the Vietcong and forced to play Russian roulette, a contest on this occasion to see who can avoid one shot to the head. (Quentin Tarantino, who was heavily influenced by the movies of the 1970s, praised the Russian roulette sequences as among the best scenes ever dramatized, edited, and performed in an American movie). At last, De Niro and Walken's characters kill their tormentors and escape, but they are never the same.

De Niro's Michael returns home but he is constantly ill at ease with civilian life. Meanwhile, Walken's Nick remains in Vietnam, high on heroin, and addicted to Russian roulette. The final words Nick says to Michael (who has returned to Vietnam to save him from what Brando called "the horror"), which Nick utters with a faint smile on his face, are "one shot"—before he blows his brains out.

After Nick's funeral, his friends engage in yet another obligatory social rite. There is none of the ambiguity some critics found in this clos-ing scene. The mourners gather around a table, drinking beer. No longer believing in a war that has shattered them all, they burst (as if they don't know what else to do) into "God Bless America." But the song is not a patriotic anthem or an affirmation of America's values. It is a requiem for the dead.

The Deer Hunter was an enormously controversial film, in part because of its repellent depiction of the Vietnamese, north and south. Yet
it won the Oscar for best picture, and Cimino received the Oscar for
best director. It also inspired the building of a National Memorial for
Vietnam Veterans in Washington, D.C.—perhaps the most visited and
sorrowful monument in the city.

Whatever the political disagreements about the movie, Cimino
came to be known—at least for a while—as a master of the cinematic
universe. He was hailed as the new Orson Welles. United Artists gave
him forty million dollars to make his next movie, a Western called
Heaven's Gate. Though gorgeously photographed, no one could follow
the complex story which originally ran over four hours. *Heaven's Gate*
wound up being a critical and commercial disaster that effectively destroyed Camino's career. But *The Deer Hunter* remained one of the most
extraordinary and harrowing films of the 1970s—a war baby's tormenting
valedictory, like Coppola's *Apocalypse Now*, to the debacle in Vietnam.

Of all the war baby filmmakers, the one who sustained his career
and the quality of his films over four decades was Martin Scorsese.
Scorsese had been watching, reading about, and learning from movies
since his childhood. His tastes were eclectic. On the one hand, he venerated the films of foreign directors like Ingmar Bergman, François Truffaut, Michelangelo Antonioni, and Federico Fellini (especially Fellini's
autobiographical *8 ½*, which explored the agonies and the absurdities of
a filmmaker trying to make a movie). And when Scorsese entered NYU
film school in the early 1960s, he was taught that foreign films were invariably superior to their American counterparts—a snobbery that often
prevailed at the time among movie critics and young audiences.

Yet Scorsese was equally entranced with American movies, notably
those of Orson Welles, John Ford, Howard Hawks, and Elia Kazan.
What all of these directors—American and foreign-born—instilled in
Scorsese was the sense that a filmmaker could make personal movies,
movies that reflected the director's life experiences and preoccupations.
So, from the beginning, Scorsese was a devotee of the auteur theory, the

notion that directors (not necessarily actors or writers) were the primary creators of their films, and that movies were a representation of the director's own idiosyncrasies.

Still, Scorsese understood that filmmaking was a collaborative enterprise. In 1967, he met Thelma Schoonmaker (yet another child of World War II, born in 1940), who specialized in film editing and worked with Scorsese on the Woodstock documentary in 1969. Thereafter, Schoonmaker became the editor for all of Scorsese's films from *Raging Bull* on, winning three Oscars for best editor along the way. It's also impossible to imagine Scorsese's movies without the presence of actors like Robert De Niro (who encouraged Scorsese to make certain films like *Raging Bull* and *The King of Comedy*), Harvey Keitel, and Joe Pesci.

By 1969, Scorsese was teaching at NYU. One of his students was Oliver Stone.[3] Scorsese was also making his own movies, some of them based on his observations growing up in Little Italy. As he launched his career, Scorsese was aided immeasurably by his friendships with his war baby peers—Brian De Palma (born in 1940), George Lucas, and Francis Ford Coppola. But Scorsese could never have made a movie, like Coppola, about a wealthy and potent family like the Corleones. Scorsese's world was composed of street thugs, loudmouths full of invective and threats of bloodshed, obsessed with personal honor and respect, always violent (like Joe Pesci's characters in *Goodfellas* and *Casino*).[4]

Mean Streets, released in 1973, was Scorsese's first major film. The movie starred Harvey Keitel who became like a brother to Scorsese and whose character, Charlie, was named after Scorsese' father. *Mean Streets* was also the first of eight Scorsese films in which Robert De Niro appeared. Scorsese had first met De Niro through Brian De Palma, but there was a close affinity between Scorsese and De Niro since both came from similar backgrounds and understood the rituals of Little Italy.

Mean Streets was an American version of an Italian neo-realist film, filled with wobbly handheld camera shots, though with a religious undercurrent that one rarely found in the movies of Roberto Rossellini or Vittorio De Sica. Keitel's character (like Scorsese) might well have been a priest, but instead lives in an environment of crime and brutality. His relationship with Johnny Boy (De Niro) is vaguely spiritual, as though he is Johnny Boy's father-confessor. But in the end, they are both damned—as are most of the characters in Scorsese's films.[5] Neither religion nor crime provides any consolation. In Scorsese's movies, you never make up for your sins. And you rarely find salvation anywhere—except maybe in the creepy enticements of fame.

Many of Scorsese's characters are unhinged, consumed with rage or a passion for revenge and an inchoate hunger for recognition (as in *The King of Comedy*, his remake of *Cape Fear*, and *Shutter Island*). But none of Scorsese's characters was more alarming than Robert De Niro's Travis Bickle in Scorsese's signature 1976 film, *Taxi Driver*.

By the 1970s, American cities were sinking in a sea of crime, rubble, poverty, and racial tensions. The decay was most visible in New York, and it was captured in movies like *Midnight Cowboy*, *Serpico*, and *Dog Day Afternoon*—as well as in the San Francisco of Clint Eastwood's *Dirty Harry* series. As Travis Bickle drives around the human and physical debris of Manhattan, he grumbles "someone should just take this city and . . . flush it down the fuckin' toilet." *Taxi Driver*, more than any other movie of the 1970s, encapsulated the rot of urban America.

Yet Scorsese was also heavily influenced in *Taxi Driver* by John Ford's Western, *The Searchers* (1956). Travis is a modernized and even more psychopathic version of John Wayne's Ethan Edwards. Toward the end of the film, Travis is obsessed with rescuing Jodie Foster's Iris (an up-dated version of Natalie Wood) from a pimp played by Harvey Keitel, who wears an Indian headband and is called "Sport" (a streetwise allusion to John Ford's villainous Indian chief "Scar"). Travis, as with Ethan Edwards, is bursting with inner conflicts, yet he is filled with a sense of God's justice (like Jules Winnfield, the Samuel L. Jackson character in Quentin Tarantino's *Pulp Fiction*, which owes a debt to *Taxi Driver* complete with the jovial star turn of Harvey Keitel as Winston Wolfe, the man who "solves problems").

Scorsese's feelings of being an interloper in the movie industry were reflected in Travis's sense of alienation and solitude.[6] "Loneliness has followed me my whole life," Travis acknowledges. "In bars, in cars, sidewalks, stores, everywhere. There's no escape. I'm God's lonely man." So Travis writes notes to himself in his room. And in the movie's most legendary scene, improvised by De Niro, he strikes poses in front of a mirror ("You talkin' to me?"), but he's the only one there.

Yet unlike Ethan Edwards who remains permanently alone at the end of *The Searchers*, Travis Bickle (after a bloody rampage) becomes the psychopath as celebrity, surrounded by newspaper clippings of his success in saving Iris from a life of prostitution (even though she doesn't particularly want to be saved). Travis winds up as the most bizarre hero ever to adorn a movie—Scorsese's way of commenting on the madness of notoriety.

The connection between psychosis and glory remained an issue for Scorsese in *Raging Bull*, released in 1980. This was, however, a movie inspired as much by De Niro as by Scorsese. They had become not only collaborators but soul mates, each intuiting the other's fixations and aspirations. De Niro had read Jake LaMotta's autobiography of his career as a middleweight boxer, *Raging Bull: My Story*, published in 1970. De Niro understood that LaMotta was not just a fighter but a man of enormous complexity, oscillating between the extremes of violence and the desire to be appreciated and loved. De Niro ultimately managed to persuade Scorsese to make a movie of LaMotta's adult life.

Scorsese himself envisioned the film as a tribute to all the illustrious boxing movies of the past: *Body and Soul, The Harder They Fall, Requiem for a Heavyweight*, and above all *On the Waterfront*. Hence, Scorsese shot the film in black and white at a time when almost all movies (except for Woody Allen's *Manhattan* and *Stardust Memories*) were made in color. Moreover, De Niro (as he had in *The Godfather: Part II*) would be reinterpreting one of Marlon Brando's most iconic roles, as Terry Malloy in *On the Waterfront*.

It was therefore appropriate that in the film's closing scene, an aging obese LaMotta should stand alone before a mirror (like Travis

Bickle) and recite Brando's "I coulda been a contender" lines before going on stage in a seedy nightclub. De Niro deliberately spoke Brando's lines in a monotone so as not to attempt an unnecessary imitation of Terry Malloy. But symbolically, De Niro (who won his second Oscar, this time for best actor) and Scorsese were reproducing the relationship between Brando and Elia Kazan.[7] Thus it was fitting that De Niro and Scorsese both introduced Kazan to receive a lifetime achievement award at the Oscar ceremonies in 1999.

Scorsese was still fascinated with the lunacy of fame. And how an outsider like himself becomes an idol. So in 1983, he directed one his most unusual and least violent movies, *The King of Comedy*. In part the movie reflected Scorsese's love of the television comedy of the 1950s and early 1960s on which he grew up: Sid Caesar's *Your Show of Shows* as well as the *Tonight Show* when it was presided over by Steve Allen and then Jack Paar. In addition, despite his own artistic ambitions, Scorsese was intrigued by the conventions of show business and the machinery of stardom. Hence the film was Scorsese's private meditation on how one achieves success in the feral world of celebrities, agents, and demented fans.

In *The King of Comedy* Robert De Niro for once is not a vicious maniac but a loser whom no one takes seriously. He plays an aspiring but untalented comic named Rupert Pupkin who concocts a scheme to kidnap a television talk-show host in order to force the producers to give him a spot on the show for his monologue (which he practices incessantly in his basement while upstairs his mother—who was actually Scorsese's mother—screams at him about what he's doing). The TV host was modeled on Johnny Carson, who was originally offered the part, as was Dick Cavett, but both turned it down. So in what turned out to be a brilliant instance of casting, an abnormally recessive and sullen Jerry Lewis played the role in the movie, as Jerry Langford.

Improbably, Pupkin's plan works. His appearance on the show makes it seems possible, at least in this movie, to achieve every frenzied fan's and autograph-seeker's thirst for applause. As Pupkin observes at the end of his monologue that is more embarrassing than witty, "better to be a king for a night than schmuck for a lifetime." For different reasons, Pupkin has attained the same renown, with photos of himself in all the newspapers and magazines, as does Travis Bickle.

The King of Comedy was Scorsese's quirkiest film. This may be why the movie was a failure at the box office.[8] So Scorsese decided to direct an intentionally commercial picture. In 1986, he released *The Color of Money*, a sequel to *The Hustler* (1961), with an older Paul Newman again in the role of Fast Eddie Felson. Scorsese, however, did not want to replicate *The Hustler* which he considered a masterpiece (although he did try, unsuccessfully, to persuade Jackie Gleason to reprise his role as Minnesota Fats). *The Color of Money*, which also starred a brash young Tom Cruise, was a commercial triumph, at last earning Paul Newman a best actor Oscar.[9] Yet it bore little resemblance to the style and themes of Scorsese's previous films.

Scorsese returned to more familiar, and more personal, territory in *Goodfellas* (1990) and *Casino* (1995). Both films starred Robert De Niro and Joe Pesci, though Pesci stole almost all the scenes he was in (and won an Oscar for best supporting actor for his performance in *Goodfellas*). The most chilling moment in *Goodfellas* occurs when Pesci as the volatile killer Tommy DeVito confronts Ray Liotta, playing the real-life Henry Hill who ultimately informs on the crime family of which he's a member. In a scene that was improvised, Pesci keeps asking Liotta "how am I funny?.... You said I'm funny. How the fuck am I funny, what the fuck is so funny about me? Tell me, tell me what's funny!" Everyone sitting at the table where this altercation occurs, and in the audience as well, thinks Pesci is about to pull out a gun and blast Liotta's head off. But the entire scene, however ominous, turns out to be a joke.

Yet in Scorsese's movies, no one can really trust anyone else. The humor is always intimidating. Whether Scorsese is dealing with Italians in New York or Irish-American mobsters in Boston, as he does in *The Departed* in 2006, the aura of treachery is omnipresent.[10] Cops and criminals are the same breed, and they're all potential stool pigeons. *The Departed* starred Leonardo DiCaprio, Matt Damon, Jack Nicholson,

Martin Sheen, and Alec Baldwin, but it's impossible to know who's honest or who to believe. And the inevitable result is that nearly all the characters meet violent deaths. There is no redemption, as there was in *Raging Bull* and of an eerie sort in *Taxi Driver.*

Over the decades, Scorsese had been nominated for best director Oscars for many of his films: *Raging Bull, The Last Temptation of Christ, Goodfellas, Gangs of New York,* and *The Aviator.* But he did not win the Oscar until *The Departed.* As so often happens in Hollywood, a director or actor is finally honored not necessarily for his best work but for the entirety of his career. Still, Scorsese was given the award by his closest colleagues and fellow auteurs: Francis Ford Coppola, George Lucas, and Steven Spielberg (who just missed being a war baby himself, having been born in 1946).

Of the four directors (Coppola, Spielberg, Scorsese, and Lucas), only Lucas never won an Oscar. But he had as much impact on the history of American movies and culture as any of his contemporaries did.

Lucas graduated from the USC film school in 1967. Like Coppola and Scorsese, Lucas was cynical about the commercialism of Hollywood movies and yearned to be a director of art films. But his first movie in 1971, *THX 1138,* was an experimental and futuristic thriller that few people saw. So Lucas reluctantly decided to adapt to the studios' desire to make money.

His next movie, *American Graffiti* (1973), was a much more auto-biographical (and more popular) film rooted in his experiences growing up in California in the 1950s and early 1960s. *American Graffiti* was crammed with the images and sounds of the era's adolescent culture that Lucas himself had internalized: drag racing, cruising through drive-in restaurant parking lots, searching for girls, all accompanied by rock music and the barking voice of the famed disc jockey Wolfman Jack.

At the end of the movie, we're told what happens to the four main characters. One becomes an insurance agent, another is killed in an auto accident, and a third is listed as missing in action in Vietnam. The fourth character, Curt (played by a young Richard Dreyfuss), is described as a writer living in Canada. Anyone in the audience in 1973 would have known what that meant: Curt has fled to Canada to escape the draft and the Vietnam War.

Yet Lucas's first two movies only hinted at the film that made him rich and transformed the movie business. The first *Star Wars* epic, released in 1977, was reminiscent of the popular culture Lucas had always cherished: the comic books and science fiction movie serials of the 1930s. But the movie was full of avant-garde special effects that buttressed an adventure infused with the mythology of outer space and other worlds.

The movie featured Harrison Ford (a war baby born in 1942) as Han Solo. Ford had already had small roles in Coppola's *The Conversation* and Lucas's *American Graffiti*. And he would go on to star in Steven Spielberg's *Indiana Jones* trilogy in the 1980s, for which Lucas was both a writer and executive producer.

If Michael Cimino's *Heaven's Gate* demonstrated to the studios how much money might be lost on a movie, *Star Wars* showed how profitable a Hollywood film could be. *Star Wars* became the highest-grossing American movie until *Titanic* in 1997. More important, by the early 1980s, *Star Wars* had made $1.5 billion from the sale of spin-off products. Most of these earnings went directly to Lucas, whose contract with Twentieth Century-Fox gave him the merchandising rights. The money enabled Lucas to launch his own company, Lucasfilm, with its subsidiaries Industrial Light and Magic and the THX sound system, each of which provided the technology indispensable to Hollywood's blockbusters from the 1980s on. Lucas was now a filmmaker whose freedom exceeded the fantasies of all the other American auteurs.

Star Wars, together with Steven Spielberg's *Jaws* in 1975, changed the way American movies were debuted (in as many cities as possible both in the United States and around the world) and marketed. From this point forward, Hollywood operated on a two-tier system, making movies for a younger audience full of cartoon characters, car chases, and ear-shattering explosions, and more serious lower-budget movies for people who still cared about films as a form of art as well as entertainment.

Yet for all the accolades bestowed on war baby directors like Coppola, Cimino, Scorsese, and Lucas, none of them could have fundamentally altered American movies without the presence in their films—and those that came later—of a new generation of actors, most of them also born during World War II. Despite the auteur theory, movies were as much an actor's, as a director's, medium. And the performances delivered by actors like Faye Dunaway, Al Pacino, Robert De Niro, Christopher Walken, Lily Tomlin, Joe Pesci, Harvey Keitel, and Harrison Ford were as crucial to the success of America's movies from the 1960s through the remainder of the twentieth century as was the artistic genius of the war baby directors.

The New Actors

One of the myths about the American films made from the late 1960s to the early 1980s is that there were no good roles for women. Yet if you remind yourself of the powerful performances delivered by actresses during this period, it is astonishing how many of them made the movies in which they appeared unforgettable. The list of noteworthy roles for women is striking: Anne Bancroft in *The Graduate*; Jane Fonda in *Klute* and *Julia*; Lily Tomlin and Ronee Blakely in *Nashville*; Diane Keaton in *Annie Hall* and *Manhattan*; Jill Clayburgh (a war baby born in 1944) in *An Unmarried Woman*; Meryl Streep in *The Deer Hunter*, *Kramer vs. Kramer*, and *Sophie's Choice*.

For ten years, though, the most riveting of all the American actresses was Faye Dunaway. She starred in some of the most innovative and influential films of the era—none more so than *Bonnie and Clyde* in 1967, the movie that showed a young generation of American directors that they could now tell any sort of story in any way they wanted on the screen.

Like her war baby cohorts, Al Pacino and Robert De Niro, Dunaway was a quintessential Method actor who projected her own personality, painful past, and memories onto a role. Like them, she was an heir of the first monumental Method actors in the 1940s and 1950s: Marlon

Brando, Montgomery Clift, and James Dean. It was hardly surprising, therefore, that of all her teachers, Dunaway learned most about acting from Elia Kazan. Kazan taught Dunaway that exceptional acting was always interior, that an actor didn't simply say the lines in a script but explored what was behind the words, what emotions created a character. As a consequence, Dunaway was driven to investigate a character's background, her psychology, her subconscious (as if she had to know more about the character than the character knew about herself).

In a fashion typical of Method actors raised on the techniques taught originally by Constantin Stanislavski and then by Lee Strasberg, Dunaway drew on her own troubled childhood and adolescence in interpreting a role. She could never play a woman who was innocent or lighthearted because she had never experienced these feelings when she was young. Dunaway always felt as if she were a girl from the impoverished underclass, filled with a sense of being an outcast, and yet who hungered to be a celebrity.[11]

All of these conflicting passions coalesced in Dunaway's complex performance as Bonnie Parker. Until Warren Beatty and the director Arthur Penn chose her to play Bonnie, Dunaway had been in a few mediocre movies, none of which brought her any attention. So essentially she was an unknown who had been given, out of nowhere, the role of a lifetime.

Dunaway understood Bonnie perfectly: her longing to escape her dismal and tedious surroundings in West Texas, her hunger to see the world or at least more of America (as Clyde tells Bonnie early in the film, "You got somethin's better than bein' a waitress. You and me travelin' together, we could cut a path clean across this state and Kansas and Missouri and Oklahoma and everybody'd know about it…. Hell, you might just be the best damn girl in Texas"). Indeed, from the first moment of the film, when we see the camera caressing Bonnie's face and body as she inspects her lips in a mirror, and wanders around her bedroom naked, we know that we're watching a star being born.

Dunaway as Bonnie feeds on the fame of the Barrow gang. She

sends their photographs to newspapers, and she writes poems eulogizing their exploits before their demise. But Dunaway's mood constantly shifts from exultation to frustration and anger, almost as if she can barely conceal her hysteria. As Bonnie, she knows that she and Clyde have no future, no fantasy of a happy ending. Lying in bed in the scene before they are ambushed, Bonnie asks Clyde "What would you do if some miracle happened and we could walk out of here tomorrow morning and start all over again clean?" Clyde replies: "Well… I guess I'd do it all different. First off, I wouldn't live in the same state where we pull our jobs." Bonnie turns over on her side, Dunaway's face enveloped in regret that Clyde does not comprehend the point of her question, and she desolately accepts their fate.

Just before their slaughter at the end of the movie, Dunaway and Beatty look at each other in their car, knowing that imminently they will die. It is one of the most intimate scenes between the two actors in the film. And then their bodies are perforated with bullets, Dunaway quivering as if she's filled with uncontrollable tremors.[12]

Bonnie and Clyde was a worldwide sensation. Nothing like it had ever been seen before in American movies. Bonnie's beret and sweater became a fashion statement for women throughout the world. More significant for Dunaway's career, *Bonnie and Clyde* made her a movie icon at the age of twenty-seven. By 1968, she had graced the covers of *Newsweek*, *Look*, and *Life* magazines. In addition, Dunaway was nominated for an Oscar for best actress, but lost to Katharine Hepburn in *Guess Who's Coming to Dinner*.

In the meantime, Dunaway—who had until now been engrossed with her career—was becoming more aware of the upheavals in American life, particularly after the assassination of Robert Kennedy.[13] Her ability as a star to select what roles she wanted to play, combined with her growing sensitivity to the malevolence of power in America, led her to a film that was even more disturbing than *Bonnie And Clyde*.

In 1974, Dunaway assumed (and identified with) the character of Evelyn Mulwray in *Chinatown*. Just as *Bonnie and Clyde* was a 1960s reinterpretation of the gangster movies made in the 1930s, so *Chinatown* was a reincarnation of film noir in the 1940s. *Chinatown* starred Jack Nicholson as J. J. Gittes, an archetypal private eye reminiscent of Humphrey Bogart in *The Maltese Falcon* and *The Big Sleep*. In an even uncannier reference to the cinematic past, the archvillain of *Chinatown*, with the biblical name of Noah Cross, was played by John Huston, the director of *The Maltese Falcon* and one of the American inventors—thematically and stylistically—of film noir. Yet *Chinatown*, directed by the Polish émigré Roman Polanski, was also a commentary on the conspiracies and deceits that seemed to flourish in America in the age of Watergate.

Nicholson urged the producers of the films to cast Faye Dunaway as the troubled and jittery Evelyn Mulwray. Nicholson told Dunaway that Evelyn was one of the most spellbinding roles for a woman he had ever encountered. And indeed it was. For much of the movie, neither the audience nor Nicholson's Gittes knows who Evelyn really is. As performed by Dunaway, she is alternately rich and sophisticated (for Dunaway, Evelyn was another version of F. Scott Fitzgerald's Daisy Buchanan in *The Great Gatsby*, her voice full of money), neurotic and frightened, haunted by memories she can't reveal. She personifies a universe of mystery and chaos, of puzzles and sleaze, all of it symbolized by "Chinatown"—a place as well as a metaphor, where Gittes once tried to keep someone he cared about from being hurt and miserably failed. Like Harry Caul in *The Conversation*, Gittes is entrapped in a world he can neither fathom nor decode. "You may think you know what you're dealing with," Noah Cross cautions Gittes, "but, believe me, you don't."

As it turns out, Evelyn is the daughter of Noah Cross, with whom she has had an incestuous relationship that produced a child. Every time Dunaway says "father," she pauses before she utters the word, her voice tremulous, as if she's recalling a venomous reptile. When Gittes finally learns the truth, it does no good. His best intentions—to save Evelyn and her daughter ("my sister, my daughter")—accomplish nothing except to provoke another catastrophe.

The movie concludes, as do many 1970s films, with a shrug and a sense of defeat. "Forget it Jake," says one of Gittes's colleagues in the film's most famous line. "It's Chinatown." So the audience is left with no happy ending, no sense of resolution, only a perception of regret and helplessness. Though also with an appreciation of the bravura acting of Dunaway, Nicholson, and Huston.

Dunaway herself came to loathe Roman Polanski. Unlike Elia Kazan, he gave her no direction or advice.[14] Hence, she had to create the character of Evelyn out of her private emotions, drawing on her recollections of her tortured relationship with her own father. But Evelyn Mulwray, like Bonnie Parker, would become one of the roles that typified Dunaway's originality as an actress. Again, she was nominated for an Oscar, but lost to Ellen Burstyn in Martin Scorsese's *Alice Doesn't Live Here Anymore*.

After watching the Senate Watergate hearings in 1973, and Richard Nixon's resignation from the Presidency in 1974, Dunaway felt an even greater sense of sorrow and rage at America's (and her own) loss of innocence. Some of these reactions she poured into her next character, Kathy Hale, in Sidney Pollack's *Three Days of the Condor* (1975). As in the case of *The Conversation* and *Chinatown*, *Three Days of the Condor* reflected the terror of a country at the mercy of unseen and unknown conspirators. But here, the source of evil is not some anonymous corporation (as in *The Conversation)* or a malevolent lunatic (as in *Chinatown*) but the government itself, particularly in the form of the CIA.

Dunaway's performance in *Three Days of the Condor* was similar to her interpretation of Evelyn Mulwray. Her Kathy is lonely, isolated, and fearful.[15] She photographs barren trees in winter, in scenes empty of people, a visual exemplification of her own seclusion from most of humanity. And her connection with Robert Redford's character, Joe Turner (a low-level CIA analyst who happens upon the murder of his colleagues) is semi-hysterical—not only because he briefly kidnaps her but because she doesn't think he's "going to live much longer." In this film as well, Dunaway's acting is magnetic; she elevates the movie from a spy thriller to a psychological study of personal paranoia.

Dunaway at last won the best actress Oscar for her performance in Sidney Lumet's *Network* in 1976. Playing a television executive, Diana Christensen, Dunaway (as she was in most of her roles, and in her own life) is both driven and vulnerable. But the Oscar signified the success she had dreamed of since her childhood. And from 1974 to 1978, she was among the top twenty-five box-office stars in the movies, an achievement by a woman equaled only by Barbra Streisand.[16]

Yet as was too often the case for actresses in Hollywood, when Dunaway neared her forties, she was offered fewer gripping roles. As a result, she moved to England to act in the theater, and began to appear in television roles in America in the 1990s.[17] Meanwhile, Meryl Streep emerged as the preeminent American actress from the late 1970s on, playing characters (as in *Kramer vs. Kramer* and *The Hours*) that might once have gone to Dunaway. Nevertheless, in her prime, Dunaway was as compelling and unconventional an actress as her male war baby colleagues, Al Pacino and Robert De Niro.

Dunaway, Pacino, and De Niro were all disciples of the Method. As such, they were the "offspring" of Marlon Brando. And they became (along with Dustin Hoffman who was born slightly earlier, in 1937) the dominant actors of their generation.

With the exception of Dunaway, none of them looked like traditional movie stars, in the mold of a Clark Gable or Cary Grant. In an earlier time, they would have been character actors, cast in roles that called for idiosyncratic talents but not for glamor or heroism. But in the 1970s and afterwards, they personified the transformation of Hollywood movies, and the idea of what constituted a model for both cinematic and (distinctly non-heroic) social behavior. In this way, they too helped change America.

I first saw Al Pacino at the beginning of his career, when he was an unknown. In 1967, the Charles Playhouse in Boston mounted a revival of Clifford Odets's *Awake and Sing!*, first put on by the Group Theater in 1935. Since I was working at Harvard on a doctoral dissertation (which eventually evolved into my first book) on the culture of the 1930s,

I decided I'd better go see the play. *Awake and Sing!* takes place during the nadir of the Depression, but it is essentially a family drama about a conflict in a Jewish family between a grandfather, a mother, and her son. The cast, all professionals, was adequate if bland. Apart from Pacino, the young actor who played the son. Every time he took the stage, he was mesmerizing; he seemed as if he were on another planet from the rest of the cast. As I left the theater, I felt that I should remember Pacino's name since I might hear of him in the future. I soon did.

In 1971, in only his second movie, Pacino starred as a heroin addict in *The Panic in Needle Park*. His charismatic performance in the film caught the attention of Francis Ford Coppola who was searching for an actor to play Michael Corleone in *The Godfather: Part I*. Over the objections of the executives at Paramount who wanted a "big name" to play Michael in what was, after all, an expensive film, Coppola chose Pacino (though he also considered for a while Robert De Niro, who was equally untested in a lead role in a major movie).

Not surprisingly, Pacino was nervous before his initial scene with Brando in *The Godfather: Part II*. When a friend asked him why, Pacino replied that he was "acting with God." Yet Pacino wound up in the *Godfather* saga acting with another divinity as well. Before the filming of *The Godfather: Part II*, Pacino and Coppola were trying to decide who should play the part of the Jewish gangster Hyman Roth. At first, they approached Elia Kazan, who declined the role. Then they made an inspired choice, asking Lee Strasberg—the guru of the Actors Studio and Pacino's one-time teacher—to play Roth. In Strasberg's scenes with Pacino, there was a not-so-hidden subtext. Strasberg became not just a teacher acting with his former student but a surrogate (if Machiavellian) father figure, dispensing what turns out to be treacherous advice to his symbolic son. In this sense, Pacino was acting with two gods, Brando and Strasberg, each of whom had helped guide him in his own techniques as a Method performer.

Pacino's Michael Corleone, however, is truly the main character in both *Godfathers*. As Pacino plays him, Michael is undemonstrative in his ruthlessness. He listens more than he talks. Pacino permits Michael to communicate mostly with his jaw muscles and his pitiless gaze. In some of his later films, Pacino often overacted, particularly if the script or plot was pedestrian. But here, his power as an actor is expressed almost inaudibly, in the intensity of the silences between his words and his sentences. In the two Coppola films, Pacino is the personification of an icy killer.

As Michael, Pacino gave the most arresting performances of his career. And he helped make it possible for other unpredictable war baby actors—De Niro, Christopher Walken, Joe Pesci, Harvey Keitel—to alter our notions of what constituted indelible acting on the screen.

Pacino himself went on to star in two of the most memorable films of the 1970s: *Serpico* (1973) and *Dog Day Afternoon* (1975), both movies directed by Sidney Lumet. *Serpico*, based on a true story about an honest cop in an otherwise corrupt New York police force, was entirely Pacino's movie. He appears in practically every scene, and he holds the film together with his soft and gloomy voice, and his evolution from a clean-cut rookie policeman to a bearded undercover and rebellious detective bent on exposing the cops who are taking cash from drug dealers. The movie would never have been as nerve-racking as it is without Pacino's enigmatic appeal; we are engrossed by Pacino's character and his acting prowess from the beginning of the film to the end.

The same capacity to beguile an audience was evident in *Dog Day Afternoon*, another movie based on a real event. Here, Pacino plays a bank robber (the actual thief had been inspired, ironically, by *The Godfather*) who wants the money to pay for his male lover's sex-change operation. And who takes hostages and tries to negotiate with the police and ultimately the FBI for a plane to take himself and his accomplice Sal (John Cazale) to a foreign country. Almost all the dialogue was improvised, including the famed scene when Pacino, outside the bank, waves a white handkerchief and starts chanting (as the crowd joins in) "Attica! Attica! Attica!" Pacino also improvised a telephone conversation with his lover, a brilliant amalgam of affection, frustration, and sorrow at the knowledge that this whole caper will end badly (as it does).

It is now impossible to conceive of both *Godfathers*, *Serpico*, and *Dog Day Afternoon* without the presence of Pacino. Moreover, the last two movies resonated in the culture long afterwards. In Spike Lee's *Inside Man* (2006), a fake bank robber played by Clive Owen keeps calling Denzel Washington, the detective trying to coax him out of the bank, "Serpico." And at one point Washington tells Owen: "Whoever heard of a bank robber escaping on a plane with fifty hostages. You've seen *Dog Day Afternoon!*"

An actor's job, however, is to keep working, even when the movie or the play is second-rate. Pacino kept working constantly from the 1970s through the early twenty-first century, though often in movies that were mediocre. Rather than succumb to the limitations of the roles, Pacino tended to chew the scenery, as if the explosiveness of his behavior on screen could compensate for the weaknesses of the material. So he was always fun to watch.

But when Pacino had the opportunity to appear in a superlative film, he could subordinate himself to the role and the rest of the cast. He was especially persuasive in the movie adaptation in 1992 of David Mamet's Pulitzer Prize-winning play *Glengarry Glen Ross*. Surrounded by an all-star group of actors (Jack Lemmon, Kevin Spacey, Ed Harris, Alan Arkin, and Alec Baldwin), Pacino plays Ricky Roma, a latter-day but successful Willy Loman, a slick salesman who knows how to talk prospective customers into buying worthless real estate. Here, Pacino often recedes into the background as the other actors argue, boast, and grumble about having no decent "leads." In fact, *Glengarry Glen Ross* was the first of Pacino's movies since *The Godfather: Part I* in which he yields the limelight to another actor, in this case Jack Lemmon as Shelley "the machine" Levine. Yet when the office manager (Spacey) screws up one of Roma's sales, Pacino grabs the audience's attention and the movie's central theme. "What you're hired for, is to help us," he bellows. "Does that seem clear to you? To help us, not to… fuck us up." And then Pacino delivers the salesman's ultimate motto: "You never open your mouth until you know what the shot is."

During the course of his career, Pacino was nominated for four best actor Oscars in *The Godfather: Part II*, *Serpico*, *Dog Day Afternoon*, and… *And Justice for All*. But he did not win until 1992 for his role as a blind, retired army colonel contemplating suicide in *Scent of a Woman*. As frequently occurred in Hollywood, an actor was awarded an Oscar not necessarily for his finest performance, but for his long history of films. This was true for Pacino. Still, he continued to make many movies and appear in plays in New York, particularly as Shylock in *The Merchant of Venice* and *Richard III*. As a result, he was acclaimed as the leading and most influential actor of his generation—his preeminence equaled only by his war baby comrade, Robert De Niro.

Of all the younger Method actors, De Niro in the 1970s came the closest to being Marlon Brando's heir. In no movie was this more evident than in *The Godfather: Part II*. Previously De Niro had made only two films in which he had major roles: *Mean Streets* and *Bang the Drum Slowly*, both released in 1973. So he was regarded as a promising actor but certainly not a star.

Now, in *The Godfather: II*, Francis Ford Coppola cast De Niro as the youthful Vito Corleone in the early twentieth-century segments of the film. De Niro confronted the challenge both of invoking and erasing the audience's memory of Brando's performance in the first *Godfather*. De Niro didn't want to imitate Brando. Yet he needed to provide viewers with a hint of how Brando sounded as the aging Don, complete with Brando's reliance on delicate hand gestures, but at the same time to put his own stamp on the role of Vito Corleone. In addition, De Niro had to play the part almost entirely in Sicilian. He rarely speaks English except to utter *The Godfather*'s most unforgettable line: "I made him an offer he don' refuse." De Niro's complex rendition of Vito as an immigrant and affectionate family man, but at the outset of his career in crime, was a stunning achievement—one that earned him an Oscar for best supporting actor.

In many ways, De Niro was a more versatile actor in the 1970s and

1980s than Brando had been in the 1950s. Unlike Brando, De Niro had an inexplicable ability not only to portray an assortment of characters, but to look like a different person from one role to the next. So he could be lean and elegant in *The Godfather: Part II*, a squat backwoods baseball catcher afflicted with leukemia in *Bang the Drum Slowly*, a twitchy near-adolescent in *Mean Streets*, hard-bodied in *Taxi Driver*, bearded and initially unrecognizable in *The Deer Hunter*, muscular as well as corpulent in *Raging Bull* (he gained nearly sixty pounds to play Jake LaMotta in retirement), a sleek Catholic priest in *True Confessions* (1981), and an impatient outlandishly-clothed show-business wannabe in *The King of Comedy*.

De Niro won a best actor Oscar for his impersonation of LaMotta in *Raging Bull*. Yet his most powerful and sensitive performance occurred in *The Deer Hunter*. De Niro plays a working-class character named Michael who with two of his friends is physically and psychologically devastated by the Vietnam War. Michael's personality is reminiscent of Ernest Hemingway's Jake Barnes, the damaged victim of World War I. Like Jake, however, Michael is a survivor, emotionally maimed but unbroken. Still, when he returns home, he feels a similar nausea and sense of embarrassment that Hemingway's veterans so often demonstrate.

In one of the moments of the film that most evokes this estrangement, De Niro's Michael, just off the train, rides by his house in a taxi. His friends have prepared a party, complete with American flags and welcome-home banners to greet the hero back from the war. Michael instinctively decides to avoid the celebrations. He orders the cab driver to take him to a motel.

There, alone in his room, in silence, with only the haunting guitar music on the soundtrack, Michael deals with himself. He sits on the bed, crouches against the wall, holds his head in his hands, and gazes at a photo of one of his friend's lovers, soon to be his own. Nothing is said or can be said. De Niro, in a dazzling piece of acting, has communicated everything we need to know about what it means to feel "distant" with the same (visual) economy and precision of Hemingway's prose.

It is difficult to imagine any other actor playing that scene with as much hushed eloquence as De Niro summoned. And it is the reason that, in his prime, De Niro was considered the most absorbing of the war baby actors.

Later in his career, though, De Niro seemed to cede the spotlight to other actors (like Joe Pesci in Martin Scorsese's *Goodfellas* and *Casino*), and his performances became more routine. In Michael Mann's *Heat* (1995), for example, there is a scene between Al Pacino and De Niro in a coffee shop in which Pacino dominates their conversation while De Niro, with hooded eyes, withdraws into his own thoughts. One problem with the Method as an acting technique is that it forced actors to dig as deeply as possible into their own psyches—until they had nothing left to offer. This is what happened to Brando after *The Godfather: Part I* and *Last Tango in Paris*, and it seemed to occur with De Niro as well. By the 1990s, he was appearing in more commonplace films, sometimes giving a parody of his past roles.

Occasionally, De Niro could recapture some of the power he had shown in the 1970s—in Quentin Tarantino's *Jackie Brown* in 1997 and *Silver Linings Playbook* in 2012. But, as yet, he has never managed to replicate the characters that made him astonishing to audiences: Johnny Boy in *Mean Streets*, the young Vito Corleone, Travis Bickle, Michael in *The Deer Hunter*, Jake LaMotta, and Rupert Pupkin in *The King of Comedy*.

Nonetheless, Faye Dunaway, Al Pacino, and Robert De Niro changed American movies, and altered the audience's assumptions of what they could see onscreen. Together with the inventiveness of directors like Francis Ford Coppola, Martin Scorsese, and George Lucas, they helped convert films from mass entertainment to personal works of art. That accomplishment was one of the war babies' most momentous contributions to American culture.

The Impact of the War Babies' Movies

None of the changes that occurred in American movies and in movie acting during the late 1960s and 1970s meant that Hollywood had abandoned its desire to make huge profits on blockbuster films choked with special effects. George Lucas, after all, demonstrated in *Star Wars* how much money could be piled up in a big-budget extravaganza. But it did mean that newer directors could use their war baby predecessors as models for the eccentric or autobiographical films they themselves wanted to make.

Indeed many of the directors of the 1990s and early twenty-first century were not only influenced but encouraged by the directors and actors born during World War II. Quentin Tarantino might never have been able to make his first movie, *Reservoir Dogs* in 1992, without the intervention and support of Harvey Keitel, who served as a co-producer and lead actor in the film.

Before he became a screenwriter and director, Tarantino had worked in a video store in California. So his head was crammed with countless scenes and snatches of dialogue from classic as well as modern films. His movies were often tributes to the techniques and icons of the cinematic past.

With *Pulp Fiction* in 1994, he created a movie that was at once esthetically intricate (like the films of the 1970s) and saturated with allusions to popular culture and the history of moviemaking. When Vincent Vega (John Travolta) gets up to dance in a restaurant filled with employees who look like Ed Sullivan, Buddy Holly, and Marilyn Monroe, we can't help smiling because we're being transported back to Travolta's performance as Tony Manero in *Saturday Night Fever* in 1977, though with the still-captivating Travolta now seventeen years older and thirty pounds heavier. And when Christopher Walken shows up as a slightly deranged Vietnam veteran, it's as if his character in *The Deer Hunter* has been resurrected, having somehow survived the carnage of Russian roulette.

Tarantino's hit men in *Pulp Fiction*, however, do not resemble the taciturn mobsters in *The Godfather*. Nor are they similar to the hooligans in Martin Scorsese's *Mean Streets* (despite the presence again in a Tarantino film of Harvey Keitel). Tarantino's gangsters, like the characters in most of his films, are garrulous, constantly chattering about life and philosophy as they go about their violent business.

Yet at one point, the connection between religion and crime does remind one of the themes in a Coppola or Scorsese movie. As Jules Winnfield (Samuel L. Jackson) acknowledges to two would-be robbers: "Normally both your asses would be dead... but you happened to pull this shit when I'm in a transitional period so I don't wanna kill you, I wanna help you.... I'm tryin' real hard to be a shepherd." Presumably for Jules, salvation is possible as it is not for Michael Corleone.

Tarantino won a best screenplay Oscar for *Pulp Fiction*, as he did again for *Django Unchained* (2012). In between, he directed one other movie that reflected both his personality, his zany humor, and his love of idiosyncratic 1970s-style filmmaking: *Inglourious Basterds* in 2009. All these films reflected his debt to the irrationality and acerbic dialogue of movies like *Mean Streets* and *Chinatown*. Furthermore, just as Coppola and Scorsese had discovered unheralded actors like Al Pacino and Robert De Niro, so Tarantino found Christoph Waltz, a previously undistinguished Austrian television actor who delivered two entrancing performances for which he won Oscars for best supporting actor in *Inglourious Basterds* and *Django Unchained*.

Yet if any contemporary director carried in her veins the artistic inclinations of the war baby filmmakers, it was Sophia Coppola, Francis's daughter. Her movies, though—especially *Lost in Translation* in 2003—were both funnier and more heartbreaking than those of her father.

Lost in Translation was also one of the most discerning movies ever made about the culture shock Americans experience when they confront the rest of the world. An aging actor, Bob Harris (played by Bill Murray who by this time was taking on more serious roles) has arrived in Tokyo to film a whisky commercial ("For relaxing times, make it Suntory time"). The premise of the movie was inspired by Francis Ford Coppolas's actually having shot a Suntory commercial in the 1970s with the Japanese filmmaker Akira Kurosawa.

But Bob is no master of the cinema. His career is fading; he's jet-lagged and surrounded by Japanese counselors and guides who are eager to please, bemused by his inability to fathom their version of English, nodding and smiling even though he's clueless about what's going on. Bob, in the midst of a midlife crisis, meets an equally baffled young woman, Charlotte (played by Scarlett Johansson). Inevitably, they fall in love—with each other and with Tokyo.

Yet *Lost in Translation* doesn't conform to the audience's expectations or the rules of a Hollywood romantic comedy. The characters don't have an affair and the movie doesn't end predictably. At the conclusion of the film, Bob and Charlotte embrace and kiss on a crowded Tokyo street. Bob whispers some words to Charlotte, but viewers don't know what he's saying. Then they part, with Bill Murray in a taxicab headed to the airport, staring at the flashing billboard signs of the city, emotionally exhausted. The final shots of the film, the sense of subdued fantasies and disappointment, are evocative of the sad finale of 1970s movies, particularly those that starred Faye Dunaway—like the aura of desolation that suffused her character's photography in *Three Days of the Condor*.

Wes Anderson's movies were as wry and wistful, and as personal, as *Lost in Translation*. But they weren't really comedies or conventional love stories either. Instead, they're filled, like Tarantino's films, with screwball dialogue and complicated plots, though without the accompanying bloodshed.

Anderson worked frequently with Roman Coppola, Francis's son. But Anderson also benefited from the support of Martin Scorsese who believed Anderson was one of the most ingenious of the modern directors. This judgment was certainly born out in some of Anderson's most unconventional films: *The Royal Tenenbaums* (2001), *The Life Aquatic with Steve Zissou* (2004), *The Darjeeling Limited* (2007), the animated *Fantastic Mr. Fox* (2009), and *Moonrise Kingdom* (2012). In most of these movies, families are dysfunctional with con-men fathers, absent or inattentive mothers, and siblings who often can scarcely tolerate their parents or one another. But all of the characters, however abnormal or self-absorbed, are charming—a trait strengthened by the regular presence in Anderson's casts of actors like Bill Murray, Owen Wilson, and Angelica Huston.[18]

Quentin Tarantino, Sophia Coppola, and Wes Anderson were carrying on the tradition of introspective filmmaking developed in the 1970s. In this sense, they were the spiritual descendants of the war babies. As such, they continued to make American movies unique and appealing to audiences throughout the world.

Still, the achievements of the war babies were hardly limited to music and movies. Their transformation of America's politics and journalism, from the 1960s to the present, was equally impressive. The politicians and political activists, as well as the journalists and pundits on both the left and the right, made the United States a different country than it would otherwise have been.

CHAPTER 7

Reshaping America: The Politics and Journalism of the War Baby Generation

BEGINNING IN THE 1960S, once they reached adulthood, the war babies reinvented America's popular music. In the late 1960s and 1970s, they also revolutionized Hollywood, making and acting in movies that were not only provocative but among the most innovative and disquieting in the history of the American film industry. Few people in the United States could listen to the war babies' music or watch the war babies' movies without being staggered by the artistic achievements of the generation born between 1939 and 1945.

The same startling effects were evident in the war babies' contributions to politics and journalism from the 1960s to the early twenty-first century. In most instances, the war babies (unlike the baby boomers) were not just participants in but leaders of the civil rights movement, feminism, the opposition to the war in Vietnam, investigative journalism, television punditry on the left as well as the right, foreign policy, and the politics of contemporary America.

In all of these cases, the war babies were more than orators, writers, and activists. They were remodeling America in their own image. For them, joining, guiding, or speaking for a cause was an existential exercise; the movements served as vehicles for their own self-expression and self-definition.

As a result, it is impossible to imagine any of the changes that took place in the United States over the past fifty years without the personal commitment and often the inner courage of the war babies themselves. For them, altering America was an emotional enterprise, a reflection of their own identities, whether they were in positions of authority or opponents of those in power. Either way, the war babies reshaped America so that it became another sort of country, less communal and with a new set of individualistic values, from what it had been during the Great Depression, World War II, or the postwar era.

Civil Rights, Feminism, and Vietnam

The first war baby activist to become famous was Mario Savio. In the early 1960s, Savio—a graduate student in philosophy at Berkeley—was growing increasingly critical of what he regarded as the elitist, programmatic, and inadequate liberalism of John F. Kennedy. Like many of the war babies at that time, Savio was gravitating toward the strategies of civil disobedience and the efficacy of moral protest. Yet whatever his disenchantment with the New Frontier, he had even less use for the sectarian brawls of the Old Left in the 1930s, many of those battles still raging among aging pro- and anti-Communists in the 1960s. In contrast, Savio's style of radicalism was anti-ideological, quasi-religious (despite his disillusion with his Catholic upbringing), and tentative, an attraction to the experimental that might or might not work in particular circumstances.

In 1964, the year Savio evolved into a star, he was twenty-four years old. During the summer of 1964, he had journeyed to Mississippi (along with other war babies like Tom Hayden, John Lewis, and Barney Frank) to help register African American voters in what was known as the Mississippi Freedom Summer. This was hazardous work. One could get beaten up, usually by members of the Ku Klux Klan or the White Citizens' Council, or murdered (as were the war babies Andrew Goodman, James Cheney, and Michael Schwerner). But the tactics of that summer and of the civil rights movement in general formed Savio's belief in personal dedication as a way of renovating America.

Returning to Berkeley in the fall of 1964, Savio was soon embroiled in a crisis that was characteristic of the student radicalism of the 1960s. For reasons that are still unclear, the administrators at Berkeley had shut down an area on campus where students could distribute leaflets for a variety of causes, not all of them political. More important, by 1964 Berkeley had become emblematic of what its president Clark Kerr called the "multiversity"—the university as a service center for the larger society, preparing students to excel in science, technology, and government as a way of fulfilling the needs of America's modernity.

Borrowing the tactics of the civil rights movements, many students at Berkeley launched a protest, complete with sit-ins, blockades, and occupations of buildings, as a revolt against both the ban on what they considered free speech and the role of the university as a training ground for America's current needs and policies. Savio himself was disturbed about the direction Berkeley, and all the country's major public universities, were taking. And so, without necessarily intending to, Savio emerged as the movement's most charismatic and eloquent speaker.

On December 2, 1964, at a demonstration, Savio gave his most renowned sermon, one that summarized both the immediate problems students perceived at Berkeley and the greater issue of where education and the social order in America were headed. "There's a time when the operation of the machine becomes so odious," Savio proclaimed, "makes you so sick at heart, that you can't take part... . And you've got to put your bodies upon the gears and upon the wheels, upon the levers, upon all the apparatus, and then you've got to make it stop. And you've got to indicate to the people who run it, to the people who own it, that unless you're free the machine will be prevented from working at all."

The imagery of a machine gone berserk summoned up memories of Charlie Chaplin entrapped in the whirling mechanisms of machinery out of control in his 1936 film *Modern Times*. But Savio wasn't joking. Nor was he referring to old, if classic, movies. What Savio called for was not just mass rebellion but personal resistance (in this sense, his speech was reminiscent of Chaplin's film). Yet Savio was arguing seriously that you have to throw your own body on the machine, on the whole structure of power and technology, in order to make them halt. No one else, separately or together, can accomplish this for you. You, individually, are at the center of the need to transform not only the contemporary university but all of America.

For a time, Savio's speech made him the poet and most eloquent spokesperson of the radicalism of the 1960s. Suddenly, he found himself thrust into the limelight, a media star of what journalists were calling the New Left and the counterculture, his celebrity linked to his forceful oratory.

But Savio himself was uneasy with his unexpected fame. He did not yearn for recognition or personal glory, as did some of his war baby contemporaries like Jesse Jackson and Muhammad Ali. Moreover, Savio grew more and more disillusioned with the rhetoric and agenda of the New Left. He abhorred the abstractions and argot of the radicals who dominated the late 1960s. By the close of the decade, Savio rarely participated in politics, even though he had been one of the most articulate of the self-styled revolutionaries of his epoch.

In addition, like Janis Joplin and Jim Morrison, Savio suffered throughout most of his life from depression, anxiety, and compulsive behavior. He was never a natural, or at least a durable, leader despite his immense influence and achievements in 1964. By the 1970s, Savio had deliberately withdrawn from public view. In 1996, he died of cardiac arrest at the age of fifty-three.[1]

Nevertheless, Savio had a monumental impact on the 1960s. He would always be revered as a prophet of rebellion. And he did manage to challenge the role of the modern university so that deans and other administrators could no longer feel comfortable in their assumptions about how their institutions should operate or what was the most effective way to serve their students. As a beacon of educational and social reform, Savio—frequently against his will—became one of the leading agents of change in modern America.

Tom Hayden was always more interested in politics than Mario Savio, yet his commitments—especially to the civil rights and anti-war movements—were just as individualistic. Hayden and Savio were not close friends, but they were members of the same generation and came from similar backgrounds. Both were lapsed Catholics with a quasi-religious though not specifically theological sensibility. And they were equally indispensable to the activism of the 1960s. Each, however, was more complex, personally and politically, than their public images intimated.

When Hayden was an undergraduate at the University of Michigan in the late 1950s and early 1960s, and editor of the student newspaper, he was profoundly influenced by James Agee's *Let Us Now Praise Famous Men*, originally published in 1941. Agee's book was as much a private meditation on the poverty of the 1930s as it was a description of the bleak lives of three sharecropper families in Alabama. Although Agee had been commissioned by Henry Luce's *Fortune* magazine to write a standard documentary on economic conditions in the South during the Great Depression, Agee and his photographer Walker Evans converted the book into a mixture of personal involvement, autobiography, and a shriek of sorrow and rage at how poor people were forced to live in America.

Let Us Now Praise Famous Men sold only 400 copies in 1941, in part because it diverged from the typical journalistic documentaries that invariably delivered "social" or ideological messages in the 1930s.[2] But in the 1960s, in the midst of the rediscovery of poverty in the United States, stimulated by the publication of Michael Harrington's *The Other America* in 1962, *Let Us Now Praise Famous Men* became something of a bible for the New Left, and for those like Hayden who wanted to be emotionally engaged in what Lyndon Johnson later called the "war on poverty."

Hayden was also deeply affected by his reading of C. Wright Mills's *The Power Elite*, published in 1956, a classic though irate polemic against America's ruling class. For Mills and his readers (including Hayden), America was governed by a self-appointed, mostly unelected, elite who made the fundamental decisions about the economy, war, and peace, decisions over which ordinary citizens had no control. In addition, Hayden—like many of the war babies in the 1960s—was inspired by the civil rights movement, especially by the Student Nonviolent Coordinating Committee (led in the early years of the decade by John Lewis) and its emphasis on decentralized endeavors, ethical responsibility, and an antipathy to the theoretical disputes of the Old Left. For these civil rights activists, the policies of the Kennedy Administration were too timid, given the militant and sadistic segregationism in much of the South.

Hayden synthesized all of these ideas when he became the principal author in 1962 of the Port Huron Statement—the essay that helped create the Students for a Democratic Society, the chief organization of the New Left in the 1960s. The statement emphasized the primacy of moral more than political or ideological commitment. It was a proclamation that merged the ideas of Agee, Mills, Harrington, Albert Camus, and SNCC. Like Mario Savio's speech at Berkeley in 1964, Hayden's Port Huron Statement was a fluent blend of personal dedication and a cry for action that characterized the radicalism of the early 1960s—not only in the political movements but also in the music of those years. As such, the Port Huron Statement became the most widely read thesis of the war baby generation.[3] For those who wanted to undermine the apparatus of racism and war, hurling one's body on the machine—metaphorically and often physically—was what Savio and Hayden advocated.

But writing a manifesto (or giving a speech) turned out to be far less thorny than trying to change the country's policies—particularly in the context of the brutality against civil rights workers in the old Confederacy and the escalating war in Vietnam. Hayden himself, as a civil rights activist rather than an author, was beaten up when he traveled to McComb, Mississippi in 1962.

Moreover, Hayden was hardly a partisan of the counterculture. He married Jane Fonda in 1973 (they were divorced in 1989) but Hayden was not the type of person to experiment with drugs or to identify with Jane's war baby brother, Peter, perched fearlessly atop a motorcycle in the middle of redneck country as Captain America in *Easy Rider*.

And while Hayden was fervently opposed to the war in Vietnam, he was (like Joan Baez) ultimately appalled by the totalitarianism of the North Vietnamese regime, the exodus of the boat people from South Vietnam, and the mass murders by the Communists in Cambodia. As a consequence, in late 1967, Hayden met with Robert Kennedy, urging him to challenge Lyndon Johnson for the Democratic Party nomination in 1968. This was not what one would normally consider a revolutionary act. But Hayden shared Bobby's existential temperament, and he believed the election of Kennedy was the only way to appeal to African Americans as well as the white working class, and to end the war. Hayden was therefore distraught by Kennedy's assassination in June of 1968; the sole hope for positive change had been obliterated.

In the meantime, Hayden, like Savio, was increasingly unhappy with the New Left as it became more militant and violent in the late 1960s. Nevertheless, Hayden participated in the convulsions outside the Democratic convention in Chicago in 1968. As one of the purported leaders of the demonstrations, Hayden was indicted and convicted (along with others branded as the "Chicago Eight") though the convictions were overturned in 1971.[4]

Where Mario Savio withdrew from politics by the end of the 1960s, Hayden remained involved but mostly as a liberal Democrat. Never an avid or doctrinaire radical, he turned eventually to more traditional electoral activities. He served in the California State Assembly for ten years, from 1982 to 1992, and then in the State Senate from 1992 to 2000.

Yet both Savio and Hayden were, at least for a time, the most persuasive proponents of an activism that was more personal than political, more psychological than abstract. They were the white leaders of a movement whose primary engine, in civil rights, was black. Whatever their skepticism about the New Left and the complicated implications of their own philosophies, they galvanized the baby boomers who may not have understood their ideas or their motivations, but were goaded by a similar passion in the 1960s to refurbish America.

The participation of white people, like Mario Savio and Tom Hayden, in civil rights organizations grew increasingly controversial as the 1960s wore on. But from the start, African American war babies were in the vanguard of the civil rights movement. None more so than John Lewis.

Lewis was a man of multiple talents. He was a preacher, an organizer, an activist who was willing to risk his own life (and sometimes did) to defy segregation, and ultimately one of the new black politicians from the South. But he was never an orator (unlike his contemporary Jesse Jackson); Lewis led by his own example rather than with speeches that aroused audiences to commit themselves to an integrated America.

By the late 1950s, as a result of his experiences growing up poor in Alabama and meeting Martin Luther King in 1957, Lewis was fully devoted to the civil rights movement. But as a young man irritated by the caution of traditional civil rights leaders, Lewis was more attracted to the tactics of direct if non-violent rebellion. Hence, he was fascinated by the potential of sit-ins at lunch counters that refused to serve blacks—and by the example of the student demonstration at Woolworth's in Greensboro, North Carolina, in 1960. The rules of the sit-ins were elementary but unalterable: the demonstrators were not to engage in any aggressive or retaliatory conduct, refrain from strident conversation, bring school-books to study, and above all be prepared to be arrested and jailed.

Lewis followed the model of Greensboro in Nashville, sitting in at W. T. Grant's in 1960. Inevitably he was arrested. Indeed, in the course of his civil rights activities, Lewis would be jailed on forty occasions, spending time in some of the most desolate prisons in the South, like the infamous Parchman Farm in Mississippi. But the Nashville sit-in was covered on television and in the *New York Times*, as well as by a young reporter named David Halberstam in the *Nashville Tennessean*. The result of these sit-ins was that lunch counters throughout the South began to serve black customers.

The sit-ins were accompanied by "freedom rides," the first one (in which Lewis participated) in 1961. The purpose of the freedom rides was to protest segregation in interstate transportation. Lewis was arrested in Birmingham by the corpulent Bull Connor, who looked and sounded as if he had been sent over by central casting in Hollywood to play the role of a redneck sheriff, a much more malign version of the Mississippi police chief impersonated by Rod Steiger in *In the Heat of the Night* in 1967. The freedom riders were also attacked by whites in Montgomery, and Lewis was knocked unconscious by a blow to his head. This initial freedom ride was followed by many others, all of them challenging the mores and police power in the South. In effect, the young civil rights workers, black and white, were literally hurling their own bodies on the machine of segregation, as Mario Savio would recommend to students at Berkeley in 1964.

Meanwhile, as the leaders of the civil rights movement began to focus on voter registration rather than acts of symbolic dissent, Lewis helped launch the Student Nonviolent Coordinating Committee, and became its chair in 1963. The Kennedy Administration was at last responding to the turmoil in the South, sending federal marshals to protect black students seeking to integrate previously all-white universities, and proposing civil rights legislation (which was eventually passed after Kennedy's assassination by Lyndon Johnson in 1964 and 1965).

As chair of SNCC, Lewis spoke at the March on Washington in August 1963—a march attended by a quarter of a million people including celebrities like Jackie Robinson, Marlon Brando, Paul Newman, Sidney Poitier, Lena Horne, Harry Belafonte, Joan Baez, Bob Dylan, and Peter, Paul, and Mary. Lewis's speech was less ferocious than he would have wished, toned down out of deference to the older organizers of the march. What Lewis could not have known, though, was that the march represented the zenith of the civil rights movement in the early 1960s.

The bombing of a black church in Birmingham in September 1963, killing four little girls, and the refusal of Lyndon Johnson to seat all of the Mississippi Freedom delegation at the Democratic convention in 1964, intensified the antagonism within the movement (and especially in SNCC) toward whites. Furthermore, the strategy of non-violence was giving way to calls for self-defense.

Self-defense was hardly an abstract issue for Lewis. In 1965, joining a civil rights march from Selma to Montgomery, Lewis and other
activists were assaulted with clubs and night sticks by Alabama State
Troopers on the Edmund Pettus Bridge in Selma. Lewis was severely
injured, his skull fractured.

After Selma, the movement could no longer hold together. The
distrust of whites was too acute, accentuated by the riots in the late
1960s in northern cities like New York, Philadelphia, Newark, Cleve-
land, and the Watts district of Los Angeles. Lewis himself—always a
zealous integrationist—was ejected as chair of SNCC, replaced by the
black power advocate Stokely Carmichael (another, but more incendi-
ary, war baby, born in 1941). Lewis was only twenty-six years old when
he was forced out of SNCC, and he found himself having to restart his
life in some other capacity.

Like Mario Savio and Tom Hayden, Lewis was never truly a radical. So Lewis, as did Hayden, gradually turned to electoral politics, while
always maintaining a moral dimension to his personality and policies.
In 1968, Lewis worked for Bobby Kennedy's nomination—and he was
traumatized by the murders within weeks of one another of both Martin
Luther King and Kennedy. Yet Lewis remained in politics and by 1986
he was elected to Congress from Atlanta.

Lewis had become a symbol of what the early civil rights movement
promised. At one point in his career, *Time* magazine called him a "living saint."[5] But Lewis was embarrassed by that label. He did not regard
himself as a savior or a hero. Yet he had helped—with his mind, his
body, and his bravery—to make America what he described as a "different country" from the one in which he was a child and teenager. In that
sense, his personal valor did help alter the United States.

In a different and more dramatic form, Jesse Jackson played a comparable role in transforming America. Jackson was a more controversial
figure than Lewis—not only for white people but also for the other leaders of the civil rights movement. In addition, Jackson (unlike Lewis)

came late to civil rights activism; initially, based in Chicago, he was not a part of the sit-ins, freedom rides, and voter registration drives that characterized the movement in the South.

Indeed, Jackson was always more focused on the economic and social problems of African Americans in the North—a far more intricate dilemma than toppling the Jim Crow laws and customs in the South. As an example, I joined the Congress of Racial Equality (CORE) in 1963 during the midst of its campaign to end segregation in the public schools of Kansas City, Missouri. CORE and other groups finally managed to overturn the system of blacks and whites going to separate grade schools and high schools. But this triumph was soon blunted as whites fled the city for the suburbs and their all-white schools in Kansas, leaving the Kansas City school system as segregated as (and worse off than) it had been when I graduated from high school in 1959.

In one way, however, Jackson resembled Lewis and other civil rights leaders. Both Lewis and Jackson, like Martin Luther King and his advisers, were committed to civil rights not just as a political but as a religious mission. And Jackson himself turned into a consummate preacher as well as a skilled politician. But for Jackson in particular, one could never distinguish his considerable gifts as a minister and organizer from his charismatic personality.

Jackson attended the March on Washington in 1963, but at that point he was simply a member of the crowd. This invisibility (and it's now hard to think of Jackson as ever having been Ralph Ellison's invisible man, bowing to the dictates of others) ended when Jackson met Martin Luther King, first in Atlanta and then at the march in Selma. For Jackson, King was a role model and surrogate father, especially for a young man like Jackson who never knew much about his real father. Jackson frantically wanted King's respect. In return, Jackson always deferred to King's policies, even when he disagreed with King's emphasis on segregation in the South while Jackson was more concerned with the difficulties of being black in places like Chicago. Yet more important, Jackson wanted to make himself essential as King's aide—which he became at the age of twenty-four, the youngest member of King's legion. In this way, Jackson gained admission to the inner core of the civil rights movement in the 1960s.

On his own, Jackson founded Operation Breadbasket and PUSH in Chicago and elsewhere in the North, all of these aimed at gaining more jobs for African Americans. Jackson's willingness to undertake his private crusades made him the object of suspicion, and perhaps also of jealousy, among King's assistants. For them, Jackson displayed too much swagger and too much ego to work well in anyone else's organization.

These suspicions were strengthened in the immediate aftermath of Martin Luther King's murder in Memphis in 1968. Jackson claimed he had held King's head in his hands, and listened to his last words—a prayerful act that King's other aides denied. Nonetheless, Jackson appeared on the *Today* show with what he described as King's blood on his shirt and pants, and asserted that he was the last person to talk to King. Consequently, and almost overnight, Jackson became a media superstar on television and in the *New York Times*, *Life* magazine, and *Playboy*. Jackson's behavior antagonized King's longtime lieutenants who believed Jackson was merely engaged in self-promotion and an effort to seize King's leadership for his own purposes.

Although King's aides were motivated by envy, they were correct about the path that Jackson would pursue. He became the leader of the movement, North and South, for racial and economic equality. The command of the movement did pass from King to Jackson. And Jackson became, as King had once been, the most magnetic orator for civil rights—in the end, not just for blacks but for all the groups excluded from America's affluence, the constituency Jackson started to call the "rainbow coalition."

One ambition Martin Luther King had never had was to be a politician, on either a local or national stage. Jackson's sense of theater drove him into politics; he was like an actor—a Faye Dunaway or Al Pacino—who recognized the potential of a captivating role for himself. In 1972, at the Democratic convention, he successfully challenged the seating of the Illinois delegation, traditionally controlled by Chicago's longtime mayor, Richard Daley. Yet this rebellion was just a prelude to Jackson's glory in the 1980s.

In 1984, Jackson ran for President in the Democratic Party primaries, gathering over three million votes and winning 400 delegates. In the 1988 primaries Jackson exceeded that total, winning seven million votes and twelve hundred delegates. When he defeated Michael Dukakis in the Michigan primary, newspapers and magazines speculated that for the first time in America's history a black man might actually be nominated for President. The conjecture was not inconceivable; Jackson was the first African American to be a plausible candidate for the country's highest office.

Though Jackson did not—could not at that point—win the nomination, he continued to play a public role, increasingly in the world arena, negotiating for the release of American hostages in Syria and Cuba. In 1997, President Clinton appointed Jackson a special envoy to Africa and awarded him the Presidential Medal of Freedom in 2000.[6]

Whatever his psychological flaws and his hunger for the spotlight, Jackson had made it possible for Americans to take seriously the possibility of a black man occupying the nation's highest office. So there was a direct connection between Jackson's Presidential campaigns in the 1980s and the elections of Barack Obama—also from Chicago—in 2008 and 2012.

Jackson understood, probably better than anyone, how his efforts and personality had changed America. When the television networks and cable news channels proclaimed Obama's victory in 2008, and Obama emerged to speak to thousands of people in Grant Park, Jackson was in one of the front rows, tears coursing down his face. For John Lewis and for Jesse Jackson, it had been a long and perilous voyage from Selma to the White House. But they were as responsible as anyone, personally and politically, for reaching what Martin Luther King had called in his last speech the "promised land."

Jackson was not the only African American war baby with a flair for drama, and for the assertion of self-liberation. Cassius Clay (as he was still known in the early 1960s) became as much a totem of black liberation in America as were Martin Luther King, John Lewis, and Jesse Jackson. And no one seemed to be aware of this more than Clay. He knew he could be not merely a highly skilled athlete but a leader, if not of the civil rights movement at least of the quest for African American freedom and an idiosyncratic identity. Clay was, in this respect, no more an invisible man than Jackson.

After Clay won a gold medal as an amateur boxer at the 1960 Olympics, he embarked on a professional career. As a black boxer, he had few exemplars to follow. Most African American fighters were expected to be respectful of white sensibilities, as Joe Louis had been throughout his life. Clay himself, as a swift, agile boxer, resembled Sugar Ray Robinson whose talents he greatly admired (Robinson had fought six grueling bouts in the 1940s and early 1950s with Jake LaMotta, gory fights that were chronicled in Martin Scorsese's *Raging Bull*). At the same time, Clay remained (as he had been during his amateur career) an actor, much like Jesse Jackson, who knew how to generate publicity and—in Clay's case—profits at the box office for his fights.

In 1964, at the age of twenty-two and when he was everyone's undisputed underdog, Clay astounded the boxing and American world by beating Sonny Liston for the heavyweight championship (Liston quit at the end of six rounds). Despite his achievement, Clay received only two congratulatory telegrams from black leaders: one from Martin Luther King; the other from Malcolm X. Secretly, Clay had been entranced since the late 1950s with the Nation of Islam and its proclamation of African American strength and rectitude. Meanwhile, in 1962, Clay had met Malcolm who became Clay's father figure and tutor, much as Martin Luther King had been for Jesse Jackson (although Clay would repudiate Malcolm after Malcolm's ejection from the Muslims in 1964).

Whatever the squabbling among the Muslims, immediately after his defeat of Sonny Liston, Clay announced that he was a member of the Nation of Islam, and that he should now be called Muhammad Ali.

The act epitomized Ali's refusal to bow to the expectations or stereo-types of white America. Indeed, Ali declared—in what could have been the credo of most war babies—"I don't have to be what you want me to be. I'm free to be what I want."

The white reaction to Ali's proclamation was swift and livid. Appearances on television shows and potential endorsements were canceled, while newspaper columnists denounced Ali as somehow an alien threat to America.

Much worse was to come. In 1966, Ali was classified 1-A by his selective service board, and was therefore eligible to be drafted at a time when the Vietnam War had grown increasingly divisive in the United States. Ali's response was to declare: "Man, I ain't got no quarrel with them Vietcong." In 1967, at the induction office, Ali refused three times to cross a yellow line on the floor, signifying his refusal to be drafted into a war he opposed. Almost instantly, he was indicted by a grand jury for evading the draft, found guilty (though the conviction was reversed by the Supreme Court), stripped of his heavyweight title, and banned from the ring for over three years.

Ali's instinctive disobedience made him a hero of the anti-war movement, both in America and overseas. Indeed, he had become the most momentous black athlete in America since Jackie Robinson integrated major league baseball twenty years earlier. In fact, no athlete—black or white—was more personally involved in the crises of his era than Ali. During his ban from boxing, Ali was defended by such luminaries as Michael Harrington, Sidney Lumet, George Plimpton, Truman Capote, James Earl Jones, and especially the sportscaster Howard Cosell. Ali also spoke before adoring audiences at universities throughout the United States and in other countries, particularly in Africa, at every juncture denouncing the Vietnam War.

But as Ernest Hemingway's Jakes Barnes ruefully remarks in *The Sun Also Rises*: "The bill always came. That was one of the swell things you could count on."

For Ali, the bill was expensive. During the years of his banishment from boxing, he would have been in his prime. When he returned to the ring in the 1970s, even though he regained the heavyweight championship three times, he was slower, less balletic, and less able to elude punches (especially in his three blood-spattered fights with Joe Frazier). By the time Ali retired at the start of the 1980s, he had fought too long and been hit too often. Toward the end of his career, he was already showing signs of brain damage—his speech slurred, his walk slowed, his physical reactions uncertain. His doctors at last diagnosed Ali's illness as "Parkinson's syndrome." This was a singular disaster for Ali since he had always depended on his mobility, his eye-catching facial expressions, and his aura of playfulness. Now his face was a mask; often, he seemed half asleep.

Yet Ali could rouse himself when necessary. On one occasion, being interviewed by Ed Bradley on *60 Minutes*, Ali looked as if he had dozed off. Then, suddenly, he threw a fake punch at the obviously startled Bradley, and a faint smile appeared on Ali's face at the joke. In sum, Ali had not lost his feel for showmanship—never more evident than when he appeared at the 1996 Olympics, struggling up the stairs with a torch in his hand, to light the Olympic flame.[7] The crowd cheered—not only for Ali's brief moment of physical triumph, but for his long career as a man who refused to be typecast, who followed his own impulses, and whose personality transcended his politics and his athleticism. In his own fashion, he represented the values the war babies cherished.

Civil rights was a generic term, applying mostly to freedom for African Americans. But civil rights also pertained to women and gay Americans. And the leaders of those last two movements were often war babies as well.

The women's movement of the 1960s and 1970s certainly had its older heroines, like Betty Friedan (author in 1963 of the best-selling and enormously influential *The Feminine Mystique*), and Gloria Steinem who co-founded *Ms.* magazine in 1969. Yet the woman war baby who had as much of an impact on the crusade for sexual equality was Billie Jean King—in many ways the Muhammad Ali of tennis.

King grew up in the suburbs of California but she was never a stereotypical blonde, sun-dappled California girl, ready for her close-up in the movies. King had short dark hair and hefty glasses; she looked as though she could have been at home in Greenwich Village. On the other hand, sports was a family tradition; her older brother, Randy Moffitt, was a major league pitcher.

King herself began playing tennis in the fifth grade, at the age of eleven. Traditionally, tennis was considered an elite country-club game. King, however, was an interloper in the sport, learning how to play on public courts and disdaining the mostly male rituals of the professional tennis circuit.

By 1963, after having withdrawn from college, King managed to ascend to the finals at Wimbledon—the most stately venue in the chronicles of tennis. She won her first Wimbledon singles championship in 1966. The following year, she defeated all her opponents in singles, doubles, and mixed doubles. As a result, she was ranked number one in women's tennis. In effect, her rise was as swift and as extraordinary as Muhammad Ali's initial conquests in boxing.

Nonetheless, the women's game was regarded as inferior to men's tennis, and this was accentuated by the fact that women received far less prize money than men. In 1968, for instance, Rod Laver's victory at Wimbledon earned him $4800, while King—the women's champion—received a paltry $1800. Indeed, it was not until 1973 that the United States Open tournament awarded equal prize money to men and women. It was the only major tournament at the time to grant financial equality to both genders.

Given these lopsided conditions between men and women, King was not only a superlative tennis player; she was also an intrinsic rebel. And she was as perceptive as Ali to the larger symbolism of athletic contests. The opportunity to demonstrate the equality, if not the superiority, of women's tennis confronted King in 1973.

In May of that year, a fifty-five year old ex-tennis professional and current con artist, Bobby Riggs, had challenged the Australian Margaret

Court to a match on the grounds that no woman could compete with a male tennis player, even one years past his prime. Riggs defeated Court badly, apparently upholding the inherent superiority of the men's game.

So in September, King responded to Riggs's assertions by agreeing to play him in a nationally televised contest on ABC, a match which was half a sporting event and half a circus. I remember Howard Cosell, who was broadcasting the game, telling viewers that this was a once-in-a-lifetime spectacle, and that they could therefore ignore the first showing of a major movie on another television network. The movie happened to be *Bonnie and Clyde*. But forty-eight million people (including me) took Cosell's advice and watched King demolish Riggs.

The match confirmed King's stature as America's female sports superstar. Along with the passage of Title IX in 1972, which mandated equal participation for men and women in high school and college athletics, the King-Riggs match helped to overturn the assumption of female inferiority in sports and in other facets of American life.

Thereafter, King became emblematic of the liberation of women and their changing status in American society. In this role, she was the leader of a revolution in sports and an icon of modern feminism.

By the end of her career, King had won six Wimbledon and thirty-nine other grand slam titles, in both singles and doubles matches. In the course of her career, she had turned women's tennis players into celebrities, able to win substantial amounts of money (as Venus Williams acknowledged when, after winning a championship, she called King the "mother" of all women tennis players, a woman who had made their successes and parity with men possible).

After King's retirement, the honors and recognition continued to accumulate. In 1990, *Life* magazine named King one of the 100 most influential people, male or female, in the twentieth century. In 2006, the United States Tennis Association named its leading setting in Flushing Meadows the Billie Jean King National Tennis Center. In 2009, President Obama presented King with the Medal of Freedom.

Yet "freedom" meant something more for King than just her accomplishments in tennis. For decades, she had denied or kept secret her bisexuality. Finally, in the late 1990s, she conceded that she was gay.[8] King had not been a leader of the gay rights movement, but her willingness—however belated—to acknowledge her sexual proclivities assisted in the campaign for equity at all levels of American society. In this manner, she was emulating Muhammad Ali's pronouncement that she didn't have to be what her fans or sportswriters wanted her to be; she was free to be what she herself desired.

Besides King, no war baby in public life knew better the risks of announcing one was gay than Barney Frank. Barney—no one ever called him Mr. or Congressmen Frank—had known he was gay since childhood, but he had kept the knowledge secret for decades. He had gone out with women throughout high school and college at Harvard, and for a time when he was a graduate student in government at Harvard he had dated Doris Kearns (later Goodwin), another war baby, born in Brooklyn in 1943, who won a Pulitzer Prize in 1995 for her book *No Ordinary Time: Franklin and Eleanor Roosevelt*. Indeed Barney went to graduate school in the first place not because he was a natural scholar but because he thought it would be easier to be gay in the academic world.

As a graduate student, Barney was a tutor in government in Winthrop House. I was also a Winthrop House tutor, in history, and it was here that I met Barney in 1966. By this time, Barney had discovered that he adored practical politics; he loved holding court in the Winthrop House dining room, encircled by undergraduates who were spellbound by his political anecdotes and analyses.

Barney has changed very little over the past fifty years. In the 1960s, he had more and darker (rather than grey) hair. Otherwise, he was a cigar-chomping, fast-talking, pol who looked and sounded as if he could have been imitating Groucho Marx's Rufus Firefly in *Duck Soup*. Except that Barney was from Bayonne, not Freedonia, though he had some of Groucho's scorn for the niceties of American political sacraments. In fact, his New Jersey accent was so thick and often indecipherable that when he traveled to Mississippi in 1964 to help register African American voters, most black Mississippians had no clue what he was saying (some Mississippi natives thought his name was Benjamin Franklin), and eventually he was relegated to office work.

Like most students—graduate as well as undergraduate—at Harvard in the late 1960s, Barney turned against the Vietnam War. In fact, when I started teaching full-time at Harvard in 1968, it was impossible to have a discussion with students in my classes about the war since everyone was opposed; there was nothing left to say.

Yet Barney was not a radical. He believed in working within the Democratic Party. And he was willing to be civil towards, if critical of, members of Lyndon Johnson's administration. When Secretary of Defense Robert McNamara visited Harvard in 1966, the Harvard administration asked Barney to escort him around campus and make sure McNamara wasn't assailed by protestors (a task which Barney accomplished by enlisting some football players at Winthrop House as McNamara's guardians). Barney's role in this episode did not endear him to the New Left at Harvard.[9] But he never viewed himself as a demonstrator or occupier of buildings.

The truth was that Barney could hardly be mistaken for a student revolutionary; he was not even really an academic. He never completed his Ph.D. dissertation. Instead he left Harvard in 1968, and started working for Boston politicians—especially Kevin White who became the mayor of the city. By 1980, Barney himself won a seat in Congress, representing the liberal Boston suburbs of Brookline and Newton. He held the seat, defeating all challengers, until his retirement from Congress in 2012.

As a professional politician, Barney was—like so many war babies—an instinctive nonconformist. He was utterly different from the suave, polished, blow-dried politicians who started to win seats in the Senate or House of Representatives in the 1980s. Barney's take-no-prisoners personality, his rumpled clothes, and his high-octane verbal style, as much as his ideas, made him a leading spokesperson for liberal values. No one wanted to debate him, either on the floor of the House or on television, because he could make his adversaries sound brainless.

But Barney still had one vulnerability. In the midst of a scandal in his house involving a male prostitute running an escort service, Barney finally acknowledged in 1987 that he was gay. There is a story, perhaps apocryphal, that when Barney told "Tip" O'Neill, the Speaker of the House, that he was gay, O'Neill replied: "I'm sorry to hear that. I'd hoped you'd be the first Jewish Speaker." Whether or not the tale is true, Barney was always too acerbic, too witty, and too ill-tempered to be the leader of his fellow Democrats. He did, however, along with Senator Chris Dodd of Connecticut, author the Dodd-Frank law to better regulate Wall Street after the stock market crash of 2008. And Barney was always in favor of civil rights for blacks, women, and gays, and he was pro-choice and concerned with environmental issues. So in many ways, he was among the most effective and lucid Congressional leaders of the late twentieth and early twenty-first centuries.

Though they were both liberal Democrats and war babies, and they represented Massachusetts, it's hard to visualize two more dissimilar political types than Barney Frank and John Kerry. Where Barney was disheveled and blunt, with a biting sense of humor, Kerry always seemed to be impeccably dressed with no strand of hair out of place and a solemnity of speech that gave one the impression that anything he was talking about was supremely important. Essentially, he was always careful about what he said and how he said it.

Yet Kerry, like Barney Frank and many other war babies, turned out to be a rebel. Especially when it counted, in a public, potent, and moving denunciation of the war in Vietnam.

His full name was John Forbes Kerry. The initials JFK were significant to him because they, along with his patrician voice, reminded everyone in the early 1960s of John F. Kennedy. The young Kerry could have been a prototype for what C. Wright Mills had in mind when he was describing the making of the "power elite." Kerry's father was a diplomat, stationed mostly in Europe, and particularly in Berlin, the city that was the symbol of the Cold War. The Kerry family constantly discussed politics and foreign policy around the dining room table. Kerry himself was continuously relocating, and spent most of his adolescence at boarding schools in Germany, Norway, and Switzerland, as well as a preppie for five years at St. Paul's in New Hampshire.

By 1962, when Kerry entered Yale, he was an ardent acolyte of the Kennedy clan. He believed in President Kennedy's pronouncement about bearing any burden and paying any price to defend liberty around the world. Kerry also thought that Kennedy's advisers—men like McGeorge Bundy and Robert McNamara—were indeed (in David Halberstam's indelible phrase) the "best and the brightest" in America, managers filled with the requisite expertise to rule the planet. In 1962 as well, Kerry handed out leaflets for Teddy Kennedy's first successful campaign for the Senate. So the President's assassination in November 1963 was a harrowing event—as it was for most Americans—in Kerry's early life.

Still, Kerry flourished at Yale. His classmates viewed him as someone who, inevitably, had political and maybe even Presidential aspirations. These ambitions were highlighted by his extensive knowledge of American foreign policy, his participation on the Yale debate team, and his election as president of the Yale Political Union. In 1966, Kerry gave the senior class oration which was mildly critical of Lyndon Johnson's escalation of the Vietnam conflict, but not a speech that would have labeled him a robust opponent of the war. Thus, it was predictable that Kerry would be "tapped" for Skull and Bones, the secret society at Yale that selected and legitimized America's future political and economic leaders (George W. Bush was a member at around the same time as Kerry).

In sum, Kerry was entering the American establishment, or what a Tom Hayden would have called America's ruling class. Kerry was no leftist or denizen of the counterculture. Nor did he feel comfortable in the folk and rock music environment of America in the 1960s. He favored Broadway musicals and, like President Kennedy, James Bond movies.[10] It's doubtful that he ever bought a Bob Dylan album, much less a Janis Joplin one. And even more unlikely that he could have identified with Alec Leamas, John le Carré's embittered, alcoholic, and cynical Cold War operative in *The Spy Who Came in from the Cold*.

After Kerry graduated from Yale in 1966, and despite his reservations about Vietnam, he was ready to serve America, to follow John F. Kennedy's dictum that you should "ask not what your country can do for you—ask what you can do for your country." Kerry enlisted in the Navy; by 1968, he had become a lieutenant, commanding "swift boats" that patrolled the treacherous rivers and jungles in South Vietnam.

It was in Vietnam that Kerry's world changed—in fact, capsized. Until early 1968, Kerry's life had been relatively comfortable and predictable, as it was for most Americans not involved in any cultural or political disruptions. Then came the North Vietnamese Tet offensive which showed that America's troops had no real control even over South Vietnam's cities, including Saigon where the American embassy was itself attacked. This shock was followed by others: the murders of Martin Luther King and Robert Kennedy, and the anti-war riots on the streets of Chicago at the Democratic convention.

For Kerry, the experience in Vietnam propelled him from the serenity of and his upward mobility in American life to the disarray and brutal anarchy of Vietnam. Here, Kerry encountered free-fire zones where American troops were permitted to machine-gun anyone or anything that moved; search-and-destroy operations; carpet bombings of North Vietnamese cities and the South Vietnamese countryside; the burning of South Vietnamese villages and the torture of North Vietnamese prisoners; and the incessant danger of ambushes, mines, trip-wires attached to bombs, and sniper attacks. It was as if Kerry and his fellow soldiers had been hurled from the solidity of their lives in the United States into the bedlam of another planet—just like the characters in *The Deer Hunter* (the Vietnam movie with which Kerry himself most identified was Oliver Stone's *Platoon* in 1986).

As Kerry's year in Vietnam wore on, he was increasingly distressed by the rising American casualties, the habitual reliance on napalm, and the notion that American soldiers were "liberating" South Vietnam from the Communists. In Kerry's eyes, the unrelenting mendacity from the Johnson and Nixon administrations about the success of America's efforts, and the sanguine pronouncements of U.S. officials in Saigon, were inane. There was no "light" Kerry could discern at the end of any tunnel. The South Vietnamese, Kerry believed, viewed Americans not as liberators but as conquerors who were ignorant about the land, the culture, and the people they had allegedly come to "save."

Kerry returned to the United States in 1969. In addition to his dismay about the war, he was now shocked by how badly America's war veterans were being treated at home. Both perceptions turned Kerry into an anti-war activist, and a leader of the Vietnam veterans opposed to the war. Though Kerry remained uncomfortable with the New Left (like Barney Frank, Kerry still wanted to work for change within the Democratic Party), he could not keep silent about how much the war had sickened and transformed him.

On April 22, 1971, at the age of twenty-seven, Kerry appeared before the Senate Foreign Relations committee to express the agony of his generation that had either directly experienced or dissented from the war in Vietnam. What was remarkable, and original, about Kerry's condemnation of the war is that he spoke from the perspective of the veterans themselves. Until his testimony, most Americans had ignored the Vietnam veterans, when they did not revile them as war criminals. Now, Kerry was describing not just the harm imposed upon the Vietnamese people, but the damage—physical and psychological—the war was inflicting on American soldiers themselves. This was the first occasion when someone was paying attention to how destructive the war was for the Americans who fought in it, as it was for all of the Vietnamese.

Kerry concluded his testimony with a question that made him famous. "How," he inquired, "do you ask a man to be the last man to die for a mistake?"

The question was unanswerable. As it would be in future American wars, like those in Iraq and Afghanistan.

The question, however, converted Kerry from a dissident to a celebrity. He was quoted on all of the nightly news broadcasts; his photograph was displayed and his testimony was summarized in *Time*, *Newsweek*, and the *New York Times*; he was interviewed on *Meet the Press* and *60 Minutes*; and he debated one of the Nixon administration's handpicked defenders of the war on the *Dick Cavett Show*. What made Kerry so effective was that he reminded no one of a long-haired hippie or a strident radical.[11] He was the archetype of a courageous war veteran who had won three purple hearts, a bronze star, and a silver star. And he remained unflappable and eloquent, with his anger always under control, throughout his media tour. Here was a young man, born during World War II, a survivor of a much more dubious conflict, who knew what he was talking about.

Inevitably—though not in the way Kerry or his colleagues anticipated when he was at Yale—Kerry became a politician. He was elected for the first time to the Senate from Massachusetts in 1984. No doubt, Kerry's condemnation of the Vietnam War a decade earlier was a catalyst for his entrance into politics.

Yet somewhere along the way, Kerry seemed to have forgotten what made him a champion in the first place to millions of Americans. When he won the Democratic nomination for President in 2004, Kerry ran a perplexing and almost incompetent campaign. Worse, he presented himself solely as a war hero rather than as the compelling critic of the war, the role that had originally propelled him to prominence and power. And so he lost the Presidency, though not badly, to George W. Bush—the proponent of yet another war that all-too-often resembled the struggle in Vietnam.

Finally, at the start of 2013, President Obama appointed Kerry to replace Hillary Clinton as Secretary of State. This was a job Kerry seemed born for. But though being Secretary of State was the capstone of Kerry's career, he had not pursued the path one might have expected for a man who evolved from a member of the "power elite" to a survivor of the madness portrayed in *Apocalypse Now*.

As Martin Sheen's Captain Willard muses in Francis Ford Coppola's film: "Everyone gets everything he wants. I wanted a mission, and for my sins, they gave me one. Brought it up to me like room service. It was a real choice mission, and when it was over, I never wanted another." It's difficult to contemplate Kerry exhibiting the same sense of embittered irony, however much he despised the Vietnam and other American wars.

Whatever their reservations or self-doubts, the war babies—men and women, whites and blacks—who were leaders of the student revolts of the 1960s, the civil rights and feminist movements, and the resistance to the Vietnam War had indeed made the United States a "different country" (as John Lewis observed) from the kind of nation America was when the 1960s began. They had navigated as best they could the crises their parents, the members of the "greatest generation," never experienced—and that the baby boomers would not have known how to confront without the guidance of the war babies.

Yet there was one more crisis over which the war babies presided. This one shook America to its very foundations because it involved not the upheavals in the streets or a lunatic conflict in a foreign land, but criminality in the White House itself.

"They're Hungry.
Remember When You Were Hungry?"

On the pre-dawn of June 17, 1972, five men with an array of bugging equipment broke into the headquarters of the Democratic National Committee at the Watergate hotel and office complex. They were discovered by a security guard, arrested by the Washington, D.C. police, and charged with burglary and the attempt to intercept telephone conversations and other communications at the Democrats' offices, especially the messages of the Committee's chair and longtime Democratic operative, Larry O'Brien. It became quickly apparent that the burglars had financial links to the Republican Committee to Re-Elect the President (an organization with the unfortunate but fitting acronym of CREEP), and that at least two of the men—including one who had supervised the plot—had formerly worked for the CIA.

Two young reporters, both working at the *Washington Post*'s Metro desk, were assigned to what seemed like a local, if peculiar, incident. They were born a year apart, during World War II. Their names were Bob Woodward and Carl Bernstein. What neither Woodward or Bernstein could have guessed at the time was that they were about to pursue a story that would transfigure American journalism, destroy the Presidency of Richard Nixon, and undermine America's faith in the power and integrity of its leaders. In short, they were going to unearth the most astonishing political story of the twentieth century, and change the country in ways no one could foresee.

As a child and teenager, Bob Woodward—though the offspring of a respectable Republican family—developed a ravenous curiosity. He loved to discover secrets about people he knew, particularly people in positions of authority. In 1961, Woodward enrolled at Yale (around the same time as did John Kerry) on a Naval ROTC scholarship. And so, again like Kerry, Woodward entered the Navy, serving as a junior officer for a five-year tour after his graduation from Yale in 1965.

Yet where Kerry always harbored political ambitions, Woodward had no idea what he wanted to do with his life. Then, in 1969, Woodward met a man who would have an immense impact on Woodward's later journalistic career. He encountered him in of all places (given future events) the White House. Woodward—detailed to the Pentagon— was delivering documents to the White House where he happened upon Mark Felt, a high-level official at the FBI, awaiting a meeting. They began to talk about Woodward's future, once he left the Navy. Quite by accident, Felt became over the next few years Woodward's mentor— even a father-figure for a young man with no plan for how to fulfill his vast ambition.

In the end, Felt turned into something far more than just an adviser to Woodward. He became Woodward's clandestine source for the mysteries of Watergate, and he was called by the *Post*'s editors (after the notorious porn film of the early 1970s) "Deep Throat."

Once Woodward left the Navy in 1970, and partly at Felt's sugges-
tion, he began to contemplate a career in journalism—even though at
the time he didn't know how to write a story. Nevertheless, he applied
for a job at the *Washington Post*, which turned him down but sent him
to the *Montgomery Sentinel*, a small Maryland weekly where Woodward
could start to learn his trade. Woodward developed into a tireless reporter and an indefatigable interviewer—qualities that would be invalu-
able when, after being hired by the *Post* in 1971, he plunged into the
morass of Watergate.[12]

Carl Bernstein's background and personality could not have been
more different from Woodward's. A year younger than Woodward,
Bernstein was saturated in the leftist politics of his parents. In certain
ways, he was a dropout from society before the rebellious counterculture
of Woodstock and *Easy Rider* became popular in the late 1960s.

Bernstein graduated from high school in 1961, went briefly to the
University of Maryland, but soon left. Yet, like Woodward, Bernstein
had an intense inquisitiveness. Additionally, having grown up in Washington, Bernstein was street-wise, and he developed contacts with the
police and bureaucrats in the Justice Department. More important, he
knew (unlike Woodward at the beginning) how to write a newspaper
story, how to focus on the most significant facts and to convey the flavor
of an episode he was describing.

As a result, the *Post* hired Bernstein in 1966 when he was only twenty-two—though the editors nearly fired him on several occasions because
of his long unruly hair, his slapdash clothing, his nonstop smoking, and
his general aura of an office hippie. Thus, Woodward and Bernstein were
an incongruous pair: the careful, well-groomed Woodward who wanted
to get ahead, and the unkempt Bernstein who had a facility for alienating
his superiors. Still, they had one feature in common (as Robert Redford
discovered when he was trying to figure out how to "play" Woodward in
the movie version of *All the President's Men*): Woodward had, like Bernstein, a "killer instinct" as a reporter.[13] And it was their lethal impulse
that ultimately helped bring down Richard Nixon.

Even before Watergate, journalism in America was changing. In the 1960s, largely as a result of the growing skepticism about the Vietnam War, what became known as the "new" journalism was emerging—created by writers (many of them novelists) like Truman Capote in *In Cold Blood* (1966), Norman Mailer in *The Armies of the Night* (1968), Joan Didion in *Slouching Towards Bethlehem* (also 1968), and in numerous essays by Tom Wolfe. Theirs was a reportorial style that was autobiographical, adversarial, and often deliberately inflammatory. But their works were not so much investigative as personal and either satirical or morose; they were meditations on the political and moral deterioration of postwar America.

Meanwhile, most readers still depended on newspapers, mass circulation magazines like *Time* and *Newsweek*, and the network newscasts for "objective" information about what was happening in the United States and the world. And by the early 1970s, Ben Bradlee, the executive editor of the *Washington Post*, and Katharine Graham, the *Post*'s owner and publisher, yearned to convert the *Post* into a national newspaper, comparable to and an indisputable rival of the *New York Times*.

The opportunity to achieve this ambition arrived with the Watergate scandal. The *Post*, as Washington's hometown newspaper, owned the story. Indeed, the Post was almost alone, originally, in its coverage of Watergate. After Richard Nixon's landslide re-election in November 1972, it appeared that the tale of the break-in would vanish. In the movie, Jason Robards playing Bradlee says to Bob Woodward (Robert Redford) and Carl Bernstein (Dustin Hoffman), "You know the results of the latest Gallup poll? Half the country never even heard of the word Watergate. Nobody gives a shit."

But Woodward, Bernstein, and Bradlee did give a shit. For the two youthful reporters, it was imperative to keep the story alive—not just for their own careers but because they believed that Watergate was more than just a baffling mystery; it was the most visible symbol concealing the possibility of massive corruption emanating from the White House.

The *Post*'s other editors were not as persuaded that the story made any sense. Their doubts were summarized in the movie when the veteran editor Howard Simons (played by Martin Balsam) wants to turn the investigation over to his "top" political reporters. But he is dissuaded when another senior editor, Harry Rosenfeld (Jack Warden), defends Woodward and Bernstein. He tells Simons "they're hungry. Remember when you were hungry?" Equally vital, Bradlee and Katharine Graham were willing to "stick with the boys."

One reason for the determination of Woodward and Bernstein was that, following the money, they had traced the cash found on the Watergate burglars to CREEP and the Nixon campaign. But their other, more important, motivation was what Woodward was learning from Deep Throat.

Woodward and Mark Felt met sporadically in an underground garage in Rosslyn, Virginia. The setting was chilling, as the movie makes clear in its shots of a dark, deserted locale with Deep Throat's haunted face (he was played by Hal Holbrook) mostly hidden in shadows except when he lights a cigarette. By this time, Felt had risen to become the FBI's Associate Director. After J. Edgar Hoover's death in May 1972, Felt believed he deserved to be appointed director of the Bureau. So he was incensed when Nixon chose L. Patrick Gray to replace Hoover, and he was even angrier at the way the Nixon Administration was trying to use the FBI to stifle the investigation of Watergate. Consequently, Felt became Woodward's covert informant, in exchange for Woodward's promise that Felt's identity would never be exposed, at least not until Felt gave his permission or after his death.

Felt—with full knowledge of Nixon's machinations—kept Woodward asking the right questions and interviewing the right people. Eventually, Felt revealed that Watergate was only the most public of Nixon's felonies, that Nixon and his men had engineered an entire cycle of spying, break-ins, and illegal wire-tapping, in effect subverting the Constitution they were sworn to defend.

Bernstein was always more intuitive about Watergate and its related offenses than Woodward, who remained cautious and restrained.

But at one point Bernstein gasped to Woodward: "Oh my God. This president is going to be impeached." Woodward agreed. As we know, they were both right.

By 1973, with the rest of America's newspapers and television networks now covering the scandal and the Senate Watergate Committee hearings, Nixon's men (H. R. Haldeman, John Ehrlichman, John Mitchell) were resigning or being fired (John Dean). Eventually they, and others, would all serve time in prison. At the same moment, one of Nixon's aides, Alexander Butterfield, disclosed the existence of an elaborate tape recording system in the Oval Office. The tapes, on which Nixon discussed a cover-up of the Watergate burglary, were the final confirmation that the President had engaged in obstruction of justice. On August 9, 1974—with no hope that the Senate would exonerate him—Nixon resigned the Presidency.

Neither Woodward nor Bernstein expressed any joy at Nixon's departure. They did not feel victorious though they were responsible for the *Washington Post* winning a Pulitzer Prize for its reporting on Watergate. Yet their work had transformed the country and their own lives—which would soon become evident in the movie that dramatized their successful investigation of the most disgraceful political crimes of the century.[14]

In the midst of their reporting, Woodward and Bernstein signed a contract with Simon & Schuster to write a book about Watergate. Neither had ever written a book before. They decided to call the book *All The President's Men*. The title was an allusion to Robert Penn Warren's 1946 novel, *All the King's Men*, based on the career of the Louisiana demagogue Huey Long, and the most engrossing political fable in the history of American literature.

But Woodward and Bernstein did not know how to proceed with their own book, or what to emphasize. In the middle of their efforts, Woodward received a telephone call from Robert Redford, who was interested in turning Woodward and Bernstein's narrative into a movie. Redford suggested that the book should not concentrate on the events of Watergate (which by now most people were familiar with), but on the reportorial techniques, the collaboration, and the diverse personalities of Woodward and Bernstein themselves. In Redford's mind, the book (and therefore the movie) ought to be a detective story in which the two reporters, as if they were private eyes, compulsively worked the phones, followed the leads, interviewed frightened people, and immersed themselves like Sam Spade in a milieu of deception and absurdity, with their own lives not only chaotic but (as Woodward is told by Deep Throat) in danger.

Woodward and Bernstein took Redford's advice. Their book, as personal as it was political, was published in 1974 and immediately became a best-seller. Both the book, and later the movie, sensationalized the role of the investigative reporter. From this point on, nearly every journalist wanted to be the next Woodward and Bernstein, the next sleuth to expose a scandal or misdeed in American public life.

Redford, however, was likely influenced by more than the saga of two investigative reporters. In the early and mid-1970s, in the wake of Vietnam and Watergate, there were a number of movies that dealt with illicit plots concocted by the American government and America's corporations. These films included *The Parallax View* (directed by Alan J. Pakula, who also directed the film adaptation of *All the President's Men*) and Francis Ford Coppola's *The Conversation*, *Chinatown*, and *Three Days of the Condor* in which Redford himself starred.

In none of these films is the "hero" able to obstruct the crime; all the movies end in doubt or disaster. In *Condor*, Redford plays Joe Turner, a low-ranking CIA analyst who uncovers a conspiracy at the highest levels of the agency. But the best he can do is give the story to the *New York Times*. In response, his CIA control officer asks: "Hey, Turner! How do you know they'll print it?" Turner doesn't know and neither do we.

At the *Washington Post*, they do print it. At least they do in *All the President's Men*, the only movie of the 1970s in which the protagonists succeed in sorting out the mystery and dethroning the criminals.

One of the reasons for the movie's vividness when it opened in 1976 was its superb cast. While Redford, always an underrated actor because of his blond handsomeness, impersonated the smoothness of Woodward's "good cop," Dustin Hoffman spent months hanging around with Bernstein, copying his impertinence, his sloppy appearance, and his incessant smoking. The two actors captured the divergence, even the ludicrousness, of Woodward and Bernstein working as a team.

Indeed, there is one point in the film when they are summoned into a furious Ben Bradlee's office. Redford and Hoffman are shot from behind, Redford walking briskly but dispassionately and Hoffman bouncing along hyperactively beside him. Looking at their different gaits, we can't help being reminded of Hoffman's Ratso Rizzo and Jon Voight's Joe Buck in Midnight Cowboy—two disparate and disreputable con men, but not all that dissimilar from Woodward and Bernstein who sometimes have to dupe people in order to get information.

Although he was only on the screen for ten minutes, Jason Robards seemed an exact replica of the sarcastic, crusty Ben Bradlee (there was a story that after the movie's release, Bradlee strode around the Post's office imitating Robards playing Bradlee). For his performance, Robards won an Oscar for best supporting actor. At the same time, Hal Holbrook as Deep Throat—croaking his laconic and enigmatic answers to Redford/Woodward's questions—actually resembled Mark Felt, though only Woodward knew this and he couldn't tell anyone.

In reality as well as in the movie, Woodward and Bernstein are not supermen. They make mistakes, print stories that are inaccurate, get the newspaper into trouble. Near the close of the film, Robards as Bradlee sardonically summarizes the pressure they're all under: "Nothing's riding on this except the... first amendment to the Constitution, freedom of the press, and maybe the future of the country. Not that any of that matters, but if you guys fuck up again, I'm going to get mad."

The guys don't fuck up again. At the end of the movie, they're clattering away on their typewriters while a parade of the President's men are convicted and jailed, ending with Nixon himself abandoning his cherished office. For once, the private eyes have prevailed.

All the President's Men was one of the two most astute movies ever made about the newspaper business—the other film being *Citizen Kane.* Pakula and his cohorts were aware of the parallels between the two movies. At one juncture, Woodward and Bernstein are pouring through the check-out cards at the Library of Congress, seeking to find out who was rummaging through books that might subvert the Democrats. The camera slowly rises to the ceiling of the library, as the audience gazes down at the two journalist-detectives. This shot from above is nearly identical to one in *Citizen Kane* where we look down from another ceiling on the nameless reporter reading the diary of Mr. Thatcher, Kane's guardian and banker.

Orson Welles's Charles Foster Kane, however, is a charming megalomaniac, where Richard Milhous Nixon, particularly on his tape recordings, was nasty and paranoid. *Citizen Kane's* journalist, moreover, never finds the key to Kane's ambiguous life or his thirst for power. Yet by the end of their labors, Woodward and Bernstein located their "Rosebud." As a consequence, they became celebrities; if you're a reporter, you know you're a deity when you're played in the movies by Robert Redford and Dustin Hoffman.

Woodward and Bernstein wrote one more book—*The Final Days,* published in 1976, about Richard Nixon's tormented, almost psychotic, last weeks in the White House. After that, though they published a number of best-sellers on their own, they never worked together again. Still, they remained friends. And like the periodic reunion concerts of Simon and Garfunkel, Woodward and Bernstein frequently reappeared jointly, whenever Watergate was a topic.

Then, in 2005, *Vanity Fair* notified Woodward and Bernstein that the magazine was about to publish an article identifying Mark Felt as Deep Throat. Woodward was still reluctant to acknowledge who Deep Throat was. But by this time, Felt was suffering from dementia; he could remember only the names of Woodward and J. Edgar Hoover, but nothing about Watergate or his role as Woodward's mole inside the FBI. Ben Bradlee, now retired, and other *Post* editors convinced Woodward that this was their newspaper's story, and that they couldn't be scooped by another publication. So the *Post* issued a statement confirming that Felt was Deep Throat. Besides, Woodward had already written a draft of a book about his relationship with Felt, called *The Secret Man* (which he published, with an "afterword" by Bernstein, in 2005 after Felt's identity was revealed). So the last mystery of Watergate was unveiled.

Watergate made Woodward and Bernstein the most illustrious print journalists, and among the most influential war babies, of the twentieth century.[15] They had become archetypes for those reporters who followed them in all the forms of the media over the next several decades.

Yet at the height of their fame, journalism—particularly the centrality of newspapers—was about to diminish. And for this decline, the war babies were as responsible as they had been for the brief, glorious ascendancy of the *Washington Post*.

The Revolution in Television News

Just as television, when it was introduced to the public in the late 1940s and early 1950s, shrank the audiences for movies, so the evening news broadcasts (originally fifteen minutes in the 1950s but expanded to half an hour in the 1960s) provided increasing competition for newspapers. Although television could not offer the extensive coverage of news events found in newspapers, it was able to bring the nation together in moments of crisis. No newspaper had the visual impact on Americans that television exerted during the assassinations and funerals of John F. Kennedy, Martin Luther King, and Robert Kennedy. Nor could newspapers impart images as forcefully as television of police dogs leaping at the throats of civil rights demonstrators, or of American soldiers maimed or killed in the jungles of Vietnam.

In fact, one of the most spellbinding episodes in the Watergate scandal was the televised testimony before the Senate Watergate Committee in 1973 of John Dean, the former White House Counsel to Richard Nixon. Dean testified for four days, sitting at a table, reading his prepared statement for two of those days in a nasal monotone, with the camera focused mostly on his impassive face. But the meticulous account he gave of a "cancer" growing on the Presidency—and of all the interrelated crimes of the Nixon Administration—was mesmerizing. Viewers, including me, could not pull themselves away from their television sets. Not even Woodward and Bernstein could convey in their stories the authority or the ghastliness of Dean's deposition.

From the 1960s to the 1990s, the national arbiters of what was newsworthy were not so much print journalists as the network anchors—starting with Walter Cronkite on CBS, and Chet Huntley and David Brinkley on NBC. The last and most versatile of those gurus was the war baby Tom Brokaw.

Brokaw joined NBC in 1966, reporting and anchoring the local news at NBC's affiliate in Los Angeles. Thereafter, Brokaw rose rapidly through the ranks of the network. By 1973, he had become NBC's White House correspondent, covering Watergate. From 1976 until 1982, he was the main host of the *Today* show. In 1983, Brokaw was anointed the sole anchor of NBC's *Nightly News*, a post he held until 2004. His presence and unruffled manner helped the NBC newscast soar to number one in the ratings from 1996 on. After the sudden death of Tim Russert in 2008, Brokaw temporarily served as moderator of *Meet the Press*, keeping the program dominant over its Sunday morning rivals through the Presidential election in November. In sum, during the course of his career, Brokaw presided over all the major news shows on NBC—a feat no one else in television news had ever achieved.

Brokaw was also the first American television journalist to broadcast live in front of the Berlin Wall when it was being chipped away by East Germans in November 1989. Again, no newspaper reporter could have conveyed as spectacularly as television the euphoria that characterized the symbolic demise of the Cold War.

Yet on a much more horrendous occasion, after anchoring NBC's coverage all day of the assault on the World Trade Towers on September 11, 2001, Brokaw returned home at night, traumatized and exhausted.

From the window of his apartment, he could gaze south at the ravaged Manhattan skyline, watching black clouds of smoke still billowing in the distance, and the evening sky bathed in a fiery glow.[16]

Three years before the terrorist attack on American and other civilians, Brokaw had published in 1998 a best-selling book titled *The Greatest Generation*. In the book, he had celebrated those, like his parents, who had endured the Great Depression and World War II, and built the prosperity of postwar America. But that generation had given way to the Americans born during the war, who (like Brokaw himself) had reshaped the nation according to their own needs and aspirations, creating the country the baby boomers inherited.

Among those changes was a nation no longer so unified as it had been during World War II, a nation whose politics were more polarized, whose culture was more fragmented. And the impartial style of a journalist like Tom Brokaw was giving way to a televised punditry that was more personal, less dispassionate or genial, more reflective of the war babies' unpredictable egoism.

One of the pioneers of that punditry was another war baby, George Will. Will was born in 1941 in Champaign, Illinois. His father was a professor of philosophy at the University of Illinois, and Will himself—even when young—always had a philosophical cast of mind. After graduating from Trinity College in Hartford in 1962, Will studied philosophy, politics, and economics at Oxford, and received a Ph.D. in politics from Princeton in 1968. So if he wished, he could have pursued a career as an academic. And he did teach political philosophy for a time at Michigan State, the University of Toronto, and Harvard.

But Will wanted to have an effect on America outside the cloistered, increasingly left-wing, enclaves of the university. Although Will had matured during the radicalism of the 1960s, he was—unlike most of his war baby cohorts—a conservative, unmoved by or at least uninvolved in the civil rights turbulence or the opposition to the Vietnam War. It's difficult to conceive of Will, with his detached demeanor, marching in the streets or occupying university buildings. Thus for two years, from

1970 to 1972, Will served as an aide to the relatively undistinguished Republican Senator from Colorado, Gordon Allott. Will then joined William Buckley's *National Review*, the preeminent conservative magazine in the United States. While at the *National Review*, Will was an editor and occasional contributor. More significantly, he learned a lot from Buckley about how to influence public opinion, not only in columns but on television (Buckley hosted *Firing Line*, in which he "debated" but more often skewered liberals, from 1966 to 1999).

In 1974, Will began writing columns for the *Washington Post* and later for *Newsweek*. Eventually, his columns were syndicated in 450 newspapers. In 1977, Will won a Pulitzer Prize for his political commentary.

Yet it was on television that Will became a "star," reaching an audience of politicians, intellectuals, and opinion-molders. In 1981, Will joined ABC's *This Week with David Brinkley* as a panelist; he remained a permanent fixture on the Sunday morning program, a competitor of *Meet the Press*, throughout the changes in hosts, until he moved to Fox News in 2013.

As a televised pundit, Will exposed audiences to the verbal pyrotechnics and stylistic tics that replaced the more aloof prose of the legendary print editorialists of the past like Walter Lippmann and James Reston. What Will conveyed was not only his opinions but his distinctive personality. He delivered his observations in a stern, almost deadpan, manner, but one that masked a scathing sense of humor (though he never smiled, not even at his own mockery of some politician's stupidity).

Philosophically and temperamentally, Will was more a traditionalist than a typical conservative. He could be as disparaging of Republicans as of Democrats. He really abhorred anyone with some ostentatious scheme to change or rescue America or the world. So his favorite targets were the neoconservatives (pseudo-revolutionary activists like his contemporary Dick Cheney, Bill Kristol of the *Weekly Standard*, the self-designated seers of the George W. Bush Administration) who wanted, like that other misguided missionary Woodrow Wilson, to make the world safe for America's brand of democracy and freedom. Will was particularly skeptical of America's wars in Iraq and Afghanistan, and its efforts to convert the Middle East to Western-style values.

Will may have been a child of World War II. But he was essentially an eighteenth-century man, a disciple of Edmund Burke, for whom change was usually ruinous. People were, in Will's view, on earth not to tinker with society or the universe, but to enjoy some happiness, yet more often to accept the burdens that all humans confronted in their lives.

As a jaundiced pundit on network television, Will was an anomaly even to his fellow conservatives. In their eyes, the networks and the newspapers—what they liked to label the "mainstream media"—were overflowing with liberals. Hence, their errand by the 1990s was to invent a conservative alternative to NBC, CBS, ABC, the *New York Times*, and the *Washington Post*. Their vehicle would be cable television.

Strictly speaking, Roger Ailes—yet one more war baby, born in 1940 in Ohio—was not a journalist. But he had a transformative impact on television news, making it both more personal and rancorous.

As a child Ailes—like Francis Ford Coppola, Martin Scorsese, Judy Collins, and Joni Mitchell—was sickly, not with polio or asthma but with hemophilia, a disease that afflicted him throughout his life. Nonetheless, Ailes was ambitious, and he understood early in his life the political implications of television and other forms of mass communication. He graduated from Ohio University in 1962, with a degree in radio and television. From the beginning, Ailes (like George Will) was a conservative—even during an era like the 1960s when the majority of his peers were on the left.

In 1968, Ailes—after working at local TV stations—was asked by Richard Nixon to become Nixon's chief television consultant and general media adviser. Ailes's unenviable task in the 1968 campaign was to make Nixon a more "pleasant" candidate, not an easy assignment for a counselor who had to somehow revise Nixon's persona from an occasionally venomous politician to an amiable human being voters might want to have a beer with. It's not clear that Ailes ever succeeded in this makeover, even briefly and certainly not during Watergate. But Nixon did win the presidency by a slender margin in 1968 and in a much greater rout in 1972.

In the 1970s and 1980s, Ailes continued to work as a consultant for Republican candidates. One of his clients in the 1980s was Ronald Reagan. Although Reagan, a veteran of Hollywood and television, knew how to perform before a camera and charm an audience, he still needed assistance in 1984 after his dreadful, inarticulate first debate with the Democratic Presidential candidate, Walter Mondale. Ailes helped make Reagan more polished and humorous in the second debate, thereby insuring that Reagan would effortlessly win a second Presidential term, sweeping every state but Mondale's Minnesota and the District of Columbia. Ailes also aided Reagan's Vice President and successor, George H. W. Bush, in the Republican primaries and general election in 1988.

Yet Ailes's supreme talent was not as a political consultant but as a visionary when it came to television news. In 1993, Ailes became president of a struggling cable business channel, CNBC. Ailes proved himself a master at hiring on-air talent, like Maria Bartiromo, and turning them into stars. Because of the CNBC anchors that Ailes and his successors selected, what could have been a dull recounting of market trends turned into a spirited, often droll analysis of Wall Street. CNBC was apolitical though irreverent in its coverage of the stock market. So it turned into the channel everyone—from market professionals to ordinary investors—had to watch if they wanted to know what was happening not only to their own stocks but to the American economy in good times and bad.

Ailes, however, remained a Republican, and one who aspired to design a conservative alternative to what he regarded as the liberal bias of the network news broadcasts and the major newspapers in the United States. In 1996, he got his chance. He was appointed by Rupert Murdoch—the global, and politically conservative, media entrepreneur—to create a new cable channel with a right-wing tilt, called Fox News.

Ted Turner (born in November 1938) had created CNN, the first cable news network, in 1980. CNN was politically centrist, and prided itself on its impartial reporting of news events. What Ailes and Murdoch had in mind was a news channel that would scorn the neutrality of CNN, and present both news and opinion from a conservative perspective.

At Fox News, Ailes made personal commentary the hallmark of his on-air luminaries (like Bill O'Reilly and Shawn Hannity) especially in the evening. And Ailes stocked even his "straight" news shows with conservative pundits like Charles Krauthammer and Bill Kristol.

There is no question that Ailes instigated a fundamental insurrection in how the news was delivered and interpreted. Fox News took pride in its divergence from the "neutral" stance of network television reporters like Tom Brokaw. Indeed, Fox News became a new model for cable news, supplanting CNN and all the other cable channels (like the liberal MSNBC) in popularity, often beating the networks in the ratings on primary and election nights. Fox and Ailes—in their approach to the news—were captivating and idiosyncratic. Fox News therefore reflected the personality of Ailes—and the channel represented another invention of the individualistic war baby generation.

News, however it was presented, was largely about domestic politics and American foreign policy. In this sense, Fox News was only more vociferous in its opinions than NBC or the *New York Times*. And many of the most important politicians and diplomats that the networks, cable channels, and newspapers reported on were also war babies themselves.

Contemporary Politics and Foreign Policy

By the beginning of the twenty-first century, most of the Americans born during World War II were now in their sixties and nearing retirement. Yet some of them—notably Dick Cheney, Joe Biden, and Nancy Pelosi, along with Barney Frank and John Kerry—were at the peak of their political power. At the same time, Richard Holbrooke remained a leading expert and practitioner of American diplomacy, which he had been ever since the Vietnam War. Far from leaving public life, all of these war babies molded the country's destiny, for better and worse, throughout the first years of the new century.

From his adolescence, Dick Cheney was a natural politician, drawn to power wherever he could find it. And to mentors who could teach him how to wield influence when it mattered. As early as high school, Cheney was elected president of his senior class. He entered Yale in 1959, a predecessor in New Haven of John Kerry. But unlike Kerry, Cheney disliked the liberal elitism of the university, and dropped out in 1962, finishing his undergraduate education in his home state at the University of Wyoming. While he was at Wyoming, Cheney got his first exposure to pragmatic politics as an intern in the Wyoming state legislature.

Although Cheney's parents were Democrats, Cheney broke with the family tradition and became a conservative Republican (like George Will and Roger Ailes) during the 1960s. Cheney championed the Vietnam War, though not enough to serve in the conflict as did John Kerry; Cheney managed to obtain five draft deferments during the course of the war. Cheney also opposed the Vietnam War protestors and voted for Richard Nixon in 1968 and 1972. In this sense, Cheney was out of step with most of his war baby colleagues. But his conservatism, by the 1970s, was about to unlock the door to political ascendancy.

Starting in 1969, Donald Rumsfeld—an influential assistant to Richard Nixon and then Gerald Ford—offered Cheney a series of increasingly potent positions. All of these culminated in Cheney's appointment as President Ford's chief of staff in 1975, and as his campaign manager in Ford's unsuccessful effort to be elected in his own right in 1976.

After Ford's defeat, Cheney returned to Wyoming and won Wyoming's lone Congressional seat, which he held until 1989. Cheney emerged as one of the most influential Republican Congressmen, an unwavering conservative but with a sure grasp of how to count votes and wield power in the House. During this time, Cheney became as commanding a Republican presence in Congress as Nancy Pelosi would be for the Democrats.

Cheney left the House in 1989 when George H. W. Bush appointed him Secretary of Defense. In that capacity, Cheney presided over the first Iraq War, and agreed that American troops should not march to Baghdad and topple the Saddam Hussein regime.

But during the 1990s, Cheney's views on issues—foreign and domestic—appeared to harden. When he became George W. Bush's Vice President in 2001, Cheney had adopted a tough-guy persona, as if he were a character resembling Luca Brasi in *The Godfather*.

Moreover, Cheney had learned during his variety of positions that influence was often better exercised if one was silent until the end of debates. After everyone was finished arguing, Cheney would present his views in an imperturbable manner, exuding certainty, as if only he was in possession of the truth and only he knew how to solve a problem.[17] He adopted this confident tone in speeches and television interviews as well, particularly when he asserted that there was "no doubt" that Iraq possessed weapons of mass destruction, and that any invasion would be a "cakewalk" in which the Iraqis would instantly greet the Americans as liberators.

Perhaps Cheney should have experienced Vietnam. Then he might have known how toxic interventions can be in foreign countries about which Americans know nothing. Cheney's policies in Iraq turned out to be a calamity—for the Iraqis as well as for American soldiers who were killed or mutilated in a war that lasted a decade. And by his second term as Vice President, Cheney was no longer guiding American policy overseas or being listened to with deference at home.

Still, for the majority of his tenure, Cheney was the most dominant, and intimidating, Vice President in American history. No one who previously held the office could match him in his certitude and self-confidence. He may have done more damage than any of his precursors, but his temperament would not permit him to admit that he was ever wrong.

Cheney's successor as Vice President, Joe Biden, could not have been more antithetical, either in his policies or his personality. Where Cheney was frequently gruff and succinct, Biden was voluble, with a tendency to meander from one thought to the next. And where Cheney was not conspicuously forthcoming about his private life, Biden persistently invoked his autobiography and working-class background as a paradigm for his political positions. In short, Cheney was respected but feared by his colleagues, both in the House of Representatives and in the White House. Biden was always popular if not taken entirely seriously.

Biden was born in 1942, a year after Cheney. Biden grew up in Scranton, Pennsylvania, a coal-mining town with a proletarian atmosphere, before his family moved when he was ten years old to the more affluent Wilmington, Delaware. Biden's parents were ingrained Democrats, particularly his father who detested rich people who considered themselves superior to less fortunate Americans. Biden inherited these instincts, and carried them with him throughout his personal and political life.

As a child and a teenager Biden—like Mario Savio and Jesse Jackson—stuttered, an unusual burden for men who later conquered their verbal difficulties and were known as enthralling speakers. By the time he was in high school and then entered the University of Delaware in 1961, Biden had emerged as a student leader, already interested in pursuing a political career. As in the case of John Kerry and Barney Frank, Biden was heavily influenced by John F. Kennedy and Robert Kennedy. He was also deeply concerned about civil rights for African Americans, and he opposed the war in Vietnam. Still, again like Kerry and Frank, Biden believed in struggling for change within the existing political system. Biden was a classic liberal, for whom the radicalism of the 1960s was never an option.

Nevertheless, no one—not Biden or even Cheney in far-off Wyoming—could evade the cataclysms of the 1960s and early 1970s: the assassinations, the riots in the streets of American cities, the demonstrations against the war, and the crimes of Watergate and its attendant illegalities. In the midst of all this pandemonium, Biden suffered a personal tragedy that nearly derailed his political ambitions.

In 1972, when he was twenty-nine, Biden was elected to the Senate from Delaware. Once he turned thirty and was able to be sworn in, he would have been one of the youngest Senators in America's political history. Yet he almost declined to serve because, just after the election, his wife and one of his babies (his one-year-old daughter) were killed in an automobile crash. Politics was now the last item on Biden's mind. But Mike Mansfield, the Democratic Majority Leader in the Senate, persuaded Biden to take his seat—both because the Democrats needed his vote, and because politics in Washington might lessen Biden's misery.

Biden never stopped recalling his heartbreak, and he referred to it in speeches even after he remarried and had another child. Again, the references to the death of his first wife and child were an example of the way Biden merged the emotional and the political strands of his life.

Biden's own private deficiencies, or careless verbosity, sometimes wrecked his political aspirations. In 1988, he ran for the Democratic Presidential nomination. But he had to withdraw when he was confronted with having plagiarized some lines from a speech by the British Labor Party leader, Neil Kinnock.[18]

Twenty years later, in 2008, Biden ran again for the Democratic nomination. This time, he was more effective and truthful about his life. Yet Biden lacked the financial support or the organization of Barack Obama or Hillary Clinton—and once more, he had to drop out.

On this occasion, however, Obama chose Biden as his Vice Presidential running mate—largely because of Biden's knowledge of foreign policy and because of his warm personal relationships with his colleagues in the Senate, a conviviality that Obama seemed to lack. Biden turned out to be exactly the right mediator, able to negotiate with Democrats and Republicans on issues like the budget at a moment when political and ideological differences in Washington were often poisonous. Dick Cheney once told Patrick Leahy, the Democratic Senator from Vermont, to "go fuck yourself"—on the floor of the Senate. It's impossible to envisage Joe Biden ever saying that to anyone, much less to a fellow politician.

On the other hand, Nancy Pelosi could be much more prickly than Biden. But, like Biden, she was an expert politician—a talent she'd learned from her father when he was Mayor of Baltimore and a U.S.

Congressman—even before she held any office.

Just as significant, Pelosi was a product of the women's movement that first arose in the 1960s with the publication in 1963 of Betty Friedan's *The Feminine Mystique*. The book had its roots in the stereotypical lives and shrunken opportunities for women in the 1950s, the sort of women who became a negative example for their more assertive war baby daughters. So Pelosi developed as a politician whose style and personality were shaped by her dream of becoming, like her contemporary Billie Jean King, a woman who could be a formidable leader in her own vocation, while at the same time retaining a strong commitment to the idea of sisterhood.

All of these qualities were visible from her childhood on. In high school, she was an imposing member of the debate team. Pelosi graduated in 1962 from Trinity College, a Catholic women's college in Washington D.C. at just the moment when Catholic women, like others of their gender, were grasping the restrictions of being a female in American political and economic life.

Yet there were Catholic men in the 1960s who influenced Pelosi's views as well—particularly John F. Kennedy and Pope John XXIII. Kennedy's commitment to civil rights and the Pope's devotion to church reform enlarged her interest in the role she could play in politics and social change.

In 1963, Pelosi married and moved with her husband to San Francisco. Over the next two decades, she not only concentrated on her family and raising her children, but also on fundraising and volunteer work for the Democratic Party in California. As a liberal, she opposed and marched against the Vietnam War. By 1981, her political activities and personal stamina resulted in her being selected chairwoman of the California Democrats and finance chair for Democrats running for the Senate.

Finally, in 1987, Pelosi ran for office herself, seeking a seat in the U.S. House of Representatives from San Francisco. She won her campaign with sixty-two percent of the vote.[19] Afterwards, she climbed swiftly through the male-dominated hierarchy of the House. Almost like a female Lyndon Johnson when he was Senate Majority Leader in the 1950s and during the early years of his Presidency in the mid-1960s, Pelosi knew the strengths and vulnerabilities of her Congressional colleagues, how to marshal support for Democratic legislation, and whom to reward or punish for their votes. Her political acumen was both admired and dreaded; she could determine the difference between a Congressman's clout or irrelevance.

As a result of her political and personal shrewdness, in 2007 Pelosi became the first woman in America's history to be chosen Speaker of the House. During the next four years, before the Republicans regained control of the House in January 2011, Pelosi was instrumental in steering President Obama's agenda through the complexities of the House. She was especially crucial in cobbling together a bill and assembling a coalition in the House that could pass Obama's controversial health care program. If anything, Pelosi was as responsible for "Obamacare" as was Obama himself; there were some in Congress and in the press who believed the law should really be called "Pelosicare."

Even when she descended to House Minority Leader following the Republicans' winning the majority in the House in 2011, Pelosi remained—with the possible exception of Hillary Clinton—the most powerful woman in America. And certainly the most dominant war baby in American politics.

Only in foreign policy was Pelosi an extraneous figure. In the world of diplomacy—despite the recent appointments of Madeleine Albright, Condoleezza Rice, and Hillary Clinton as Secretaries of State—men were still prominent as advisers and veterans of America's foreign policy triumphs and misfortunes, from the Vietnam War to the present.

No diplomat was more involved in all of these foreign policy predicaments than the war baby Richard Holbrooke. From his early adulthood, Holbrooke was present at, and often in command of, the efforts to resolve civil wars, the menace of terrorism, and the intricacies that accompanied the end of the Cold War.

Holbrooke graduated from Brown University in 1962. As was the case with John Kerry, Holbrooke heeded President Kennedy's entreaty for young people to decide how they could best aid their country. So a few weeks after his graduation, Holbrooke enlisted in the foreign service. He spent the next six years in South Vietnam—an experience that molded his attitudes about the prospects and limitations of American foreign policy for the remainder of his life.

In Vietnam, Holbrooke initially specialized in what was called, euphemistically, rural "pacification" and economic development. But his skills were noticed speedily by his superiors, and he became an assistant to American ambassadors Maxwell Taylor and Henry Cabot Lodge, and to Averell Harriman at the first negotiations with the North Vietnamese in Paris in 1968.

At the age of twenty-seven, in 1967, Holbrooke also wrote a chapter of the Pentagon Papers, a secret and classified study commissioned by Secretary of Defense Robert McNamara to evaluate the origins and failures of American policy in Vietnam. In 1971, Daniel Ellsberg, who had worked on the project as well, leaked excerpts of the Pentagon Papers to the *New York Times*, the *Washington Post*, and the *Boston Globe*. The leak so enraged the Nixon Administration (even though the Papers had nothing to do with Nixon's Vietnam policies) that several of Nixon's operatives broke into Ellsberg's psychiatrist's office in an attempt to find incriminating evidence on Ellsberg's mental health—one of the multiple crimes that preceded the Watergate burglary.

By this time, Holbrooke didn't need an official analysis to decide for himself what was appalling about the war. From his own experiences, and from his conversations with journalists (with whom Holbrooke was always close) covering the war in the field, away from the optimistic pronouncements of the U.S. Embassy in Saigon, Holbrooke learned lessons that he tried to apply to future American interventions. In his eyes, the "pacification" program was a pretext for uprooting Vietnamese peasants, destroying their villages, and killing anyone suspected of cooperating with the Viet Cong or the North Vietnamese. In addition, Holbrooke was dubious about the concept of "counter insurgency," especially when the South Vietnamese people could not be expected to support a government in Saigon that was corrupt and despised.

Holbrooke deduced from Vietnam that American power should be applied abroad only after careful contemplation. And that grand strategies, like "nation building," were an exercise in hubris—the notion that the United States could reconstruct a foreign country in its own image was a fool's errand. In sum, like the characters in *The Deer Hunter*, Holbrooke concluded that America did not belong in Vietnam or in any comparable situation where the impenetrability of a foreign land made our strategies futile.

Holbrooke's congenital misgivings about the uses of American power—a skepticism he shared with members of his war baby generation—did not prevent him from holding other key positions in the foreign policy establishment. During the administration of Jimmy Carter, Holbrooke served as Assistant Secretary of State for East Asian and Pacific Affairs. For two years, starting in 1993, President Clinton appointed Holbrooke ambassador to the newly reunified Germany. Among his accomplishments there was the creation of an American Academy in Berlin, an institution where scholars and journalists could write and discuss the post-Cold War relationship between the United States and Europe.

Holbrooke's supreme achievement as a diplomat was to negotiate an end to the war in Bosnia in 1995. This was a war whose Serbian slaughter of Bosnian civilians reminded Holbrooke of the Nazi genocide that had prompted his Jewish parents to flee Europe in the 1930s, before they could be gassed in the concentration camps.

As a reward for his role in ending the Bosnian war, Holbrooke served as Ambassador to the United Nations from 1999 to 2001, the uppermost diplomatic title he was ever to hold. But despite his diplomatic experience and political connections, Holbrooke never attained his most cherished ambition: to be Secretary of State. No one disputed Holbrooke's brilliance. Yet he could be abrasive and egotistical, continually exasperating his superiors with what he obviously considered his superior wisdom on foreign affairs. Thus, unlike Joe Biden or Nancy

Pelosi whose individuality abetted their political influence, Holbrook's personality hindered his effectiveness.

Possibly if Hillary Clinton had won the Presidency in 2008, she might have given Holbrooke the position he longed for. Instead, President Obama appointed him a "Special Representative" to Afghanistan and Pakistan—another thankless job of nation building in countries with crooked or incompetent governments, and alienated populations, all of this far too reminiscent of Vietnam. Moreover, Obama and his White House staff often ignored Holbrooke's advice, and excluded him from discussions about the two countries. Finally, at a meeting at the State Department, Holbrooke suffered a ruptured aorta. He was rushed to the hospital, but died on December 13, 2010.[20]

In many ways, Holbrooke was among the most talented of the war babies. He may not have had the same dramatic impact on American domestic life as Bob Dylan or Joan Baez, Paul Simon and Art Garfunkel, Francis Ford Coppola or Martin Scorsese, John Lewis or Jesse Jackson, Muhammad Ali or Billie Jean King, Bob Woodward and Carl Bernstein. But Holbrooke shared with them, and with other war babies active in both culture and politics, the searing memories of World War II and the Cold War, a rebelliousness against the norms of middle-class life, a healthy mistrust of those in power, an emphasis on individuality and self-expression, and a desire to change the values of modern America. In all of these areas, the war babies were as unique and consequential as any generation in the history of the United States.

The Legacy of the War Babies

OBVIOUSLY, THE MAJORITY OF THE CHILDREN born between 1939 and 1945 did not turn out to be outstanding singers, composers, filmmakers, actors, journalists, civil rights and antiwar activists, or political leaders. But that is true of every generation. It's often far too easy to mythologize the most visible members of a generation—whether we're talking about the novelists and artists of the 1920s (as Woody Allen did in *Midnight in Paris*), the survivors of the Depression and World War II (as Tom Brokaw did in *The Greatest Generation*), or the baby boomers (as numerous historians have done, whether they were discussing people born in the late 1940s or in the early 1960s, people whose early years were unrelated except that they were infants in a two-decade stretch of postwar America).

Like those in other generations, most of the war babies led unexceptional lives even if they were successful as lawyers, doctors, business people, nurses, primary and secondary school teachers, or university professors. They did not set out to change America; they simply relished its prosperity and endured its traumas.

Yet we focus on the eminent members of a generation because they did share in the experiences of their illustrious cohorts, and because they amended our values and the way we thought about ourselves. So if Ernest Hemingway and F. Scott Fitzgerald defined the America of the 1920s in *The Sun Also Rises* and *The Great Gatsby*, the foremost war babies restructured American culture and politics from the 1960s to the present.

The war babies were born, grew up, and became adults during the most stressful years of the twentieth and early twenty-first centuries. Their lives were formed not just by World War II, but also by the Cold War, McCarthyism, the turbulence of the 1960s (including the murders of John F. Kennedy, Martin Luther King, and Robert Kennedy), Vietnam, Watergate, ideological schisms, cultural and social discord, and terrorist assaults on the United States. There were few prior generations in American history—not even those who outlasted the butchery of the Civil War, or suffered through the Great Depression, or fought in Europe and the Pacific during World War II—that witnessed as many cataclysms over so many years, indeed throughout their lifetimes, as did the war babies.

Their response to the crises they faced was ingenious. And personal. Musicians like Bob Dylan, Paul Simon, Joan Baez, Judy Collins, and Joni Mitchell created a new music that reflected their private reactions to the convulsions of the 1960s. Film directors like Francis Ford Coppola, Martin Scorsese, and George Lucas drew on their own pasts in spawning a renaissance in the American cinema in the 1970s. Lily Tomlin, Faye Dunaway, Al Pacino, and Robert De Niro all used the techniques of Method acting to incorporate their psyches into the characters they played on screen or stage.

But the war babies did not just craft a cultural revolution. They altered the politics of the country as well. The civil rights movement could not have prevailed without the bravery of John Lewis or the oratory of Jesse Jackson, each drawing on their youthful wrath at their exclusion from the public institutions of a segregated America. The discontent with the bureaucratic model of university education, and the need to intervene personally to challenge the notion that universities were merely servants of the government, the corporations, and the military, could not have occurred without the eloquence of Mario Savio at Berkeley.

In the meantime, the opposition to the Vietnam War might have been more fragile had it not been for the efforts of Tom Hayden to challenge the configuration of power in America, or Muhammad Ali's distinctive refusal to step across a line and be drafted into the military, or John Kerry's emotional testimony before the Senate Foreign Relations Committee about the degree to which the war was turning American soldiers into mindless killers. Nor would Richard Holbrooke's own encounter with the failures of American strategy in Vietnam have persuaded him in later wars like Iraq and Afghanistan to question Washington's efforts to remake other societies in America's image. In addition, the free-fire zones in Vietnam that executed peasants indiscriminately motivated Holbrooke to negotiate a resolution to the Bosnian civil war that was similarly exterminating thousands of innocent civilians.

The war babies also used the media to transform both American culture and American politics—mostly by bringing their own personalities to bear on the issues they were probing. The demise of the Nixon Administration, because of Watergate and other subversions of the Constitution, was engineered—in large part—by the investigative doggedness of Bob Woodward and Carl Bernstein, each a different human being with a different past but with a shared determination to unearth the secrets of an illicit Presidency. Though Woodward and Bernstein, like Tom Brokaw, kept their own ideological beliefs out of their journalism, they were followed increasingly by pundits and news executives—none more so than George Will and Roger Ailes—who employed their personal allegiances to shape political debate in America.

Not all the war babies who influenced modern America were men. Besides the female singers and actresses of the 1960s and 1970s, there were at least two women who changed the way gender roles were perceived. Billie Jean King maximized her individuality, and not just as a tennis player, to bring about more financial and athletic equality for women. Nancy Pelosi took advantage of her background and instincts as the daughter of a politician to become Speaker of the House, and thus a model for other women with leadership ambitions. Pelosi was as influential a politician as her male contemporaries like Dick Cheney, Joe Biden, and Barney Frank.

What the majority of these war babies had in common was a suspicion of traditional American institutions and assumptions. Their parents—whether they were immigrants themselves, or the children of immigrants, or the descendants of slaves—conveyed to the war babies an awareness of the world outside the United States. So war babies like Joan Baez, Bob Dylan, Paul Simon, Tom Hayden, John Kerry, Joe Biden, Richard Holbrooke, Muhammad Ali, and Jesse Jackson all had a global sensibility, a recognition that their art or political actions and attitudes transcended America's boundaries.

But the war babies' parents also believed, from the 1930s through the 1950s, in the beneficence and honesty of the American government, as well as in the virtues of other pillars in American life. The Great Depression and World War II had taught them the advantages of working together for communal ideals—building labor unions in the 1930s, cooperating on the home front to help win the war, remaining loyal to the postwar organizations that gave them employment, affluence, and a sense of collective identity.

The war babies, however, had been reared in the 1940s and 1950s on radio and television comedy, much of it satirical (it was hard to revere the army while watching Phil Silvers as Sergeant Bilko swindling his colleagues and superiors, or Sid Caesar, Mort Sahl, Mike Nichols and Elaine May, and Lenny Bruce excoriating the values of the liberal middle class). The war babies had been raised as well on the movies of the 1950s, films like *On the Waterfront*, *Rebel Without a Cause*, and *East of Eden* that dramatized a mistrust of authority figures of all types. And they were reading, either in the 1950s or early 1960s when they were in college, novels like J. D. Salinger's *The Catcher in the Rye*, or works of social criticism like David Riesman's *The Lonely Crowd*, William Whyte's *The Organization Man*, C. Wright Mills's *The Power Elite*, John Kenneth Galbraith's *The Affluent Society*, and Paul Goodman's *Growing Up Absurd*—all of which disputed the idea of America as a contented nation.

As a result of these influences, the war babies came to doubt the majesty of institutions like the Catholic Church (Mario Savio, Tom Hayden, Martin Scorsese). Or they rebelled against the norms of the old

Hollywood studio system (Francis Ford Coppola, George Lucas, Scorsese, Michael Cimino). Or they marched against the century-old existence of segregation and racism, and the way African Americans were supposed to behave (John Lewis, Jesse Jackson, Muhammad Ali). Or they asserted the power of women in what had been a male-controlled society (Billie Jean King, Nancy Pelosi). Or they devised a more autobiographical musical idiom (Bob Dylan, Paul Simon, Joni Mitchell). Or they revolted against the liberal outlook of the established news media (George Will, Roger Ailes).

Above all, the war babies no longer had faith in the integrity or intelligence of the American government—not after the Vietnam War and Watergate, or later Iraq and Afghanistan. This disillusion with the wisdom of people in power was the most notable contribution the war babies made to the overhaul of modern America.

Not all of these changes have been positive. The war babies' creativity in music and movies, as well as in investigative journalism, is undeniable. But American politics has become more divisive, more partisan, and less capable of resolving the social and economic difficulties the country faces. The loss of a communal spirit that Americans enjoyed during the Depression and World War II has paralyzed the government and made political discourse more belligerent.

On the other hand, the war babies constructed a more personal culture and politics whose reverberations we have been living with throughout the past fifty years. Moreover, the war babies are the children of Pearl Harbor and the adults of 9/11. They have lived through all the catastrophes of contemporary life. So they have had to develop new ways of coping with the upheavals they have experienced since World War II.

Their response has been more psychological than programmatic. But because of their emphasis on self-expression and their efforts to achieve some private autonomy in a complex society, the war babies have managed to reshape the culture and politics of America from the 1960s until now.

Yet the most crucial lesson the war babies have taught us is both frightening and liberating. Unlike the war babies' parents, we can no longer rely on institutions like the government, or even on other people, to save us or solve all of our problems. Whether we like it or not, whether we prefer it or not, we are most of the time on our own.

Notes

Chapter 1: A Child Eye's View of World War II

1. On Coppola's ability to rely on his own inner strengths as a result of his polio, see Robert Casillo, *Gangster Priest: The Italian American Cinema of Martin Scorsese* (Toronto: University of Toronto Press, 2006), 80.

2. Ibid., 77, 79; Vincent LoBrutto, *Martin Scorsese: A Biography* (Westport, Conn.: Praeger, 2008), 12-16; Richard Schickel, *Conversations with Scorsese* (New York: Knopf, 2011), 5-6.

3. David Thompson and Ian Christie, eds., *Scorsese on Scorsese* (London: Faber and Faber, 1989), 3; Schickel, *Conversations with Scorsese*, 16; LoBrutto, *Martin Scorsese*, 25.

4. Faye Dunaway with Betsy Sharkey, *Looking For Gatsby: My Life* (New York: Pocket Books, 1998, c. 1995), 14-17, 19, 25-26, 29, 37; Allan Hunter, *Faye Dunaway* (New York: St. Martin's, 1986), 14-15. Hereafter, a publication date given in the fashion of *Looking For Gatsby* means that the page references are from the 1998 edition of a work copyrighted in 1995.

5. For Collins's memories of childhood and her father, see Judy Collins, *Trust Your Heart: An Autobiography* (Boston: Houghton Mifflin, 1987), 5, 8-9, 11-12, 14, 16, 19-21; and Judy Collins, *Sweet Judy Blue Eyes: My Life in Music* (New York: Crown, 2011), 16-17, 30.

6. Howard Sounes, *Down the Highway: The Life of Bob Dylan* (New York: Grove, 2011, c. 2001), 4, 19-20, 23, 29; Sean Wilentz, *Bob Dylan in America* (New York: Anchor, 2011, c. 2010), 32, 34; Bob Dylan, *Chronicles: Volume One* (New York: Simon & Schuster, 2004), 29; Anthony Scaduto, *Bob Dylan* (New York: Grosset & Dunlap, 1971), 5-7.

7. Joan Baez, *And a Voice to Sing With: A Memoir* (New York: Simon & Schuster, 2009, c. 1987), xxv, 17-19, 22, 24, 29; David Hajdu, *Positively 4th Street: The Lives and Times of Joan Baez, Bob Dylan, Mimi Baez Fariña, and Richard Fariña* (New York: Farrar, Straus and Giroux, 2001), 3, 6.

8. Marc Eliot, *Paul Simon: A Life* (Hoboken, N.J.: Wiley, 2010), 9-10, 13; Joseph Morella and Patricia Barey, *Simon and Garfunkel: Old*

Notes to pages 27-33

Friends: A Dual Biography (New York: Birch Lane, 1991), 5-6.

9. Eliot, *Paul Simon*, 12; Morella and Barey, *Simon and Garfunkel*, 3-4.

10. Carole King, *A Natural Woman: A Memoir* (New York: Grand Central, 2012), 9, 13, 16, 34-35.

11. Sandy Troy, *Captain Trips: A Biography of Jerry Garcia* (New York: Thunder's Mouth, 1994), 1-3, 36; Blair Jackson, *Garcia: An American Life* (New York: Viking, 1999), 7-8, 13.

12. Tom Brokaw, *A Long Way from Home: Growing Up in the American Heartland* (New York: Random House, 2002), 5, 7, 16-17, 61, 63-64, 82.

13. On the disparate backgrounds of Woodward and Bernstein, see Alicia Shepard, *Woodward and Bernstein: Life in the Shadow of Watergate* (Hoboken, N.J.: Wiley, 2007), 5; and Carl Bernstein, *Loyalties: A Son's Memoir* (New York: Simon & Schuster, 1989), 17, 35, 50, 52, 54, 60, 69, 77, 107, 167.

14. For Lewis's and Jackson's childhoods, see John Lewis with Michael D'Orso, *Walking with the Wind: A Memoir of the Movement* (New York: Harvest, 1999, c. 1998), xv, 10, 17, 21, 31, 34, 36; Marshall Frady, *Jesse: The Life and Pilgrimage of Jesse Jackson* (New York: Random House, 1996), 114, 116; and Roger Bruns, *Jesse Jackson: A Biography* (Westport, Conn.: Greenwood, 2005), 11.

15. David Remnick, *King of the World: Muhammad Ali and the Rise of an American Hero* (New York: Random House, 1998), 81, 87; Michael Ezra, *Muhammad Ali: The Making of an Icon* (Philadelphia: Temple University Press, 2009), 9.

16. Susan Ware, *Game, Set, Match: Billie Jean King and the Revolution in Women's Sports* (Chapel Hill: University of North Carolina Press, 2011), 17-18.

17. On Hayden and Savio, see Tom Hayden, *Reunion: A Memoir* (New York: Random House, 1988), 4-5, 7; and Robert Cohen, *Freedom's Orator: Mario Savio and the Radical Legacy of the 1960s* (New York: Oxford University Press, 2009), 7, 19-20.

18. For the early political experiences of Cheney and Pelosi, see Dick Cheney, *In My Time: A Personal and Political Memoir* (New York:

Notes to pages 33–45

Threshold, 2011), 17, 42; and Vincent Bzdek, *Woman of the House: The Rise of Nancy Pelosi* (New York: Palgrave Macmillan, 2008), 16, 22, 28-29.

19. Stuart Weisberg, *Barney Frank: The Story of America's Only Left-Handed, Gay, Jewish Congressman* (Amherst: University of Massachusetts Press, 2009), 22, 26-29, 34.

20. Douglas Brinkley, *Tour of Duty: John Kerry and the Vietnam War* (New York: Morrow, 2004), 18-19, 22-23; Michael Kranish, Brian Mooney, and Nina Easton, *John F. Kerry: The Complete Biography by the Boston Globe Reporters Who Know Him Best* (New York: Public Affairs, 2004), xxii. 2-4, 7, 17.

21. Roger Cohen, "Holbrooke, A European Power," in Derek Chollet and Samantha Power, eds., *The Unquiet American: Richard Holbrooke in the World* (New York: Public Affairs, 2011), 165.

22. Collins, *Trust Your Heart*, 15; Brokaw, *A Long Way from Home*, 66.

23. Dylan, *Chronicles: Volume One*, 230.

24. Dunaway, *Looking For Gatsby*, 25-26.

Chapter 2: Growing Up in Cold War America

1. On Scorsese's interest in the Catholic Church and the Mafia, see Vincent LoBrutto, *Martin Scorsese: A Biography* (Westport, Conn.: Praeger, 2008), 19, 21, 32, 34, 39-40; Richard Schickel, *Conversations with Scorsese* (New York: Knopf, 2011), 5, 23, 56; David Thompson and Ian Christie, eds., *Scorsese on Scorsese* (London: Faber and Faber, 1989), 1, 9-10; and Robert Casillo, *Gangster Priest: The Italian American Cinema of Martin Scorsese* (Toronto: University of Toronto Press, 2006), 70-71, 79, 93-95, 97.

2. For Scorsese's adolescent love affair with movies, see LoBrutto, *Martin Scorsese*, 23, 26, 36, 50, 52, 55; Schickel, *Conversations with Scorsese*, 40-41, 55, 58, 60, 62, 64; and Casillo, *Gangster Priest*, 59, 96.

3. I have discussed at greater length the Method and its transition from Russia to the United States in my book *Modernist America: Art, Music, Movies, and the Globalization of American Culture* (New Haven: Yale University Press, 2011), ch. 12.

Notes to pages 46-53

4. On Dunaway's youthful training as an actress, see Faye Dunaway with Betsy Sharkey, *Looking For Gatsby: My Life* (New York: Pocket Books, 1998, c. 1995), 38, 41-43, 48-51, 58, 63-64; and Allan Hunter, *Faye Dunaway* (New York: St. Martin's, 1986), 14-16.

5. On Presley and Freed, see Joseph Morella and Patricia Barey, *Simon and Garfunkel: Old Friends: A Dual Biography* (New York: Birch Lane, 1991), 14; David Hajdu, *Positively 4th Street: The Lives and Times of Joan Baez, Bob Dylan, Mimi Baez Fariña, and Richard Fariña* (New York: Farrar, Straus and Giroux, 2001), 11; and Carole King, *A Natural Woman: A Memoir* (New York: Grand Central, 2012), 27, 41.

6. Hajdu, *Positively 4th Street*, 10, 12, 73; Judy Collins, *Trust Your Heart: An Autobiography* (Boston: Houghton Mifflin, 1987), 67; Blair Jackson, *Garcia: An American Life* (New York: Viking, 1999), 37.

7. Sean Wilentz, *Bob Dylan in America* (New York: Anchor, 2011, c. 2010), 59; Hajdu, *Positively 4th Street*, 15-16; Sandy Troy, *Captain Trips: A Biography of Jerry Garcia* (New York: Thunder's Mouth, 1994), 20-21.

8. On Baez's teenage years, see Joan Baez, *And a Voice to Sing With: A Memoir* (New York: Simon & Schuster, 2009, c. 1987), 25, 27-28, 32, 40-41, 49, 52, 59; and Hajdu, *Positively 4th Street*, 13, 23, 31.

9. Collins, *Trust Your Heart*, 20, 29, 31, 33-35, 37, 42-44; Judy Collins, *Sweet Judy Blue Eyes: My Life in Music* (New York: Crown, 2011), 15, 17-18, 20-21, 25, 39-40.

10. For Dylan's adolescence and origins as a folk singer, see Hajdu, *Positively 4th Street*, 66-73; William McKeen, *Bob Dylan: A Bio-Bibliography* (Westport, Conn.: Greenwood, 1993), 5-7, 11, 13-14; Bob Dylan, *Chronicles: Volume One* (New York: Simon & Schuster, 2004), 29-30, 34; Anthony Scaduto, *Bob Dylan* (New York: Grosset & Dunlap, 1971), 3, 6, 8, 26, 41, 51-53, 56; Howard Sounes, *Down the Highway: The Life of Bob Dylan* (New York: Grove, 2011, c. 2001), 27-28, 34, 38, 47, 49-50, 58, 64, 71, 88; Wilentz, *Bob Dylan in America*, 33, 41-42, 64; and Collins *Sweet Judy Blue Eyes*, 55.

11. On Simon and Garfunkel's early years, see Victoria Kingston, *Simon and Garfunkel: The Biography* (New York: Fromm International, 1998),

Notes to pages 53–61

5, 7, 9, 11-13, 15; Marc Eliot, *Paul Simon: A Life* (Hoboken, N.J.: Wiley, 2010), 15, 17-20, 22-23; and Morella and Barey, *Simon and Garfunkel*, 7, 10-11, 16-17, 23-24.

12. King, *A Natural Woman*, 78.

13. For Joplin's formative years in Texas, see Alice Echols, *Scars of Sweet Paradise: The Life and Times of Janis Joplin* (New York: Holt, 2000, c. 1999), 3-4, 9, 12, 17, 21, 39, 41, 45, 53, 64-66; and Myra Friedman, *Buried Alive: The Biography of Janis Joplin* (New York: Three Rivers, 1992, c. 1973), 16, 38, 40-41.

14. On Garcia, see Troy, *Captain Trips*, 11-13, 16-17.

15. Stephen Davis, *Jim Morrison: Life, Death, Legend* (New York: Gotham, 2004), 7, 14, 48-49; James Riordan and Jerry Prochnicky, *Break on Through: The Life and Death of Jim Morrison* (New York: Morrow, 1991), 25, 30, 32-33, 47-50.

16. John Lewis with Michael D'Orso, *Walking with the Wind: A Memoir of the Movement* (New York: Harvest, 1999, c. 1998), 31, 34, 37-41, 43, 45, 53, 66, 68, 78, 85.

17. Roger Bruns, *Jesse Jackson: A Biography* (Westport, Conn.: Greenwood, 2005), 16-17, 25; Marshall Frady, *Jesse: The Life and Pilgrimage of Jesse Jackson* (New York: Random House, 1996), 91, 131.

18. E. Benjamin Skinner, "Reporting Truth to Power" and Jonathan Alter, "That Magnificent Hunger," in Derek Chollet and Samantha Power, eds., *The Unquiet American: Richard Holbrooke in the World* (New York: Public Affairs, 2011), 46-47, 58.

19. On Frank's interest in politics and his need to conceal his homosexuality, see Stuart Weisberg, *Barney Frank: The Story of America's Only Left-Handed, Gay, Jewish Congressman* (Amherst: University of Massachusetts Press, 2009), 23, 26, 33, 35, 37-39, 42-43, 48-49.

20. Robert Cohen, *Freedom's Orator: Mario Savio and the Radical Legacy of the 1960s* (New York: Oxford University Press, 2009), 22, 24-28, 30-32.

21. Tom Hayden, *Reunion: A Memoir* (New York: Random House, 1988), 10, 12-19, 26, 32-33, 35.

Notes to pages 62–70

22. Tom Brokaw, *A Long Way from Home: Growing Up in the American Heartland* (New York: Random House, 2002), 90, 92, 130-131, 154, 156, 166, 168, 188, 191, 216, 219, 222, 225.

23. Mike Marqusee, *Redemption Song: Muhammad Ali and the Spirit of the Sixties* (London: Verso, 1999), 50-52; David Remnick, *King of the World: Muhammad Ali and the Rise of an American Hero* (New York: Random House, 1998), 87-88, 120; Michael Ezra, *Muhammad Ali: The Making of an Icon* (Philadelphia: Temple University Press, 2009), 10.

Chapter 3: The Limits of McCarthyism

1. I have analyzed McCarthyism extensively in my book *The Liberal Mind in a Conservative Age: American Intellectuals in the 1940s and 1950s* (New York: Harper & Row, 1985), ch. 5.

2. Judy Collins, *Trust Your Heart: An Autobiography* (Boston: Houghton Mifflin, 1987), 32; Faye Dunaway with Betsy Sharkey, *Looking For Gatsby: My Life* (New York: Pocket Books, 1998, c. 1995), 52.

3. Stuart Weisberg, *Barney Frank: The Story of America's Only Left-Handed, Gay, Jewish Congressman* (Amherst: University of Massachusetts Press, 2009), 34.

4. Carl Bernstein, *Loyalties: A Son's Memoir* (New York: Simon & Schuster, 1989), 16, 21, 99, 101-102, 107, 110, 141, 162, 165, 198-202, 224, 258-259, 261.

5. I have described the influence of European modernism on American culture in my book *Modernist America: Art, Music, Movies, and the Globalization of American Culture* (New Haven: Yale University Press, 2011).

6. William McKeen, *Bob Dylan: A Bio-Bibliography* (Westport, Conn.: Greenwood, 1993), 9; Sean Wilentz, *Bob Dylan in America* (New York: Anchor, 2011, c. 2010), 50-51; Bob Dylan, *Chronicles: Volume One* (New York: Simon & Schuster, 2004), 57; Howard Sounes, *Down the Highway: The Life of Bob Dylan* (New York: Grove, 2011, c. 2001), 70; Sandy Troy, *Captain Trips: A Biography of Jerry Garcia* (New York: Thunder's Mouth, 1994), 18; James Riordan and Jerry Prochnicky, *Break on*

Notes to pages 72–82
Through: The Life and Death of Jim Morrison (New York: Morrow, 1991), 35.

7. Stephen Davis, *Jim Morrison: Life, Death, Legend* (New York: Gotham, 2004), 36.

8. I have interpreted the works of the 1950s social critics at length in *The Liberal Mind in a Conservative Age*, ch. 4.

Chapter 4: The War Babies and the Postwar Media

1. Judy Collins, *Trust Your Heart: An Autobiography* (Boston: Houghton Mifflin, 1987), 34; Joan Baez, *And a Voice to Sing With: A Memoir* (New York: Simon & Schuster, 2009, c. 1987), 22; Carole King, *A Natural Woman: A Memoir* (New York: Grand Central, 2012), 19; Bob Dylan, *Chronicles: Volume One* (New York: Simon & Schuster, 2004), 50; John Lewis with Michael D'Orso, *Walking with the Wind: A Memoir of the Movement* (New York: Harvest, 1999, c. 1998), 20; Tom Brokaw, *A Long Way from Home: Growing Up in the American Heartland* (New York: Random House, 2002), 89, 100.

2. David Thompson and Ian Christie, eds., *Scorsese on Scorsese* (London: Faber and Faber, 1989), 4; Vincent LoBrutto, *Martin Scorsese: A Biography* (Westport, Conn.: Praeger, 2008), 18; Stuart Weisberg, *Barney Frank: The Story of America's Only Left-Handed, Gay, Jewish Congressman* (Amherst: University of Massachusetts Press, 2009), 26; Howard Sounes, *Down the Highway: The Life of Bob Dylan* (New York: Grove, 2011, c. 2001), 27; Sean Wilentz, *Bob Dylan in America* (New York: Anchor, 2011, c. 2010), 34; Dick Cheney, *In My Time: A Personal and Political Memoir* (New York: Threshold, 2011), 20; Brokaw, *A Long Way from Home*, 143, 172-174.

3. Lewis, *Walking with the Wind*, 58, 100.

4. Faye Dunaway with Betsy Sharkey, *Looking For Gatsby: My Life* (New York: Pocket Books, 1998, c. 1995), 34.

5. Sounes, *Down the Highway*, 99.

6. Dunaway, *Looking For Gatsby*, 68-69, 71-72.

7. For Keillor's background and career, see Michael Fedo, *The Man*

Notes to pages 83–96
from Lake Wobegon (New York: St. Martin's, 1987), 1-2, 6, 8, 11, 14-15, 32, 34-35, 37, 48, 58-59, 74, 78-79, 87, 214, 216; and Judith Lee, *Garrison Keillor: A Voice of America* (Jackson: University Press of Mississippi, 1991), 1-6, 10, 12, 41.

8. On Tomlin, see Jeff Sorenson, *Lily Tomlin: Woman of a Thousand Faces* (New York: St. Martin's, 1989), 6-7, 9, 21-23, 26, 29, 41, 43-44, 77, 80.

9. I have interpreted in more detail the movies of the 1950s and early 1960s in my book *Modernist America: Art, Music, Movies, and the Globalization of American Culture* (New Haven: Yale University Press, 2011), 269-277.

10. LoBrutto, *Martin Scorsese*, 17, 34; Richard Schickel, *Conversations with Scorsese* (New York: Knopf, 2011), 8, 19, 29, 31, 38, 42, 47, 50-51, 72, 83; Thompson and Christie, eds., *Scorsese on Scorsese*, 8.

11. Dunaway, *Looking For Gatsby*, 222; Victoria Kingston, *Simon and Garfunkel: The Biography* (New York: Fromm International, 1998), 20.

12. On the admiration of Scorsese, Dunaway, and Baez for Brando, see Thompson and Christie, eds., *Scorsese on Scorsese*, 8; Schickel, *Conversations with Scorsese*, 39; Dunaway, *Looking For Gatsby*, 13, 60, 388, 393; and Baez, *And a Voice to Sing With*, 58, 300-303.

13. For the influence of James Dean on various war babies, see Anthony Scaduto, *Bob Dylan* (New York: Grosset & Dunlap, 1971), 9; David Hajdu, *Positively 4th Street: The Lives and Times of Joan Baez, Bob Dylan, Mimi Baez Fariña, and Richard Fariña* (New York: Farrar, Straus and Giroux, 2001), 67; William McKeen, *Bob Dylan: A Bio-Bibliography* (Westport, Conn.: Greenwood, 1993), 7-8; Tom Hayden, *Reunion: A Memoir* (New York: Random House, 1988), 18; Stephen Davis, *Jim Morrison: Life, Death, Legend* (New York: Gotham, 2004), 14; Brokaw, *A Long Way from Home*, 145; and Schickel, *Conversations with Scorsese*, 12, 232.

Chapter 5: The Music of the War Babies

1. For more information on Baez's early career and image, see Joan

Notes to pages 97–102

Baez, *And a Voice to Sing With: A Memoir* (New York: Simon & Schuster, 2009, c. 1987), 15, 72; and David Hajdu, *Positively 4th Street: The Lives and Times of Joan Baez, Bob Dylan, Mimi Baez Fariña, and Richard Fariña* (New York: Farrar, Straus and Giroux, 2001), 19, 21, 54, 61, 88, 90, 104, 123-124, 190.

2. On Baez's activism, see Baez, *And a Voice to Sing With*, 107, 118-119, 125-126, 170, 180, 183, 204, 219, 254, 268, 274-275, 278-280, 285, 294-295.

3. Judy Collins, *Trust Your Heart: An Autobiography* (Boston: Houghton Mifflin, 1987), 64, 68-69, 81-82; Judy Collins, *Sweet Judy Blue Eyes: My Life in Music* (New York: Crown, 2011), 3, 11, 79, 89, 105, 107, 133, 136, 160, 191, 204, 305-306, 308.

4. On Dylan's career as a political singer, see Howard Sounes, *Down the Highway: The Life of Bob Dylan* (New York: Grove, 2011, c. 2001), 2, 127, 135; Sean Wilentz, *Bob Dylan in America* (New York: Anchor, 2011, c. 2010), 92-93; Hajdu, *Positively 4th Street*, 74; Anthony Scaduto, *Bob Dylan* (New York: Grosset & Dunlap, 1971), 111, 117, 147; and Baez, *And a Voice to Sing With*, 92-93.

5. Sounes, *Down the Highway*, 137, 141-142, 145; William McKeen, *Bob Dylan: A Bio-Bibliography* (Westport, Conn.: Greenwood, 1993), 24-25; Scaduto, *Bob Dylan*, 146, 150; Baez, *And a Voice to Sing With*, 90-91; Wilentz, *Bob Dylan in America* (New York: Anchor, 2011, c. 2010), 102; Hajdu, *Positively 4th Street*, 182.

6. For more on Dylan's retreat from political causes and protest music, see Bob Dylan, *Chronicles: Volume One* (New York: Simon & Schuster, 2004), 119; Sounes, *Down the Highway*, 4, 144, 153, 216, 263, 338; Wilentz, *Bob Dylan in America*, 72, 76, 279; Scaduto, *Bob Dylan*, 160, 170, 180; Hajdu, *Positively 4th Street*, 195, 201-202; and McKeen, *Bob Dylan*, 26, 28, 33.

7. McKeen, *Bob Dylan*, 35-36, 130; Sounes, *Down the Highway*, 165, 171, 183-185, 189, 196-197, 201; Wilentz, *Bob Dylan in America*, 104; Hajdu, *Positively 4th Street*, 210, 236, 259-261.

8. Scaduto, *Bob Dylan*, 245; McKeen, *Bob Dylan*, 40, 45; Sounes, *Down the Highway*, 236, 252-253, 292-293, 295, 298, 326-327, 347, 351-352, 382-

Notes to pages 104–113

384, 426, 427; Wilentz, *Bob Dylan in America*, 134, 176.

9. Joseph Morella and Patricia Barey, *Simon and Garfunkel: Old Friends: A Dual Biography* (New York: Birch Lane, 1991), 1, 36, 72-73, 86-87; Marc Eliot, *Paul Simon: A Life* (Hoboken, N.J.: Wiley, 2010), 4, 89-91, 190; Victoria Kingston, *Simon and Garfunkel: The Biography* (New York: Fromm International, 1998), 7, 81.

10. Morella and Barey, *Simon and Garfunkel*, 72, 96, 111, 127; Eliot, *Paul Simon*, 3, 101, 118, 173-174; Kingston, *Simon and Garfunkel*, 85, 121-124.

11. Carole King, *A Natural Woman: A Memoir* (New York: Grand Central, 2012), 119; Grace Slick with Andrea Cagan, *Somebody to Love?: A Rock-and-Roll Memoir* (New York: Warner, 1998), 101, 131-132; Blair Jackson, *Garcia: An American Life* (New York: Viking, 1999), 103.

12. Jackson, *Garcia*, 133, 173; Slick, *Somebody to Love?*, 134, 140, 145, 148-149; Sandy Troy, *Captain Trips: A Biography of Jerry Garcia* (New York: Thunder's Mouth, 1994), 110, 127, 129; Baez, *And a Voice to Sing With*, 164-165; Vincent LoBrutto, *Martin Scorsese: A Biography* (Westport, Conn.: Praeger, 2008), 107-108, 110.

13. Troy, *Captain Trips*, 29, 58, 69, 72; Jackson, *Garcia*, 67, 79, 119, 318, 455; Sounes, *Down the Highway*, 411.

14. Stephen Davis, *Jim Morrison: Life, Death, Legend* (New York: Gotham, 2004), 37, 442, 445, 463; James Riordan and Jerry Prochnicky, *Break on Through: The Life and Death of Jim Morrison* (New York: Morrow, 1991), 19, 105, 126-127, 165, 235, 285, 443, 452-453.

15. Collins, *Sweet Judy Blue Eyes*, 11; Myra Friedman, *Buried Alive: The Biography of Janis Joplin* (New York: Three Rivers, 1992, c. 1973), xiii, xvii, xxii, xxiv, 48, 61, 110, 159, 163, 228, 253, 309, 311; Alice Echols, *Scars of Sweet Paradise: The Life and Times of Janis Joplin* (New York: Holt, 2000, c. 1999), xii, xvii, 200, 223, 234, 257, 297, 308.

16. Collins, *Sweet Judy Blue Eyes*, 144, 191, 201, 219, 279, 315; Collins, *Trust Your Heart*, 83, 146, 150.

17. Kingston, *Simon and Garfunkel*, 139; Eliot, *Paul Simon*, 144, 158-159, 187, 201, 203, 233, 237, 241; Morella and Barey, *Simon and Garfunkel*, 235, 246, 250-251.

Notes to pages 116–137
Chapter 6: The Revolution in Movies

1. Scorsese's quote can be found in Richard Schickel, *Conversations with Scorsese* (New York: Knopf, 2011), 85. I have written extensively about the American films and actors of the late 1960s and 1970s in my book *Modernist America: Art, Music, Movies, and the Globalization of American Culture* (New Haven: Yale University Press, 2011), chs. 11–12.

2. Robert Casillo, *Gangster Priest: The Italian American Cinema of Martin Scorsese* (Toronto: University of Toronto Press, 2006), 63, 98.

3. On Scorsese's interests and time at NYU, see Vincent LoBrutto, *Martin Scorsese: A Biography* (Westport, Conn.: Praeger, 2008), 41, 103; David Thompson and Ian Christie, eds., *Scorsese on Scorsese* (London: Faber and Faber, 1989), 8, 14–15; and Schickel, *Conversations with Scorsese*, 27–28, 41, 75, 337.

4. Schickel, *Conversations with Scorsese*, 84, 206; Thompson and Christie, eds., *Scorsese on Scorsese*, 71.

5. Schickel, *Conversations with Scorsese*, 68, 99–100, 103–104; LoBrutto, *Martin Scorsese*, 135, 137.

6. Schickel, *Conversations with Scorsese*, 72, 113–114, 116.

7. Ibid., 141, 146, 152; LoBrutto, *Martin Scorsese*, 218–219, 223, 229; Thompson and Christie, eds., *Scorsese on Scorsese*, 77.

8. For more on *The King of Comedy*, see Schickel, *Conversations with Scorsese*, 155; and LoBrutto, *Martin Scorsese*, 257, 260.

9. Schickel, *Conversations with Scorsese*, 160–161; LoBrutto, *Martin Scorsese*, 275, 280.

10. Schickel, *Conversations with Scorsese*, 261.

11. On Dunaway as a Method actress, see Faye Dunaway with Betsy Sharkey, *Looking For Gatsby: My Life* (New York: Pocket Books, 1998, c. 1995), 23–24, 41, 58–61, 73, 77, 86, 101.

12. Allan Hunter, *Faye Dunaway* (New York: St. Martin's, 1986), 43; Dunaway, *Looking For Gatsby*, 122–124, 131–132, 136.

13. Dunaway, *Looking For Gatsby*, 107–108, 117–118, 128, 142–144, 175, 188.

14. On Dunaway in *Chinatown*, see Dunaway, *Looking For Gatsby*, 249, 252–253, 257–258; and Hunter, *Faye Dunaway*, 116.

Notes to pages 137–164

15. Dunaway, *Looking For Gatsby*, 278, 280.

16. Hunter, *Faye Dunaway*, 146-147, 152, 154; Dunaway, *Looking For Gatsby*, 293, 317.

17. Dunaway, *Looking For Gatsby*, 342, 353.

18. I have discussed the films of Tarantino, Sophia Coppola, and Anderson at greater length in *Modernist America*, 381-387.

Chapter 7: Reshaping America: The Politics and Journalism of the War Baby Generation

1. On Savio's career and personality, see Robert Cohen, *Freedom's Orator: Mario Savio and the Radical Legacy of the 1960s* (New York: Oxford University Press, 2009), 1-6, 8, 10-12, 46, 48, 76, 82, 86, 88, 178-179, 244, 246, 260, 270.

2. I have written in depth about Agee's *Let Us Now Praise Famous Men* in my book *Radical Visions and American Dreams: Culture and Social Thought in the Depression Years* (New York: Harper & Row, 1973), 246-251.

3. Tom Hayden, *Reunion: A Memoir* (New York: Random House, 1988), 39, 42-45, 58, 74-76, 78, 91, 102.

4. John Lewis with Michael D'Orso, *Walking with the Wind: A Memoir of the Movement* (New York: Harvest, 1999, c. 1998), 188; Hayden, *Reunion*, 162, 203, 244, 248-249, 264, 270, 327, 452.

5. Lewis, *Walking with the Wind*, 9, 92-93, 97, 104-105, 107, 111, 123, 130, 138, 149, 155-157, 168, 172, 176, 179, 200, 224-225, 227, 255, 290-291, 340, 343, 362-363, 385, 391, 403, 405, 479-480, 489.

6. Marshall Frady, *Jesse: The Life and Pilgrimage of Jesse Jackson* (New York: Random House, 1996), 4, 170, 190, 192-193, 199, 208-209, 217, 220-221, 223, 228-229, 234-235, 246-247, 392; Roger Bruns, *Jesse Jackson: A Biography* (Westport, Conn.: Greenwood, 2005), x-xi, 1, 28, 32, 35, 37-39, 51-52, 74, 82, 88, 92, 94-95, 119.

7. On Ali, see David Remnick, *King of the World: Muhammad Ali and the Rise of an American Hero* (New York: Random House, 1998), xii-xiv, 99, 125, 165, 214, 229, 286, 288-290, 301; Mike Marqusee, *Redemption*

Notes to pages 167-183
Song: Muhammad Ali and the Spirit of the Sixties (London: Verso, 1999),
3, 6, 8-10, 63, 75, 79, 162, 194, 219-220, 225, 247; and Michael Ezra, *Muhammad Ali: The Making of an Icon* (Philadelphia: Temple University
Press, 2009), 98, 128, 140, 149, 152, 161.

8. Susan Ware, *Game, Set, Match: Billie Jean King and the Revolution in
Women's Sports* (Chapel Hill: University of North Carolina Press, 2011),
1-5, 8-9, 11, 16, 19-20, 22, 24, 27, 29, 31, 38-39, 41-42, 181, 208, 310.

9. Stuart Weisberg, *Barney Frank: The Story of America's Only Left-
Handed, Gay, Jewish Congressman* (Amherst: University of Massachusetts Press, 2009), 48, 51-53, 55-57, 59-63.

10. For Kerry's life before Vietnam, see Michael Kranish, Brian
Mooney, and Nina Easton, *John F. Kerry: The Complete Biography by the
Boston Globe Reporters Who Know Him Best* (New York: Public Affairs,
2004), xxi, xxiii, 20-22, 25-26, 31, 38, 42, 55-56; and Douglas Brinkley,
Tour of Duty: John Kerry and the Vietnam War (New York: Morrow,
2004), 26-27, 35-36, 39, 42, 50-53, 59-63.

11. Brinkley, *Tour of Duty*, 7-8, 11, 14, 128, 342, 348-349, 353, 381; Kranish,
Mooney, and Easton, *John F. Kerry*, 109, 111, 120, 123, 131.

12. On Woodward's life before he joined the *Washington Post*, see Ali-
cia Shepard, *Woodward and Bernstein: Life in the Shadow of Watergate*
(Hoboken, N.J.: Wiley, 2007), 2, 5, 7, 9-12, 16; and Bob Woodward,
The Secret Man: The Story of Watergate's Deep Throat (New York: Simon
& Schuster, 2006, c. 2005), 15, 18, 21, 23, 31-32, 186.

13. For more on Bernstein's personality, see Shepard, *Woodward and
Bernstein*, 7, 17-18, 21, 29, 136.

14. Ibid., xiv-xv, 22-23, 48-49, 67-68, 71, 79, 105, 108, 124, 161; Woodward, *The Secret Man*, 2-3, 5, 7, 12, 34, 39, 41, 46, 51, 63-64, 66, 75, 77, 79,
104-106; Carl Bernstein, "A Reporter's Assessment," in Woodward,
The Secret Man, 229.

15. Woodward, *The Secret Man*, 108-109, 112-113, 115, 173-174, 200, 212;
Bernstein, "A Reporter's Assessment," 221, 225; Shepard, *Woodward
and Bernstein*, xii, 75, 77-78, 91, 115, 118, 136, 140, 142, 160, 187. I have
analyzed the movie of *All the President's Men* in my book *Modernist*

Notes to pages 185–198
America: Art, Music, Movies, and the Globalization of American Culture
(New Haven: Yale University Press, 2011), 313-315.

16. On Brokaw's reporting from the Berlin Wall and his view of the
World Trade Towers' collapse, see Tom Brokaw, *A Long Way from
Home: Growing Up in the American Heartland* (New York: Random
House, 2002), 174-175, 232.

17. Dick Cheney, *In My Time: A Personal and Political Memoir* (New
York: Threshold, 2011), 26, 28, 30, 33, 35-37, 43, 48, 110-111.

18. Jules Witcover, *Joe Biden: A Life of Trial and Redemption* (New
York: Morrow, 2010), 7, 12, 14, 17, 19, 21, 25; Joe Biden, *Promises to Keep:
On Life and Politics,* (New York: Random House, 2007), xvii, 13, 22,
80-82.

19. Vincent Bzdek, *Woman of the House: The Rise of Nancy Pelosi* (New
York: Palgrave Macmillan, 2008), 25, 32, 34, 46-47, 73, 75, 78.

20. For analyses of Holbrooke's career, see the essays in Derek Chollet
and Samantha Power, eds., *The Unquiet American: Richard Holbrooke in
the World* (New York: Public Affairs, 2011), xii-xiii, 5, 11, 16, 19, 21, 88,
92, 95, 105, 127, 167, 170, 199, 283. On Holbrooke's strained relationship
with the Obama Administration, see James Traub, "Who Lost Afghanistan?" *Wall Street Journal* (April 20-21, 2013), C5, C7.

Bibliography

What follows is a list, separated by topic, of the secondary sources, autobiographies, and collections of interviews that I found most useful in writing this book.

Film

Casillo, Robert, *Gangster Priest: The Italian American Cinema of Martin Scorsese* (Toronto: University of Toronto Press, 2006).

Dunaway, Faye with Betsy Sharkey, *Looking For Gatsby: My Life* (New York: Simon & Schuster, 1995).

Hunter, Allan, *Faye Dunaway* (New York: St. Martin's, 1986).

LoBrutto, Vincent, *Martin Scorsese: A Biography* (Westport, Connecticut: Praeger, 2008).

Pells, Richard, *Modernist America: Art, Music, Movies, and the Globalization of American Culture* (New Haven: Yale University Press, 2011).

Schickel, Richard, *Conversations with Scorsese* (New York: Knopf, 2011).

Thompson, David, and Ian Christie, eds., *Scorsese on Scorsese* (London: Faber and Faber, 1989).

Music

Baez, Joan, *And a Voice to Sing With: A Memoir* (New York: Summit, 1987).

Collins, Judy, *Sweet Judy Blue Eyes: My Life in Music* (New York: Crown, 2011).

Collins, Judy, *Trust Your Heart: An Autobiography* (Boston: Houghton Mifflin, 1987).

Davis, Stephen, *Jim Morrison: Life, Death, Legend* (New York: Gotham, 2004).

Dylan, Bob, *Chronicles: Volume One* (New York: Simon & Schuster), 2004.

Echols, Alice, *Scars of Sweet Paradise: The Life and Times of Janis Joplin* (New York: Holt, 1999).

Eliot, Marc, *Paul Simon: A Life* (Hoboken, N.J.: Wiley, 2010).

Friedman, Myra, *Buried Alive: The Biography of Janis Joplin* (New York: Morrow, 1973).

Hajdu, David, *Positively 4th Street: The Life and Times of Joan Baez, Bob Dylan, Mimi Fariña, and Richard Fariña* (New York: Farrar, Straus and Giroux, 2001).

Jackson, Blair, *Garcia: An American Life* (New York: Viking, 1999).

King, Carole, *A Natural Woman: A Memoir* (New York: Grand Central, 2012).

Kingston, Victoria, *Simon and Garfunkel: The Biography* (New York: Fromm International, 1998).

McKeen, William, *Bob Dylan: A Bio-Bibliography* (Westport, Conn.: Greenwood, 1993).

Morella, Joseph, and Patricia Barey, *Simon and Garfunkel: Old Friends, A Dual Biography* (New York: Carol, 1991).

Riordan, James, and Jerry Prochnicky, *Break on Through: The Life and Death of Jim Morrison* (New York: Morrow, 1991).

Scaduto, Vincent, *Bob Dylan* (New York: Grosset & Dunlap, 1971).

Slick, Grace, with Andrea Cagan, *Somebody to Love?: A Rock-and-Roll Memoir* (New York: Warner, 1998).

Sounes, Howard, *Down the Highway: The Life of Bob Dylan* (New York: Grove, 2011).

Troy, Sandy, *Captain Trips: A Biography of Jerry Garcia* (New York: Thunder's Mouth, 1994).

Wilentz, Sean, *Bob Dylan in America* (New York: Doubleday, 2010).

Journalism

Bernstein, Carl, *Loyalties: A Son's Memoir* (New York: Simon & Schuster, 1989).

Brokaw, Tom, *A Long Way From Home: Growing Up in the American*

Heartland (New York: Random House, 2000).

Shepard, Alicia, *Woodward and Bernstein: Life in the Shadow of Watergate* (Hoboken, N.J.: Wiley, 2007).

Woodward, Bob, *The Secret Man: The Story of Watergate's Deep Throat* (New York: Simon & Schuster, 2005).

Politics

Biden, Joe, *Promises to Keep: On Life and Politics* (New York: Random House, 2007).

Brinkley, Douglas, *Tour of Duty: John Kerry and the Vietnam War* (New York: Morrow, 2004).

Bzdek, Vincent, *Woman of the House: The Rise of Nancy Pelosi* (New York: Palgrave Macmillan, 2008).

Cheney, Dick, *In My Time: A Personal and Political Memoir* (New York: Threshold, 2011).

Chollet, Derek, and Samantha Power, eds., *The Unquiet American: Richard Holbrooke in the World* (New York: Public Affairs, 2011).

Kranish, Michael, Brian Mooney, and Nina Easton, *John F. Kerry: The Complete Biography by the Boston Globe Reporters Who Know Him Best* (New York: Public Affairs, 2004).

Pells, Richard, *The Liberal Mind in a Conservative Age: American Intellectuals in the 1940s and 1950s* (New York: Harper & Row, 1985).

Weisberg, Stuart, *Barney Frank: The Story of America's Only Left-Handed, Gay, Jewish Congressman* (Amherst: University of Massachusetts Press, 2008).

Witcover, Jules, *Joe Biden: A Life of Trial and Redemption* (New York: Morrow, 2010).

Activists

Bruns, Roger, *Jesse Jackson: A Biography* (Westport, Conn.: Greenwood, 2005).

Cohen, Robert, *Freedom's Orator: Mario Savio and the Radical Legacy of the 1960s* (New York: Oxford University Press, 2009).

Frady, Marshall, *Jesse: The Life and Pilgrimage of Jesse Jackson* (New York: Random House, 1996).

Hayden, Tom, *Reunion: A Memoir* (New York: Random House, 1988).

Lewis, John, with Michael D'Orso, *Walking with the Wind: A Memoir of the Movement* (New York: Simon & Schuster, 1998).

Comedians

Fedo, Michael, *The Man From Lake Wobegon* (New York: St. Martin's, 1987).

Lee, Judith, *Garrison Keillor: A Voice of America* (Jackson: University Press of Mississippi, 1991).

Sorenson, Jeff, *Lily Tomlin: Woman of a Thousand Faces* (New York: St. Martin's, 1989).

Sports

Ezra, Michael, *Muhammad Ali: The Making of an Icon* (Philadelphia: Temple University Press, 2009).

Marqusee, Mike, *Redemption Song: Muhammad Ali and the Spirit of the Sixties* (London: Verso, 1999).

Remnick, David, *King of the World: Muhammad Ali and the Rise of an American Hero* (New York: Random House, 1998).

Ware, Susan, *Game, Set, Match: Billie Jean King and the Revolution in Women's Sports* (Chapel Hill: University of North Carolina Press, 2011).

Index

Printed in the USA
CPSIA information can be obtained
at www.ICGtesting.com
LVHW020401151223
766590LV00036B/763